Her Majesty MARY

Queen of Peace

End times prophecies and warnings of Mary

Professor Courtenay Bartholomew, M.D.

PUBLISHING COMPANY
P.O. Box 220 • Goleta, CA 93116
(800) 647-9882 • (805) 692-0043 • Fax (805) 967-5133

IMPRIMATUR

Most Reverend Edward J. Gilbert C. Ss. R.
Archbishop of Port of Spain
February 15, 2002

©2002 Queenship Publishing — All rights reserved. No part of this book may be reproduced, in any form or by any means, without permission in writing from the publisher.

Library of Congress Number #2002090850

Published by:
   Queenship Publishing
   P.O. Box 220
   Goleta, CA 93116
   (800) 647-9882 • (805) 692-0043 • Fax: (805) 967-5133
   http://www.queenship.org

Printed in the United States of America

ISBN: 1-57918-192-9

Contents

Dedication	VII
Acknowledgements	IX
Foreword	XI
Introduction	XIII

1. The First War in Heaven — 1
2. Eden's First Eve; Nazareth's Second Eve — 5
3. Hail, Full of Grace — 13
4. The Second Eve Says 'Yes' — 19
5. Her Majesty's Magnificat — 23
6. The Redeemer and Coredemptrix on Calvary — 29
7. Old Testament Heralds of Mary — 39
8. 431 AD. The First Marian Dogma — 47
9. 649 AD. The Second Marian Dogma — 51
10. 1054. Disunity in the Church Christ Founded — 57
11. 1531. Her Majesty Appears in the New World — 61
12. 1571. The Battle of Lepanto — 69
13. 1830. The Medal of the Immaculate Conception — 73
14. Coredemptrix, Mediatrix, Advocate — 81
15. 1846. Her Majesty Weeps in La Salette — 91
16. 1854. The Third Marian Dogma — 97
17. 1858. "I am the Immaculate Conception" — 103
18. Lourdes and Our Lady of Mt. Carmel — 109
19. 1871. Pontmain and the Franco-Prussian War — 115
20. 1917. Our Lady of the Rosary of Fatima — 121
21. Why Did Mary Choose Fatima? — 131
22. The Meaning of Devotion to the Immaculate Heart — 135
23. 1945. Amsterdam. The Mother of all Nations — 145
24. The Political Prophecies of the Lady — 153
25. 1950. The Fourth Marian Dogma — 163
26. 1951-54. A Fifth and Final Marian Dogma? — 167
27. 1961. Mary's Warnings in Garabandal — 177
28. 1973. Akita: "Fire will fall from the sky" — 189
29. 1981. The Ten Secrets of Medjugorje — 199
30. Old Testament Marian Symbols in Medjugorje — 207

31. 2000 AD. The Third Fatima Secret Revealed 223
32. 2000 AD. Cardinal Ratzinger's Interpretation 227
33. The Apocalypse. Chapters 8 and 13 231
34. An Attempt to Interpret Further the Third Secret 235
35. 2000 AD. Millennium Entrustment to the
    Immaculate Heart 247
36. What is the Triumph of the Immaculate Heart? 255
37. Judaism, Christianity and Islam 267
38. The Palestinian Problem 275
39. God's Children at War 285
40. Her Majesty, the Queen of Peace 289

Dedication

This book is dedicated to Fr. Slavko Barbaric who wrote the foreword in my first book *"A Scientist Researches Mary Ark of the Covenant,"* and who first invited me to the room of the apparitions in the rectory of St. James' Church in Medjugorje when the "Queen of Peace" appeared to the visionaries on October 12, 1986. It was an occasion which heightened my devotion to Mary.

October 12 is a great religious day in Spain and her once Spanish colonies. It celebrates the feast of Our Lady of the Pillar (El Pilar), which commemorates the occasion when tradition has it that in the year 40 AD the Blessed Virgin bilocated to Saragossa in Spain where St. James was evangelizing. It is said that many angels accompanied her and left a pillar with an image of their Queen atop it. This pillar is still in the Basilica of El Pilar in Saragossa and has been a monument of great veneration throughout the centuries.

It is hardly a coincidence that on October 12, 1492, Christopher Columbus and his Spanish crew discovered the New World, which he called the West Indies. On the other hand, it is fortuitous that it was on October 12, 1986 that I, a West Indian, was invited to the room of the apparitions in Medjugorje on that feast day.

I will always treasure my friendship with Fr. Slavko, his many kindnesses to me and his spiritual teachings. May he rest in peace in the bosom of Her Majesty.

Acknowledgements

I wish to express my deep appreciation to Ms. Mary Pinder for reviewing and proofreading the text and Ms. Mary Alcala-Jack, Ms. Pat Virgil and Mr. Roger Moe for preparing the manuscript.

Foreword

The human battle between "the head" and "the heart" dates back to the Garden itself. Eve received a heart formed by the Creator, but allowed her head to be confused by the father of lies. Although the heart was inscribed with the truth of God, the head accepted the rationalization of the ancient dragon. Thus the mother of the living was instrumental in the loss of the greatest gift given to her earthly children: participation in the very life and the love of the Trinity.

Then in the fullness of time, the Father created the Immaculate Heart. This Heart, bursting with Trinitarian love and grace, was perfectly conformed to the Heart of God. The head of the Immaculate One, filled with the Spouse's gifts of wisdom, counsel, and knowledge, was always in perfect obedience with her heart, understanding and living the *primacy of the heart*, where God whispers to his children and directs their journey to Him, in the intimacy of the inner sanctuary; in the tabernacle of the heart.

From the "yes" of the Immaculate Heart comes the flesh of the Sacred Heart, the instrument of our redemption (cf. Heb. 10:10). The Immaculate Heart must be pierced (Lk. 2:35) so that the Sacred Heart can be pierced (Jn. 19:34-35), releasing the precious blood which restores grace to Eve's children. The Sacred Heart and the Immaculate Heart, the New Adam and the New Eve, the Redeemer and the Co-redemptrix, bringing forth a universal victory of hearts.

Now it is time for a new conquest of hearts. The Father has again sent the Immaculate Heart into the world to bring forth a second historic triumph of hearts in preparation for a new historic victory of the Sacred Heart: "God wishes to establish in the world devotion to My Immaculate Heart…in the end, My Immaculate Heart will triumph…and a period of peace will be granted to the world" (Fatima, July 13, 1917).

Such a triumph will demand a new victory of "the heart" over "the head"—a victory of faith over rationalism, of adoration over atomic bombs, of conscience over cloning, of Consecration over contraceptives, of Rosary over religious indifferentism, of a dogma of Mary Co-redemptrix over discussion of theologians, of obedience to the will of God inscribed in the heart of man over the rationalization of the dragon inserted into the mind of man. The Mother of all Peoples and Nations did not call for a "triumph of the head," but a "triumph of the heart," Her Immaculate Heart and all hearts united to Her Immaculate Heart.

Most fortunately, in the person and work of Prof. Bartholomew, we have a blessed complementarity of head and heart at full service to the Immaculate One. The holy Catholic faith has never been anti-intellectual, but rather "supra-intellectual," that is to say, the excellence of the human mind must in the final analysis always bow in humility to the sublimity of the supernatural mystery of God, which is never irrational but simply supra-rational, soaring beyond the limits of human understanding. Prof. Bartholomew's exceptional work, *Her Majesty, Mary* manifests the gifted exercise of scientific scrutiny in the pursuit of mariological truth, but always with the humility of the heart that does not seek to compete with God's revealed mind but only to embellish its beauty with the best the human mind and heart can offer and explain.

Ultimately, Bartholomew's work reveals the primacy of his own heart—a heart grafted to the truth and love of the Immaculate Heart and to its historic Triumph in our own critical moment of human history. As revered Philippines Vatican Ambassador Howard Dee was rightly nicknamed by Pope John Paul II as "Our Lady's Ambassador," so too is Prof. Bartholomew rightly nicknamed "Our Lady's Scientist."

Make the time to read *Her Majesty, Mary,* written from the golden pen of Prof. Bartholomew. This book will save souls.

> Dr. Mark Miravalle
> Professor of Theology and Mariology
> Franciscan University of Steubenville
> President, Vox Populi Mariae Mediatrici
> 2 February 2002
> Feast of the Presentation of the Lord

Introduction

"To everything there is a season, and a time to every purpose under the heaven; a time to be born, and a time to die; a time to plant, and a time to pluck up that which is planted…; a time of war, and a time of peace" (Ecclesiastes 3:1-8). Count Leo Tolstoy (1828-1910), Russian novelist and writer on ethics and religion, wrote his masterpiece *War and Peace*, one of the two or three greatest novels of world literature. In it the element of peace, of the family, prevails over that of war. My book also deals with war and peace. Indeed, the God of Peace created the universe and peace initially reigned in the empyrean heavens as it does now. But there was a time for war even in God's heaven. As Aristotle (384-322 BC) once said: "We make war that we may live in peace." In fact, it is perhaps the only moral reason for war. And so, Michael declared war on Lucifer, and the enemies of God were cast down to earth.

But so many of us appear to be completely oblivious to the reality that that spiritual warfare is continuing on earth ever since and that "we wrestle not against flesh and blood, but against principalities, against powers, against the rulers of the darkness of this world, against spiritual wickedness in high places" (Ephesians 6:12). These are the spirits who do not wish us to fill their places which have been vacated in heaven and want us to be damned like they have been.

Satan then introduced sin into the Garden of Eden. And so, first it was the angels, then man rebelled against God, and in time "God saw the wickedness of man was great in the earth, and that every imagination of the thoughts of his heart was only evil continually. And it repented the Lord that he had made man on the earth, and it grieved him at his heart. And the Lord said, I will destroy man whom I have created from the face of the earth; both man and beast, and the creeping things, and the fowls of the air; for it repented me that I have made them. But Noah found grace in the eyes of the Lord…. The earth grew corrupt in God's sight, and was filled with violence" (Genesis 6:5 -11).

But, the Mother of the Lord once said in a private revelation that "the sins of today are worse than in the time of Noah." Indeed, never in known world history has there been such universal violence, corruption and moral decay as in today's world. Before the Flood came, man was warned for decades while Noah was building the ark. And yet did not listen. In this post-Flood era, God has sent his mother, and especially since the 19th, and above all, the 20th century, she has been frequently appearing and warning her children that our wickedness is such that a punishment is to be expected if we do not convert. The Prince of Peace, Lord Jesus Christ, also gave us the signs of the end times (Mathew 24:7; Mark 13:8; Luke 21:11) — but to no avail. As the old negro spiritual warned: "God gave Noah the rainbow sign, the fire next time," and so "as it was in Noah's day, so will it be when the Son of Man comes. For in those days before the Flood people were eating, drinking, taking wives, taking husbands, right up to the day Noah went into the ark, and they suspected nothing till the Flood came and swept all away" (Matthew 24:37-39).

Now, in modern times, European society was in imminent danger of anarchy, and atheism was beginning to sweep across the continent. During World War I Pope Benedict XV, in desperation, instructed his Secretary of State to send a message, dated May 5, 1917, to the bishops of the world. After listing the horrors afflicting Europe, he called upon Her Majesty, the Queen of Heaven, for help: "Our earnestly pleading voice invoking the end of this vast conflict, the suicide of civilized Europe has remained unheard... Since all graces which the Author of all good deigns to bestow on the poor sons of Adam, by the merciful disposition of Divine Providence, are distributed through the hands of the Blessed Virgin, we desire that the earnest and confident prayer of her afflicted children, may be more than ever addressed in this dreadful hour to the August Mother of God... We order that from June 1 there shall be permanently introduced into the Litany of the Blessed Virgin the invocation, 'Queen of Peace, pray for us...' May this pious and devout invocation arise from every corner of the earth; from the great temples as from the lowliest churches, from the palaces of the rich mansions of the great as from the humblest cottages wherever dwells a faithful soul, and from the blood-stained fields and seas. May it rise to Mary, who is the Mother of Mercy and all-powerful by grace; and may it carry with it the agonizing cries of mothers and wives, the wails of innocent children, and the sighs of all hearts; may it prevail with her, in her loving motherly solicitude, to obtain for the stricken world the peace that is asked, and in the times to come remind mankind of the power of her mediations."

Just eight days after Pope Benedict's strong plea to the Blessed Mother for help, Her Majesty appeared in the Cova da Iria in the parish of Fatima, Portugal. And said that the war was going to end soon but if men did not stop offending God another and more terrible war would begin during the reign of Pius XI. Men did not stop offending God!

During World War II, on March 25, 1945, Her Majesty appeared to a visionary called Ida Peerdeman in Amsterdam, Holland once more in response to the prayers of the faithful, and promised that the war would soon end. It ended in the Netherlands on May 5, 1945, the month dedicated to Mary, "Thanks to this," she said, showing a rosary. May 5 is the feast of Pope Pius V, who called upon all Christendom in 1571 to storm heaven with rosaries for victory in the naval battle between the Christian fleet and the Islamic fleet in Lepanto. However, degeneration, corruption, and wars, civil, religious and ethnic, have continued throughout the decades, and in 1973 the Blessed Virgin then warned in Akita, Japan that the sins of man were such that "fire would fall from the sky," if men did not repent.

In fact, the evidence for the authenticity of many of her apparitions and her messages is so clear and convincing that those who do not choose to believe, or even to read about them, well-advertised throughout the world as they have been, will only have themselves to blame and would therefore have no excuse. She has, above all, appeared in most dramatic ways to Muslim crowds in various cities in Egypt, indeed, much more dramatically than in Christian apparition sites, yet only a small percentage of the world's children pay any heed to God's greatest messenger.

True Devotion To Mary by St. Louis Marie Grignion De Montfort (1673-1716) is considered to be one of the greatest books on the Blessed Virgin Mary ever written. It is a classic statement on the *"spiritual way to Jesus Christ through Mary,"* who is the "Morning Star" who leads souls to her divine son. As St. Louis said in the introduction to his book: "The more we honour the Blessed Virgin, the more we honour Jesus Christ, because we honour Mary only that we may the more perfectly honour Jesus, since we go to her only as the way by which we are to find the end we are seeking, which is Jesus."

It is therefore significant, most significant that our present Holy Father, Pope John Paul II, was greatly influenced by this 18th-century lover of Mary. He wrote in a recent edition of the book: "The reading of this book was a decisive turning-point in my life. I say 'turning-point,' but in fact it was a long inner journey… This 'perfect devotion' is indispensable to anyone who means to give himself without reserve to Christ and to the work of redemption. It is from Montfort that I have taken my motto *'Totus Tuuus'* ('I am all thine'). Someday I would have to tell you Montfortians how I discovered *De Montfort's Treatise on True Devotion to Mary*, and how often I had to reread it to understand it."

In his book St. Louis prophesied about the end-times and the latter-day apostles of Mary. Now, let me stress from the onset that by "end-times" I do not mean the end of the world, but the end of an era or epoch. The Flood, for example, was not the end of the world. De Montfort's book states: "Genesis 3:15 reads – 'I will put enmity between you and the woman and between your seed and her seed; she shall crush your head and you shall lie in wait for her heel,' that is to say, her humble slaves and her poor children, whom she will raise up to make war against him. She must be terrible to the devil and his crew, as an army arrayed in battle, principally in these latter times, because the devil, knowing that he has but little time, and now less than ever, to destroy souls, with every day redoubles his efforts and his combats. He will presently raise up cruel persecutions and will put terrible snares before the faithful servants and true children of Mary, whom it gives him more trouble to conquer than it does to conquer others."

De Montfort continues: "They [her heel] shall be chosen to match themselves against the enemies of God, who shall rage on all sides, and they shall be singularly devout to Our Blessed Lady, illuminated by her light, strengthened by her nourishment, led by her spirit, supported by her arm and sheltered under her protection, so that they shall fight with one hand and build with the other. By their words and their examples they shall draw the whole world to true devotion to Mary. They shall bring upon themselves enemies, but shall also bring many victories and much glory for God alone.... With Mary, they shall crush the head of the devil and cause Jesus Christ to triumph... They will know the grandeur of their Queen and will consecrate themselves entirely to her service as subjects and slaves of love... They will know what is the surest, the easiest, the shortest and the most perfect means of going to Jesus Christ; and they would give themselves to Mary, body and soul, without reserve, that they might thus belong entirely to Jesus Christ. Mary is the Queen of heaven and earth by grace, as Jesus is the King of them by nature and by conquest."

The Mayas and the Aztecs at the time that Her Majesty appeared in Mexico in 1531, and indeed long before that, knew that there was a Flood which destroyed the world. How did this information get to them? It is as difficult a question to answer as it is to answer who built the pyramids in Egypt. And so, there is much that is under the sun that is still to be understood. The Aztecs and the Mayas before them also believed that the time of the next cataclysmic catastrophe will occur in the year 2000 *y poco* (a little). We do not know the year, the day, or the hour, and so "y poco" is a prudent prediction! But all this is conditional. As she once said: "Prayer and fasting can change the laws of nature." And so, "y poco" can become *"y mas tarde"* (and much later), or even *"nunca mas"* (never again), if we do as she says.

Our Lady appeared in Kibeho, Rwanda, Africa to six visionaries in 1981 and her last apparition was in 1989. In those apparitions she called herself the "Mother of the Word." The apparitions were approved by the local bishop on August 15, 1988, thus allowing public devotion. In his book *Too Late?*, John Haffert quoted one of the visionaries of Rwanda who once exclaimed to Our Lady:

"I know what makes you suffer, it is because the day will come when we will wish we had listened to what you have been telling us about loving, serving, and doing what you asked… but it will be too late."

Haffert went on to say that "the world was shocked that in Rwanda over 500,000 people were brutally killed by their neighbours. However, very few seem aware that 10 years before the massacre, the Blessed Virgin appeared to warn them and to give specific requests to avoid a 'river of blood'. Her requests were not heard and the warning messages she had given came true to the letter—'a river of blood… people killing each other… bodies without their heads.' Indeed, many of the half million who died ten years later were decapitated."

He continued: "A nun in Rwanda wrote: 'It is like the end of the world here." Another said: "Hell has followed us.' It is utterly amazing that we hear the same words used to describe the horror which took place in the Balkans 10 years after Our Lady was reported to have appeared in Medjugorje (Yugoslavia)… If this happened in Bosnia and Rwanda, what will happen in the rest of the world if the Akita update of the Fatima message is ignored."

So said, in 1973, Our Lady said in Akita, Japan: "As I told you, if people do not repent and better themselves, the Father would inflict a terrible punishment on all humanity. It will be a punishment greater than the Flood, such as one has never seen before. Fire will fall from the sky and wipe out a great part of humanity, the good as well as the bad, sparing neither priests nor faithful. The survivors will find themselves so desolate that they will envy the dead…" Now, the Fatima warning of 1917 was that if her messages of conversion were not heeded, "various nations will be annihilated!" But it is not too late to prevent this.

She is shedding tears during many of her apparitions and through her images worldwide. It is Rachel weeping for her children, refusing to be comforted for her children, "because they are no more" (Jeremiah 31:15). But there are those, lay and religious, who preach the business-as-usual homilies, believing it to be prudent while the signs of the times are flashing in neon lights for all to see and warning us that time is short. But we prefer to wear dark shades and blinkers and so, like days of yore, we will be drinking wine and taking wives and husbands just before "the fire next time."

On February 11, 2001, the feast of Our Lady of Lourdes, a request was made by someone very dear to me that I should write another book which should expand on some of the themes in my earlier works and I have also included new chapters on contemporary world events as they relate to Mariology. I have attempted in this book to give a history of Her Majesty as briefly as is possible, and, above all, to evangelize her warnings to us whom she is asking so repetitively to respond to her call. It is all about war and peace. It is all about being lost and being saved. It's all about the end times. It is a book of linkages and I have tried to link all her apparitions and dogmas so that what appears to be a jumbled jigsaw puzzle will all fall into place and present a beautiful mosaic of the motherly love and tenderness of Her Majesty, the Queen of Peace, towards her children.

In this Marian journey which you will travel I have also devoted much time to a detailed interpretation of the revealed third secret of Fatima and to the triumph of the Immaculate Heart of Mary, all part of my humble attempt to unravel the great mystery and truth about Her Majesty. This book, of course, is neither Montfortian nor Tolstoyan. It is simply the humble research of a scientist who cannot comprehend the mystery of God but is trying to appreciate a little bit about the mystery of his mother, Her Majesty, the Queen of Peace.

January 1, 2002
The Feast of the Mother of God.

Chapter 1

The First War in Heaven

The story of the creation is recorded in the Book of Genesis and brief mention is made of the fall of the angels in several passages in the Old and New Testaments. The Sacred Scriptures also speak of the fall of Satan in the fourteenth chapter of Isaiah: "How did you come to fall from the heavens, Daystar, son of Dawn? How did you come to be thrown to the ground, you who enslaved the nations? You who used to think to yourself, 'I will climb up to the heavens; and higher than the stars of God I will set my throne. I will sit on the Mount of Assembly in the recesses of the north. I will climb to the top of thunderclouds, I will rival the Most High.' What! Now you have fallen to Sheol, to the very bottom of the abyss!" (Isaiah 14:12-15). In the New Testament, Luke 10:18 records the words of Jesus Himself: *"I watched Satan fall like lightning from heaven."*

But "there were many other things that Jesus did, if all were written down, the world itself, I suppose, would not hold all the books that would have to be written," says John (John 21:25). So said, *The Mystical City of God* by the Venerable Maria de Jesus of Agreda (1602-1665) is a monumental four-volume history of the life of the Blessed Virgin, as privately revealed by the Blessed Virgin herself to this seventeenth-century Spanish Franciscan nun whose body I saw lying incorrupt in the Convent of the Immaculate Conception in Agreda in Spain. It is said that this holy nun saw in ecstasy all the events recorded in her book. Indeed, the book, acclaimed by popes, cardinals and theologians, has inspired the laity and the clergy for over three hundred years. The mystic relates in great detail the account of creation of the angels and the future role of Mary, the Mother of the Word, as predestined by God.

She wrote in Book 1, Chapter 1 that in the beginning God created heaven and earth. He created heaven for angels and men, and the earth as a place of pilgrimage for mortals. The angels were created in the empyrean heavens and in a state of grace by which they might be first to merit the reward of glory. At first, they received a more explicit intelligence of the Being of God, one in substance, three in person, and they were commanded to adore and reverence him as their Creator.

Heaven and earth were hardly created when God dared to reveal his divine plan for the first time, also proposing it as a test for the angelic creatures. The angels were then informed that He was to create a human nature and reasoning creatures lower than themselves and that they too should love and reverence him as their Author. They were informed that these lower creatures were to stand in high favour, and that the second Person of the Blessed Trinity was to become incarnate and assume their nature, raising it to the hypostatic union, and that the angels were also to acknowledge him as their head, not only as God, but as God and man, the God-man, adoring Him and reverencing him.

To this command, using their free will, all the obedient and holy angels submitted themselves and they gave their full assent and acknowledgment with a humble and loving subjection of the will. But Lucifer, full of envy and pride, resisted and induced his followers to resist likewise, as they in reality did, preferring to follow him and disobey divine command.

After it was revealed to the angels that they would have to obey the Incarnate Word, a third precept was given to them, namely, that they were to admit as a superior conjointly with him, a woman in whose womb the Only Begotten of the Father was to assume flesh, and that this woman was to be their queen and the queen of all creatures. He then presented her to them, not in reality, since she did not as yet exist, but in a sign or image. It was a woman, adorned with the sun, standing on the moon, and with twelve stars on her head for a crown. St. John describes this image in the Book of Revelation (Rev. 12:1-2). This Woman was shown in her condition of motherhood, that is, in a state of maternity. The angelic spirits understood at once the role of this woman.

The mystic went on to relate that the good angels obeyed this latter command of the Lord with still increasing humility, praising the powers and the mysteries of the Most High, accepting also the woman of the sign as their queen. Lucifer and his confederates, however, rose to a higher pitch of pride and boastful insolence. In disorderly fury, he aspired to be himself the head of all the human race and of the angelic orders, and if there was to be a hypostatic union, he demanded that it be consummated in him: "It is only I who will be like the Most High. All will render me honour." Above all, the decree constituting him inferior to the mother of the Incarnate Word, he opposed with horrible blasphemies. Turning against God in unbridled indignation and calling upon the other angels, he exhorted them, saying: "Unjust are these commands and injury is done to my greatness. This human nature which you, Lord, look upon with so much love and which you favour so highly, I will persecute and destroy. To this end I will direct all my power and all my aspirations. And this woman, Mother of the Word, I will hurl from the pedestal upon which you have proposed to place her and at my hands, the plan which you set up shall come to naught."

This proud boast aroused the indignation of the Lord and to humiliate and punish him, he spoke thus to Lucifer: "This woman whom you refuse to honour, shall crush your head and by her shall you be vanquished and annihilated. And if through your pride, death enters into the world, life and salvation of mortals shall enter through the humility of this woman. Those that are of the nature and likeness of this man and woman shall enjoy the gifts and the crowns which you and your followers have lost." Then happened that great battle in heaven which St. John describes in Revelation 12. The good angels, led in battle by Michael the Archangel, cast one third of the angelic host down to earth. It was the first warfare in eternity, a war beyond human imagination. It was a disaster unparalleled in eternity and in time. It stemmed from the free will which God in his wisdom had chosen to give his creatures, both angelic and mortal.

And so, as Pope John Paul II states in *Redemptoris Mater*, in the "mystery of Christ, she is ever present, even before the creation of the world, as the one whom the Father has chosen to be the mother of his Son in the Incarnation."

Chapter 2

Eden's First Eve; Nazareth's Second Eve

In the fullness of time God said (obviously to the two other Persons of the Trinity): "Let us make man in our own image, in the likeness of ourselves... And so it was God saw all that he had made, and indeed it was very good. Evening came and morning came; the sixth day" (Genesis 1:26; 1:31). Eventually, when the earth was "user-friendly" for man, God formed Adam from the dust of the ground and placed him in the Garden of Eden. He then said to him: "Of all the trees in the garden you may freely eat, but of the tree of the knowledge of good and evil, you shall not eat, for in the day that you eat thereof, you will surely die." God then caused a deep sleep to fall upon Adam and took one of his ribs and closed up the flesh. One may well say that it was the first biblical record of anaesthesiology and surgery. A companion was given to Adam. Adam then said: "This one is bone of my bones, and flesh of my flesh. She shall be called woman, because she was taken out of man" (Genesis 2:21-23). He called her Eve, meaning "mother of all the living" (Genesis 3:20). This, of course, could also be translated "mother of mankind" or "mother of all peoples" (see chapters 11 and 23).

Now, in this play of life, let us call it Act 3, Scene 1-6 (Genesis 3:1-6). Enter the serpent. Satan then tempted Eve first and said to her: "You surely will not die. For God knows that in the day you eat thereof, your eyes will be opened and you will be as gods knowing good and evil." It was Satan's perpetual obsession to be like God. Eve then ate of the fruit and gave it to her husband and he did eat. Satan had his first victory over man. Sin had entered the world for the first time.

In Act 3, Scene 15 (Genesis 3:14 -15), God then rebuked the

ancient serpent and said to him: "Because you have done this, cursed are you above all cattle, and above all wild animals; upon your belly you shall go, and dust you shall eat all the days of your life. I will put enmity between you and the woman, between your seed and her seed. She will crush your head and you will strike at her heel." It was God's first promise to man that he will redress the situation. The woman could not be the first Eve whom he had just seduced. Satan knew that full well. He had heard this rebuke when he saw her in image form clothed with the sun before he fell from heaven! It was the woman of Revelation 11:19; 12:1 "Then the temple of God in heaven was opened, and the ark of the covenant was seen inside his temple... And a great sign appeared in heaven, a woman clothed with the sun, with the moon under her feet and on her head a crown of twelve stars..." This was the woman to crush the head of the serpent. But she was not to be born on earth until around 16 BC.

The Second Eve is Born

Once more, as we say, in the fullness of time, the "woman" of Genesis 3:15, the greatest of all women in the Bible, was born to Joachim and Anne of the tribe of David and a descendant of Abraham. According to the mystic, the Venerable Catherine Emmerich (1774—1824), a stigmatist and visionary who also received visions of the life of Our Lord and his mother, the ancestors of Anne were said to have been devout Israelites, who were called Essenes. They lived mostly on the slopes of Mt. Horeb and Mt. Carmel, the home of the prophet Elias. They stood particularly against sexual immorality, and often by mutual consent lived in continence for long periods, and when they did live together as husband and wife, it was only with the intention of producing a holy offspring. The highest members of the Essenes who lived in community did not however marry but lived in chastity. Indeed, the others who married were akin to members of the Catholic Third Orders or Tertiaries. In fact, it is said that many other Jews disliked them because of their austerity. St. Anne's grandparents belonged to this kind of married Essenes. The prophet Jeremiah was connected to them. It is said that the Maccabees also belonged to them.

Anne's ancestors, according to the mystic, also helped to carry the Ark of the Covenant with great devotion and piety. The first child born to her was a daughter but she was not the "child of the promise." For seventeen years after the birth of their first child Anne was fruitless and prayed constantly and fervently for an end to her barrenness. Indeed, it is often through initial barrenness that God produced his great leaders. It is said that the Almighty could not find more worthy parents for his chosen bride and at last Anne gave birth to the Immaculate Conception. Joachim and Anne, according to Catherine Emmerich, lived together in continence afterwards and in the greatest devoutness and fear of the Lord.

The Soul of Mary

Now, Canon Sheehan was a parish priest of Doneraile in County Cork, Ireland. Preaching on the Blessed Virgin, he once eloquently said that it was decreed by God at the fall of our first parents that as their children would have inherited grace and glory if his commands had been obeyed, so, because of their disobedience, their children were to inherit only sin and shame. This law is universal. Not even the greatest saints were exempt from it. Once and once only did God create a soul as pure and beautiful at the moment of its conception as it is now in heaven; a soul to which the Almighty could turn when weary of the deformity which sin had stamped upon mankind.

It was the time when the fullness of years had come and it was decreed that the son should leave the bosom of the Father and take flesh among men. For centuries, he said, God had not created a soul in grace. Yes, he had fashioned and formed them and sent them into the world, but they were in the power of the enemy before they left his almighty hands. But now, for an instant, the old time was to come back again when God could look upon his work and say that it was good, and that it did not repent him that he had made it. And so, the Blessed Trinity fashioned and formed and sent into the world the soul of Mary. And God admired his handiwork, while hell trembled at the conception of a woman who was destined to break the power of its prince.

This is the girl chosen from all women to give God the colour of his eyes and of his hair. She was to teach the Word to speak in her own accent. She was to help the Almighty walk his first baby steps. She was to give him the body and blood in which he would live and suffer and die to redeem us all. She was called Mary, a famous name in Jewish history, Miriam. Miriam was the sister of Moses, and in God's inscrutable, providential plan, Miriam helped Moses, the leader of the "exodus" from Egyptian slavery, grow. In the New Testament, the new Miriam, Mary, is going to help the Redeemer of the world to grow, to help to save us all. This time it was an "exodus," not from Egyptian slavery but from the slavery of sin and Satan.

This sermon of Canon Sheehan beautifully reflects "the image of our Queen," Her Majesty, the Queen of Heaven and Earth. As the Franciscan St. Bonaventure once wrote: "Mary is that being which God cannot make greater. He can make a greater earth and a greater heaven but not a greater mother." Or as Fr. Cyril Papali, O.D. once said: "God exhausted his omnipotence in creating her."

The Annunciation

In time God sent his messenger and ambassador Gabriel to the Virgin of Nazareth with a gilt-edged invitation to her to be the "Mother of the Word." As the Gospel of Luke states: "In the sixth month, the angel Gabriel was sent from God to a town of Galilee called Nazareth, to a virgin betrothed to a man named Joseph, of the house of David, and the virgin's name was Mary. And coming to her he said: *'Hail, full of grace!* The Lord is with you.' But she was greatly troubled by what was said and pondered what sort of greeting this might be. And the angel said to her, 'Do not be afraid, Mary, for you have found favour with God. Behold, you will conceive in your womb, and bear a son, and you shall name him Jesus. He will be great and will be called Son of the Most High, and the Lord God will give him the throne of David his father, and he will rule over the house of Jacob forever, and of his kingdom there will be no end. Mary said to the angel, 'But how can this come about, since I am a virgin?' 'The Holy Spirit will come upon you,' the angel answered, 'and the power of the Most High will cover you with its shadow. And so the child would be holy and would be called Son of God. Know this too: your kinswoman Elizabeth has, in her old age, herself conceived a son, and she whom people call barren is now in her sixth month, for nothing is impossible to God.' 'I am the handmaid of the Lord,' said Mary, 'let what you have said be done to me.' And the angel left her" (Luke 1:26-38).

Indeed, Gabriel in Luke would readily be associated with Gabriel in the Book of Daniel (9:20-25), where this messenger of the Lord announces to Daniel the coming day of the Lord and the dawning of the messianic era. Luke may imply that the angel bowed to Mary as Nicholas Ayo speculates in his book *Hail Mary*.

Now, angels are superior beings to men and on the occasions in the Bible when there are encounters with them, they have always been treated with awe and deep respect. For example, in the Book of Daniel, when the Angel Gabriel appeared to him Daniel prostrated himself before Gabriel: "As he approached I was seized with terror, and fell prostrate" (Daniel 8:17). However, nothing is said about the attitude of the angel upon arriving in the presence of Mary and greeting her. Indeed, "if all were written down, the world itself would not hold all the books that would have to be written" (John 21:25). So said, the more detailed lives of Our Lord and Our Lady have been given to certain privileged mystics.

Anne Catherine Emmerich (1774-1824) was a nun of the Augustinian Order at the Convent of Agnetenberg in Germany. She was told in mystic visions that her gift of seeing past, present, and future was greater than that possessed by anyone else in history. During most of her later years she rejected the simplest food or drink, subsisting for long periods almost entirely on water and the Holy Eucharist. From the year 1812 until her death she bore the stigmata of Our Lord, including a cross over her heart and wounds from the crown of thorns. In her book *The Life of the Blessed Virgin Mary*, she described the vision she saw of the Annunciation: "I saw in this light a shining white youth with *flowing* blond hair, floating down before her. It was the Angel Gabriel. He gently moved his arms away from his body as he spoke to her. Mary turned her veiled head slightly towards the right, but she was shy and did not look up..."

The Venerable Mary of Agreda (1602-1665) described the seconds after the angel was seen *floating* down before her. She was a 17th century Spanish Franciscan nun who saw in ecstasy all the events recorded in her book. The Blessed Virgin told her to write them down and the four volume book *The Mystical City of God*, acclaimed by popes, cardinals and theologians, inspired the laity and clergy for over three hundred years. She wrote on her vision of the Annunciation: "The Archangel Gabriel entered into the chamber where most holy Mary was praying. It was on a Thursday at 6 o'clock in the evening and at the approach of night. The great modesty and restraint of the Princess of Heaven did not permit her to look at him more than was necessary to recognize him as an angel of the Lord. Recognizing him as such, she, in her usual humility wished to do him reverence. The holy angel would not allow it. On the contrary, he himself *bowed* profoundly as before his Queen." In fact, it was the first time I read about the day of the week and the time that the angel appeared to Mary at the Annunciation. And so, it is Jesus Christ, conceived on a Thursday, died on a Friday!

Maria Valtorta (1897-1961) was born in Italy. At age 23, in an act of thoughtless violence, she was struck in the back by a young delinquent, an injury which confined her to bed for the rest of her life. She never became a nun but she soon pronounced the vows of virginity, poverty and obedience, and accepted her suffering, both physical and spiritual, as a victim soul. *The Poem of the Man-God* is a major work of the great life of Jesus given to her by Our Lord himself, the narration of which extends from the birth and childhood of the Virgin Mary to her assumption into heaven. She used to write in an almost sitting position in bed, and as her biographer wrote: "Christ used her as a faithful 'spokesman' and 'pen', manifesting himself in the richness of the visions to her and in the depth of the dictations. On the Annunciation she wrote : "The Archangel *prostrates* himself (before her)... She is even more startled when she sees the shining creature *kneeling* at about a meter from her and looking at her with infinite veneration, his hands crossed over his chest." In short, Mary was the exception to the angelic protocol. Gabriel bowed to Her Majesty, his Queen to be.

Her Majesty Mary, Queen of Peace

Chapter 3

Hail, Full of Grace

Hail

Now, the Archangel Gabriel's greeting began with the Greek word *Chaire*. It has been translated for centuries as the customary greeting "Hail," "Hello" or "Greetings." For example, "Hail Caesar" (*Julius Caesar*, Act II, scene 1). The original Latin Vulgate translation of the scholarly St. Jerome is "Ave," hence "Ave Maria" (Hail Mary). Another reading of *Chaire* which is used in some Bibles is "Rejoice," but this translation has been disputed by many. The New American Bible, for example, prefers "Hail."

Full of Grace

Now, in the first part of his salutation, Gabriel does not call her Mary. He gives her a new name. It is "full of grace." In Greek the word is *kecharitomene*, and the Latin Vulgate translation of *kecharitomene* is *gratia plena* (full of grace). It recalls to me the name she said that she prefers "for these times," namely, "Mother of all Nations" and simply "Mary." (see chapter 23).

As St. Alphonsus Liguori, in his classic Marian work *The Glories of Mary,* wrote: "The argument by which it is proved that Mary was more than holy in the first moment of her existence than all the saints together, is founded on her great office of mediatrix of men, with which she was charged from the beginning, and which made it necessary that she should possess a greater treasure of grace from the beginning than all other men together. It is well known with what unanimity theologians and the holy fathers gave to Mary this title of Mediatrix. It is on account of her having obtained salvation for all by her powerful intercession and merit, thereby procuring the great benefit of redemption for the lost world… St. Sophronius,

Patriarch of Jerusalem, has asserted that the reason for which the Archangel Gabriel called her full of grace, 'Hail, full of grace!', was because only limited grace was given to others, but it was given to Mary in all its plenitude. Truly was she full of grace for grace is given to the other saints partially, but the whole plenitude of graces poured itself into Mary. She received this plenitude that she might thus be a worthy mediatrix between God and men, and by whom heaven and earth are brought together and united."

It is noteworthy that none of the great women of the Old Testament has been called *"full of grace."* "This solemn and unparalleled salutation," said Pope Pius IX, "heard at no other time, shows the *Mother of God* as the seat of all divine graces, and as adorned with all the gifts of the divine Spirit" (*Ineffabilis Deus*). Indeed, most Catholic theologians agree with the Jesuit Suarez in holding that "if we add up all the graces conferred on all the saints and angels in one, it would not equal Mary's grace." Such is the excess of their interpretation of the meaning of "full of grace." May I add that my choice of the word "excess" is in no way intended to mean "undue excess." One can only speak of Her Majesty in superlatives! The great theologian and Doctor of the Church, St. Thomas Aquinas, was equally exuberant: "There is no doubt that the Blessed Virgin received in a supereminent degree the gifts of wisdom, of miracles, and even of prophecy." Augustine also justified the privilege: "We know that she has received such an abundance of grace because she was worthy to conceive and bring forth God." And so, *"full of grace"* she was.

"The Lord is with you," Gabriel later said to her. The *Dominus Tecum (*The Lord is with you) is an expression that is prominent in the vocabulary of the Old Testament. This assurance of God was first given in the promise to Isaac: "Fear not, for *I am with you* and will bless you and multiply your descendants for my servant Abraham's sake" (Genesis 26:24). And to Jacob Yahweh also said: "*I am with you* and will keep you wherever you go... for I will not leave you until I have done that of which I have spoken to you" (Genesis 28:15). When Moses at the burning bush fears going to the Pharaoh, Yahweh also fortifies him: "I am who am... *I will be with you*" (Exodus 3:11-12).

As successor to Moses and the one chosen to lead Israel into the Promised Land, Joshua is also assured: "You shall bring the children of Israel into the land… *I will be with you*" (Deuteronomy 31:23). In similar vein, Gideon, son of Joshua, was called to liberate his people from the Midianites. Yahweh promised: *"I shall be with you* and you will crush Midian as though it were a single man"* (Judges 6:11-17). It came to pass. Jeremiah, too, was called by the Lord to be a prophet to the nations but wished to decline the invitation because he was fearful. But he is consoled by the Lord: *"I am with you* to protect you" (Jeremiah 1:6-8). And so, *"the Lord is with you"* speaks of the protection of God for his chosen ones and not simply his actual presence. It was the divine assurance to those who have been called but who had to put up with difficulties in accepting the mission entrusted to them. It signifies the assistance given by God to the individual whom he deputes to accomplish a great work. And so, when Yahweh is with his people, victory is certain. As the psalm says: "With Yahweh on my side, I fear nothing: what can man do to me?" (Psalm 118:6).

After Gabriel told her that her cousin Elizabeth had also conceived a son in her old age, Mary set out at that time and went as quickly as she could to a town in the hill country of Judah. She went into Zecheriah's house and greeted Elizabeth. Elizabeth was filled with the Holy Spirit and said loudly: *"Of all women you are the most blessed, and blessed is the fruit of your womb"* (Luke 1:39-42*).* The expression *"blessed are you among women"* occurs for the first time in the canticle of Deborah (Judges 5:2-31). It was addressed to Jael, the wife of Heber, the Kenite. Jael it was who took a tent-peg and with a mallet drove a hole right through the temple of another of Israel's dreaded enemies, Sisera. It is this feat that Deborah, one of the judges of Israel, celebrated, saying: "Blessed among women be Jael, blessed among tent-dwelling women" (Judges 5:24). Over a thousand years later, Jael's story will be told afresh in Judith. Judith it was who decapitated the head of Holofernes, the evil henchman of King Nebuchadnezzar of Babylonia, after she had prayed: "Strengthen me O Lord, that I may act according to thy will" (Judith 9:18). Ozias, the prince of the people, then said to her: "Blessed are you, O daughter, by the

Lord, the Most High God, above all women upon the earth" (Judith 13:22-23).

In the New Testament, Luke 1:28 records the words of Gabriel to Mary: "Of all women you are the *most* blessed..." (Jerusalem Bible). In saying that Mary was the not only blessed but the *most* blessed among all women, Luke thereby seems to be pointing out that it is she in whom God will bring the salvation of his people to fulfillment. Once more God made a woman the instrument of victory over Israel's enemies. And so, we see in Jael and Judith heralds of the "woman" of Genesis 3:15, who will crush the head of the greatest enemy of Israel and the world, the serpent we call Satan. Indeed, Mary not only supplants Jael and Judith, she also stands on a higher plain. Mary is the woman *most* blessed among all women because only she was chosen in a unique way to become the *Mother of God* through whom salvation would be wrought. This praise is to be perpetuated down the centuries as Mary prophesized: "From now onwards all generations will call me blessed" (Luke 1:48).

"Blessed is the fruit of your womb," the Ambassador Gabriel said to Mary. Now, the great women of the Old Testament are frequently associated with fruitlessness. Indeed, an "unfruitful womb and dry breasts" (Hosea 9:14) would at first appear to be a sign of divine rejection. The "father of a multitude" of descendants, Abraham himself, and after him, his son Isaac and his grandson Jacob, had wives who were barren. Consider also Rachel with Joseph, Hannah with Samuel, and the parents of Samson. And so, the history of this people, who were to become as numberless as the sands on the seashore and the stars of heaven (Genesis 16:2; 25:21; 29:31) was destined to begin with the very barrenness of Sarah, Rebecca, and Rachel.

It is another example of the "irony" of God, who chooses the foolish things of the world to confound the wise, those whom the world thinks contemptible are the ones that God has chosen—those who are nothing at all to show up those who are everything. (1 Cor. 1:27). And so, God chose the sorrow and humiliation of the childless woman as a setting in which the promise would be fulfilled. As Lucien Deiss said in his book *Mary, Daughter of Sion:* "It is the very barrenness and sorrow of Sarah that God was trying to form into a wellspring of fruitfulness and joy for Abraham. The barren wife becomes the joyful *mother of nations"* (Genesis 17:16). That miraculous fruitfulness of Abraham and Sarah serves as a preparation for the miraculous fruitfulness of Mary, who was to become the *mother of (all) nations* (chapter 23). Sarah was unable to have children because she was barren and had passed the age of child bearing. Mary could not have a child because she "knew not man." Yet it is through Mary that the long series of generations, coming down through the entire history of the chosen people, was brought to final issue in the Son of God.

In Mary, therefore, the ancient prophecy of Moses to the Israelites in the Book of Deuteronomy is to be fulfilled: "As your reward for heeding these decrees and observing them carefully, the Lord, your God, will keep with you the merciful covenant which he promised on oath to your fathers. He will love and bless and multiply you; he will bless the *fruit of your womb…*" (Deuteronomy 7:13).

Gabriel "floats" down towards Mary

He kneels before her

Chapter 4

The Second Eve Says "Yes"

Now, when she recovered her composure and said "yes" to the invitation of Gabriel, God's ambassador, to be the Mother of the Word, the Holy Spirit overshadowed her and she immediately conceived at that moment the God—Man, the second Adam. Redemption had begun. It was the marriage between heaven and earth. The daughter of the Father then became the bride of the Holy Spirit and the mother of the Son. And so, with her, in her, and through her the Holy Spirit produced his most illustrious work, the Incarnation of the Word. The hypostatic union of the Son of God with human nature was accomplished and fulfilled. It was the most important event in human history. God so loved the world that he sent his only begotten son (John 1:4;9). Indeed, God also so loved mankind that he made one of us his mother!

God's promise of Genesis 3:15 was being fulfilled. The first Eve was born out of the rib of the first Adam. The second Adam was born out of the womb of the second Eve. The first Eve said "yes" to Satan and sin. The second Eve said "yes" to Gabriel and God. This Eve knew her Old Testament and the true mission and fate of the promised Redeemer, as written in Psalm 22. In short, she was not cajoled into something about which she was not aware. She knew what being the Mother of the Redeemer would mean and the suffering it would entail, a suffering which was confirmed by Simeon in the Temple: "And a sword will even pierce your soul too" (Luke 2:25).

Indeed, with her consent she played her part in what may be called 'God's conspiracy' to save the world from the dominion of Satan. It was the beginning of the "Good News," but it was bad news for Satan. The Woman of Genesis 3:15 had consented! And with her consent two wondrous things happened. A woman while remaining virgin became a mother, and more wondrous yet, a woman became the mother of her own Creator. As St. Francis of Assisi once said: "O humble sublimity! O sublime humility!" On earth the Word had a mother without a father as in heaven he had a father without a mother.

At that moment 'Infinity' confined himself in the womb of a mere mortal woman and the angels must have gasped in wonderment. The bodiless takes upon himself a body; the invisible makes himself visible; he who is without beginning begins; the Son of God becomes Son of Man, and prophecy is fulfilled: "Sacrifices and offerings you have not desired, but a body you have prepared for me... Lo, I have come to do your will, O God" (Hebrews 10:5-7). She was the sole human parent. No human father was involved and she alone furnished the sacred body of her son. This body would be the instrument of redemption, for redemption was to come from suffering. She gave him his hands and feet which were to be pierced (Psalm 22:16) and the rib cage to be lanced. And just as the Son came eternally from the substance of the Father alone, so, too, in time, he came from the flesh and blood of Mary alone. As Fr. Michael O'Carrol of Dublin so scientifically put it: "His very genetic substance and constitution was Marian. His DNA was totally Marian. He was the first Marian." They both had the bloodline and genes of Abraham and David.

She then became the Womb of God, the House of Gold, the Tabernacle of the Most High, the Ark of the Covenant, or more correctly, the living Ark of the Mediator of the New Covenant. And just as the ancient ark of the Old Testament was covered inside and outside with the purest gold, so is she pure, precious, and regal, for she is the Queen of heaven and earth. The ancient ark was made of an incorruptible acacia wood, so was she incorrupt and incorruptible, and, as the Church teaches, did not experience the corruption of the grave. The ancient ark contained the two tablets of the Law given to Moses on Mt. Sinai, but she contained in her womb, not the tablets of the Law but the Law-giver himself. The ancient ark contained a ciborium with some of the miraculous manna which fell from heaven to feed the Israelites on their journey to the Promised Land. With her "yes," she then contained within her womb, not the bread which the Israelites ate and yet they died, but the true Bread of Life which gives us everlasting life.

Nine months later, she gave birth to the God-Man, the second Adam, "bone of her bones and flesh of her flesh," as the first Adam said about his Eve. There was no room in the inn and so he was born in a humble stable, for where else would a lamb be born, even the Lamb of God, he, who was the most humble of all the lambs? He was born in Bethlehem, and so should it also be, for where else should the Bread of Life be born but in Bethlehem? Bethlehem means "house of bread," and from her breasts she gave milk to this Bread of Life.

The war which Satan started among the angels in heaven is still being fought among men on earth. The mission of the Word was one of "peace." She gave birth to the Prince of Peace and thereby became Her Majesty, the Queen of Peace: "For unto us a child is born, unto us a son is given, ... and his name shall be called Wonder–Counsellor, Almighty God, Eternal–Father, Prince of Peace" (Isaiah 9:6). "And the angels sang: 'Glory to God in the highest and peace on earth to men of good will'" (Luke 2:14). Two thousand years after the birth of the Redeemer that "peace" still eludes us.

Chapter 5

Her Majesty's Magnificat

The Old Testament Hannah, the wife of Elcana, was barren because "the Lord had closed her womb" (1Samuel 1:6), and she prayed to Yahweh: "O Lord of hosts, if only you will look down on the affliction of your servant and will be mindful of me, and not forget your handmaid, and will give to your servant a male child…" (1Samuel 1:11). Yahweh was indeed mindful of Hannah. She gave birth to Samuel, the last of the judges and the first of the prophets. When she came to the Temple to offer and consecrate him, her first-born, to Yahweh, her prayer of thanksgiving was:

> *My heart has rejoiced in the Lord… because I have joy in your salvation. There is none holy as the Lord is… and there is none strong like our God… the bow of the mighty is overcome, and the weak are girth with strength. They that were full before have hired out themselves for bread: and the hungry are filled… The Lord makes poor and makes rich, he humbles and he exalts…(1 Samuel 2:1-10).*

When at the "Visitation," Elizabeth said to Mary that she was "blessed" for trusting that the Lord's words to her would be fulfilled (Luke 1:45), Mary proclaimed and praised the greatness of the Lord in what may be considered the first Christian hymn. It is called the *Magnificat* (Latin for '*magnifies*'), and is the song of thanksgiving *par excellence* in the New Testament. As Pope John Paul II once said: "It is the Song of Songs of the New Testament." It is an echo of Hannah's prayer of thanksgiving in the Old Testament.

> "*Then Mary said: 'My soul magnifies the Lord, and my spirit rejoices in God my saviour; because he has re-*

> *garded the lowliness of his handmaid; for behold, from henceforth all generations shall call me blessed; because he who is mighty has done great things for me, and holy is his name; and his mercy is from generation to generation on those who fear him. He has shown might with his arm, he has scattered the proud in the conceit of their heart. He has put down the mighty from their thrones, and has exalted the lowly. He has filled the hungry with good things, and the rich he has sent away empty. He has given help to Israel, his servant, mindful of his mercy—even as he spoke to our fathers—to Abraham and to his posterity' " (Luke 1:46-55).*

There are passages in the Old Testament in which we encounter this first verse of the Magnificat: My soul magnifies the Lord, and my spirit rejoices in God my saviour; because he has regarded the lowliness of his handmaid. One of them is in the canticle of Habakkuk: "But I will rejoice in Yahweh, I will exult in God my saviour" (Habakkuk 3:18). Another verse in the Old Testament which heralds the "joy" of the first verse of the *Magnificat* is found in the first poem of Isaiah: "I exult for joy in Yahweh, my soul rejoices in my God, for he has clothed me in the garments of salvation..." (Isaiah 61:10).

Mary calls God "her Saviour" for like every other creature she too needs him. She recognizes that God, who has a preferential love for the poor, has chosen the poorest of the poor, herself, a young virgin, to make her his handmaid; she, who dwells in a little unknown village and has neither pride nor power nor riches. And so, the almighty Lord enters into the world through the porchway of humility and poverty.

From henceforth all generations shall call me blessed.

She herself can speak in all humility of how all generations will call her "blessed" for she knows that the blessing would only lead to God and never remain fixed in herself. She knows that the messianic age is beginning in her, and her song of thanksgiving is addressed to Jesus the Saviour whom she is carrying in her womb. It is because of this maternity that generations of *nations* will proclaim her "blessed." In other words, she was fully aware of the greatness of her mission, but at the same time she recognized herself to be "a lowly servant."

But a similar prophecy of "blessedness" was addressed to the entire "people of the promise" by the prophet Malachi. His name means "my messenger." Speaking of Israel, the Book of Malachi reads: "Then all the *nations* will call you *blessed* for you will be a delightful land," said the Lord of hosts" (Malachi 3:12). Was this not a herald of the Woman of Israel and the *Mother of all Nations, Mary*?

> *For he that is mighty has done great things for me and holy is his name.*

Mary is also saying here that her *Magnificat* renders all glory to Holy God for the great things which he has accomplished in her —the incarnation of her Son. She does not claim for herself any merit or glory for that would be contrary to her spirit of poverty and humility. As Leviticus 19:1 states: "Yahweh spoke to Moses; he said 'Be holy, for I, Yahweh your God, am holy.'" And so, "holy is his name."

> *And his mercy is from generation to generation on those who fear him... He has given help to Israel, his servant, mindful of his mercy—even as he spoke to our fathers—to Abraham and to his posterity forever.*

What she is saying is that the God of mercy has come to the help of Israel, his servant, and through Israel, to the help of all mankind. It began with Abraham and by extension all Israel, and through Mary this same mercy is going to be passed on to all the world in Jesus Christ and his body, the Church. It is the old saying: "Salvation comes from the Jews" (John 4:22).

This verse of the *Magnificat* also borrows words from David's psalm: "Bless the Lord; O my soul and all my being, bless his holy name... Merciful and gracious is the Lord, slow to anger and abounding in kindness... But the kindness of the Lord is from eternity to eternity toward those who fear him" (Psalm 103:1-17).

He has shown might with his arm, he has scattered the proud in the conceit of their heart. He has put down the mighty from their thrones, and has exalted the lowly. He has filled the hungry with good things and the rich he has sent away empty.

It may also be said that the Virgin Mary is here preparing us for the entry of Christ in the temple to overturn the tables of the money-changers, and for his grave indictment against the rich, "who already have their human reward." Indeed, the *Magnificat* can be seen as the herald of the eight Beatitudes and that she is thus providing a platform for the Sermon on the Mount in which her Son will proclaim blessedness to the poor, the meek, the afflicted and the needy, to those who show mercy, to the pure, to the peaceful and to the persecuted. Indeed, it is a constant theme in the Gospel.

And so, this canticle of Mary is ingeniously replete with biblical references from the Old Testament. It gives witness to one who is living in close contact with the history of her people and with the Scripture with which she is so familiar. She is "full of grace" and undoubtedly she was given the gifts of extraordinary wisdom and knowledge and therefore must have known the Scriptures page by page, verse by verse. Indeed, here we see how well-versed in the Hebrew Bible she was, and how deeply her whole being is rooted in the themes of the Old Testament. She expresses her joy in a selection of passages borrowed from the Scriptures. She tells us the story of the New Testament with the text of the Old.

Mary's magnificent *Magnificat* can therefore be seen as composed of three parts: a song of praise, a song of the poor of Yahweh, and the fulfillment of the promise made to Abraham. In fact, the whole meaning of the *Magnificat* may be summed up in one theme: God loves the poor, the Messiah wills to be born of a poor and humble Virgin, and his mercy is limitless.

And now, a surprise for many modern-day Protestants, many of whom do not seem to know that the great Protestant reformer himself, Martin Luther, had a deep appreciation of Mary's *Magnificat*. In his commentary on the *Magnificat,* Luther wrote: "O blessed Virgin and Mother of God, how have you been able to be considered as nothing, and disdained as of little consequence and yet God has nonetheless regarded you with all his grace and all his riches, and accomplished in you such mighty things? Yet, you are blessed from this hour and unto all eternity, you who have found such a God..." (*Mariae Lobgesang,* Wittenberg, March 10, 1521).

Karl Barth (1886-1968), the celebrated Swiss Protestant theologian, also added his praise of Mary: "'Behold from henceforth all generations shall call me blessed.' What unspeakable grandeur there is in this encounter!... If ever in the history of the world anything of great importance has taken place it is in this regard. Here there is no hesitation, no fear, no light, which runs the risk of being extinguished, but rather, certitude. Victory has already been won. Our calling is to be on the side of Mary... We have only one thing to do, like Mary: to let God act. Let it be unto me as you have said" (Bible Studies in the First Chapter of St. Luke in *Foi et vie,* 85-6, p. 509-10, 1936).

Chapter 6

The Redeemer and Coredemptrix on Calvary

Thirty years later, the mother and her son were invited to a wedding banquet but the bride and groom were embarrassed. There was no more wine. The guests were obviously enjoying themselves immensely! "They have no wine," she told her son. *"Woman, what have I to do with thee? My hour is not yet come,"* he replied to her. She, as it were, disregarded him and turned to the servants and said: "Do whatever he tells you." It was then that he turned water, not only into wine, but into the best wine—six jars full, about 120 gallons of it (John 2:1-11). However, she realized full well that by initiating his public ministry she would be hastening what she always feared most—his Calvary. Nonetheless, undoubtedly inspired by the Holy Spirit, she knew that the time had come. It was as though heavenly protocol demanded that it was his mother who should initiate his public ministry and hence the road which would lead her to the foot of the Cross. It was then that she initiated her role as Mediatrix with the one Mediator and as Advocate for the people.

Maundy Thursday Night

Three years later, as his ministry was approaching its end and at another banquet which we call the Last Supper, he performed his last major miracle on earth. This time he changed wine into his precious blood and bread into his sacred body: *"Take this and eat. This is my body which will be given up for you... Take this and drink. This is the cup of my blood, the blood of the new and everlasting covenant. It will be shed for you and for all so that sins will be forgiven"* (Matthew 26:26-28). It was to be the fulfillment of Psalm 40 as quoted in Paul's sermon to the Hebrews (Hebrews 10:5–

7): "Bulls' blood and goats' blood are useless for taking away sins and this is what he said on coming into the world. *You who wanted no sacrifice or oblation, prepared a body for me. You took no pleasure in holocausts or sacrifices for sin, then I said, as was written of me in the scroll of the book, 'God, here I am. I am coming to do your will.'"*

Now, she is hardly mentioned in the Gospels for it is the Gospel of her son; the Gospel of Jesus, not of Mary. She is not there, for example, on Mount Tabor where he manifested himself in all his glory to Peter, James and John (Mark 9:1-8). That was not her place. She is also not there on that Sunday when he entered Jerusalem on a humble donkey and the crowds waved palms and shouted hosannas (Luke 19:37). This too was not her place. Her place was on Calvary where she stood at the foot of the Cross for three hours and watched the bloody immolation of her Lamb, *Stabat mater dolorosa*, we say in Latin. The sacrifice of Isaac was renewed on Calvary. But whereas on the Mount of Moriah God supplied the victim (a ram) to be substituted for Isaac and spared both the life of the son and the hearts of his father Abraham and his mother Sarah, on Calvary God fully accepted both the sacrifice of his son and the broken heart of his mother, Mary, the second Eve. The ewe witnessed her Lamb who was cruelly and ruthlessly slaughtered while she stood helplessly by.

But the traditional, motionless and bloodless figure of Christ on the Cross, hanging in churches and in millions of homes, belies the true picture, plight, and punishment of that day, and fails to depict the unspeakable suffering of the living Christ 2000 years ago. It was a skin-torn, nay, ripped body; a body pinned to bars of wood and over-stretched with its joints pulled out of their sockets. It was the lacerated body of a man so immobilized and nailed, that he was able to raise his torso to breathe only by using the nail, which pierced his unbearably painful and spastic feet as a fulcrum for frequent elevations and descents. It was a cruelty which wouldn't be done to a dog and unpitifully witnessed by the jeering soldiers and Jewish high priests. With each forced inspiration the muscles between his ribs became increasingly strained, sunkened and weakened, so much so that his ribs could be clearly seen and counted. It was a pallid body, drained of all blood and serum, and a tongue and palate so dry that he was barely able to shout in a throaty voice: "I thirst!"

Now, I do not for one moment believe that this cry, as so many writers have tried to interpret, was all about his "thirst for souls." The man on that Cross was thirsty from utter and extreme dehydration. It was a physical thirst that few have ever experienced. And what did they offer him for his thirst? Vinegar! It was the price he had to pay for being the Redeemer. No bones were broken as was decreed by Yahweh for the paschal lamb which was to be eaten before the exodus from Egypt, but the nerves were pierced by the nails and the persistent shooting electric-like pains up and down the limbs were extremely excruciating. The torture endured for three long hours and it must have seemed that it would never end. Eventually, with his respiratory muscles fatigued from painful spasms and over-burdened with the forced inspirations to survive, he inspired no more. And expired! But not before shouting with surprising and inexplicable loudness for a dying man: "It is finished!" What he was saying to his God was: "Father, I have done your will. I have paid the ransom for man's sins. It is all over. No more suffering!"

But it was all prophesied in Psalm 22, 1000 years previously: "My God, my God, why have you deserted me? How far from saving me, the words I groan! Yet here am I, now more worm than man, scorn of mankind, jest of the people, all who see me jeer at me, they toss their heads and sneer, 'He relied on Yahweh, let Yahweh save him! If Yahweh is his friend, let Him rescue him!' Yet you drew me out of the womb, you entrusted me to my mother's breasts; placed on your lap from my birth, from my mother's womb you have been my God. Do not stand aside: trouble is near, I have no one to help me! A herd of bulls surrounds me, strong bulls of Bashan [a people of considerable physique who were in Palestine before Abraham] close in on me; their jaws are agape for me, like lions tearing and roaring. I am like water draining away, my bones are all disjointed, my heart is like wax, melting inside me; my palate is drier than a potsherd and my tongue is stuck to my jaw. A pack of dogs surround me, a gang of villains closes me in; they pierce my hands and feet and leave me lying in the dust of death. I can count every one of my bones, and there they glare at me, gloating; they divide my garments among them and cast lots for my clothes" (Psalm 22:1-18).

Close to his death, he made his last will and testament and bequeathed his mother to be our mother also, our spiritual mother. *"Woman, behold your son... Behold your mother,"* he said first to his mother and then to John (John 19:26-27). *"Woman, behold your son,"* he said to her. He was obviously referring to her as the "woman" first spoken of in Genesis 3:15: "I will put enmity between you and the woman, and between your seed and her seed; she will crush your head." Indeed, it was on this hill called Calvary that this verse in Genesis was fulfilled. The word Calvary is from the Latin word *Calvaria*, meaning skull. The hill was also called Golgatha, the Hebrew word from the Greek *Kranion,* a skull. The Cross of the Redeemer was firmly crushed into the ground. And so, the "skull" was "crushed" by the man on the Cross, the Redeemer ("her seed"), and beneath that rugged Cross was the Coredemptrix; one suffering woman, suffering *with* God who in turn was suffering *for* mankind and *from* them. Redemption begun at the Annunciation was completed on Calvary. It was 3:00 p.m. on a Friday. It was an hour and a day to remember. But few of us do.

World War I ended at 11:00 a.m. on November 11, 1918, and in the United States, November 11 is set aside as Armistice Day to remember the sacrifices that men and women made in World War I in order to ensure lasting *peace*. Indeed, Congress voted Armistice Day a federal holiday and at 11:00 in the morning, most Americans observe a moment of silence, remembering those who fought for *peace.* Yet in that country and in most other countries in the world, the memory of the greatest sacrifice and death of the *Prince of Peace* on that "Good" Friday is not honoured with a solemn holiday. O, such ingratitude!

But what humility! He chose to minimize the account of his suffering and his excruciating passion and, guided by the Holy Spirit, Mathew, Mark, Luke and John all summarily said: "They crucified him... then Jesus in a loud voice said: "Father, into your hands I commend my spirit." And so, one would have to read the private revelations of Maria Valtorta, Catherine Emmerich or Maria de Jesus of Agreda who were given somewhat detailed visions of his vicious execution and savage slaughter.

The Co-Sufferer

But it was as though God had predetermined that one had to be a "Mary" to have the *privilege* of standing beneath the Cross. John speaks of that congregation: "Standing by the cross were his mother (Mary), and his mother's sister, Mary the wife of Clopas, and Mary Magdalene" (John 19:25). Redemption had to come from suffering, and so, he needed a body to suffer. His mother gave him that body. No human father was involved in that conception. *"You who wanted no sacrifice or oblation, prepared a body for me"* (Hebrews 10:5). On that joyous day when he was born she wrapped his tiny body in swaddling clothes and placed him in his crib (Luke 2:12). But on that Friday at the foot of the Cross, thirty-three years later, she received a body, tattered and torn and swaddled with blood as he took upon himself the sins of the world. It was not a pretty sight but neither is sin in the eyes of God! It was the blood of the new and everlasting covenant which was shed for all so that sins may be forgiven. Her suffering too was minimized.

Words cannot fully describe and adequately measure Mary's anguish on that day. Perhaps it can be appreciated somewhat better if every mother were to contemplate her own son on the cross in place of the son of Mary. Yet, if there were a thousand such mothers standing at the feet of a thousand crosses bearing their thousand crucified sons, the sum total of their anguish could not in any way measure the pain and suffering of that *Mother of Sorrows* on that hill on that Friday that some men call "Good." She too was being crucified! So said, in 1373, Lady Julian of Norwich, in her book *Revelations of Divine Love* which records her privileged visions from God, says of Mary: "I saw part of the love and suffering of Our Lady Saint Mary, for she and Christ were so joined in love that the greatness of their love caused the greatness of her grief... for the higher, the greater, and the sweeter the love is, so the greater the grief it is for those who love, to see their loved one suffer."

What is also not appreciated by many is that spiritual and mental suffering can be as agonizing as physical pain, and at times even more so. For example, the emotional pain of a patient suffering from depression and the spiritual dryness of the "desert," the so-called "dark night of the soul," which a few prayful people experience, can parallel or exceed physical pain, albeit measured on different scales and parameters of human suffering. There are also many cases, for example, of elderly spouses of happy and long-standing marriages, dying within hours or days of each other from the sheer anguish of the death of their loved one and from the unbearable and emotional pain of the separation. So it would have been with the *Mother of Love* on that Friday had she not been preserved from death by God. Indeed, the Church recognizes her as a martyr, the Queen of the martyrs, but one who was not allowed to die!

Neither did Matthew, Mark, Luke or John record the great anguish of the mother during the Friday evening, Saturday and early Sunday morning following the Crucifixion. In her book *the Poem of the Man-God* Maria Valtorta relates what she saw when they took him down from the cross: "When on the ground, they would like to lay him on a sheet that they had spread for him, but Mary wants him. She opened her mantle, letting it hang on one side, and she sits with her knees rather apart to form a cradle for her Jesus. He is now in his mother's lap. With a trembling hand she parts his ruffled hair. She tidies it and weeps. Speaking in a low voice, her tears drop on the cold body covered with blood. She begins to clean and dry his body on which endless tears are dropping. And while doing so her hand touches the huge gash in his chest and enters almost completely into the large hole of the wound. She utters a loud cry. A sword seems to split her heart. She shouts and throws herself on her son and she seems also dead..." Valtorta then describes the vision she saw of what happened on early Sunday morning. Joseph had already died and now the God-Man, her son, was murdered and she was the only one left of the Holy Family. For her it must have been the desolation of desolations. Valtorta described Mary's longing for the company of St. Joseph to console her during those long three days when all around her, even the disciples, did not believe that he would resurrect. "Let me lean on a Joseph!... O, happy Joseph, who has not seen this day," she moaned. Valtorta then recorded her visions of the first meeting of Jesus and his mother after the Resurrection:

> *"Mary is prostrated with her face on the floor. She looks like a poor wretch. Suddenly the closed window is opened with a violent banging of the heavy shutters and with the first ray of the sun, Jesus enters. Mary, who has been shaken by the noise and has raised her head to see which wind has opened the shutters, sees her radiant son, handsome, infinitely more handsome than he was before suffering, smiling, dressed in a white garment... He calls her, stretching out his hands: 'Mother!' And he bends over his mother and places his hands under her bent elbows and lifts her up. He presses her to his heart and kisses her... With a cry, she flings her arms around his neck and she embraces and kisses him, laughing in her weeping. She kisses his forehead, where there are no longer any wounds; his head no longer unkempt and bloody; his shining eyes, his healed cheeks, his mouth no longer swollen. She then takes his hands and kisses their backs and palms, their radiant wounds, and she suddenly bends down to his feet and uncovers them from under his bright garment and kisses them. She kisses and kisses him and Jesus caresses her.*

Valtorta continued:

> *"Jesus speaks now: 'It is all over, mother. You no longer have to weep over your son. The trial is over. Redemption has taken place. Mother, thanks for conceiving me. Thanks for looking after me, for helping me in life and in death... I heard your prayers come to me. They have been my strength in my grief. They came to me on the Cross... They have been seen and heard by the Father and by the Spirit who smiled at them as if they were the most beautiful flowers and the sweetest song born in Paradise... These past days*

you have been alone, but that sorrow of yours was required for the Redemption... I will come to fetch you to make Paradise more beautiful... Mother, your kisses are a blessing, and my peace to you as a companion. Goodbye.' And Jesus disappeared in the sunshine that streams down from the early morning clear sky."

In an apparition to the saintly Berthe Petit, a visionary who was highly respected in ecclesiastic and lay societies in Belgium in the 1920s, Jesus is said to have exalted the merits of the sorrow of his mother, saying: "The title 'Immaculate' belongs to the whole being of my mother and not specifically to her heart. This title flows from my gratuitous gift to the Virgin who has given me birth. However, my mother has *acquired* for her heart the title 'Sorrowful' by sharing generously in all the sufferings of my heart and my body from the crib to the Cross. There is not one of these sorrows which did not pierce the heart of my mother. Living image of my crucified body, her virginal flesh bore the invisible marks of my wounds as her heart felt the sorrows of my own. Nothing could ever tarnish the incorruptibility of her Immaculate Heart. The title of *'Sorrowful'* belongs, therefore, to the heart of my mother, and, more than any other, this title is dear to her because it springs from the union of her heart with mine in the redemption of humanity. This title has been acquired by her through her full participation in my Calvary, and it should precede the gratuitous title *'Immaculate'* which my love bestowed upon her by a singular privilege."

The Redeemer and Coredemptrix on Calvary

The anguish of the Mother

A sword pierced her heart

The seven sorrows (swords)

Chapter 7

Old Testament Heralds of Mary

Deborah and Jael

Let us see how Mary was foreshadowed by some of the great women of the Old Testament. Now, in their prosperity and contentment, the Israelites gradually forgot the goodness of the God who had brought them out of the land of Egypt, and they turned away from him to bow down to the gods of the people who lived around them. These were the false gods called Baal and Asherah. In worshiping them "the children of Israel did evil in the sight of the Lord," and the Lord made them captives of Jabin, king of Canaan. His army was commanded by a great general called Sisera, who had 900 chariots, and for twenty years he cruelly oppressed the children of Israel.

At that time, before there were any kings, Israel was ruled by "judges." It is said that God called them to lead his people whenever they were in danger from their enemies. However, they were more than judges in today's meaning of the term for they were chieftains and heroes as well, and their influence was felt mainly in war. One of the judges of Israel was a woman called Deborah (about 1125 BC). Men at that time did not believe that women should lead the people and the only woman in the Bible who was placed at the height of political power by the common consent of the people was Deborah. Indeed, there are few women in the history of Israel who have ever attained the public dignity and supreme authority of Deborah. She may be likened to Joan of Arc of later times, who rode in front of the French soldiers and led them to victory.

Deborah's story is told in the first part of the Book of Judges, when the Israelites were about to be attacked by the Canaanites. They were fearful of Sisera and his army of 900 chariots of iron while they had none. When they paled with fear, Deborah sent for a man called Barak from his home in Kedes. He was one of Israel's most capable military men. She let him know that she was not afraid of Sisera and his army, neither was she afraid of his 900 chariots She said to him: "Go to Mount Tabor with 10,000 men and I would deliver Sisera with all his soldiers and chariots into your hands." Barak gave a conditional acceptance: "I would go if you accompany me, but not otherwise." Spoken by a man to a woman, this is one of the most unusual passages in the Bible. Deborah agreed to go with him, but she prophesied and warned him that he would gain no honour from the expedition for the Lord will sell Sisera into the hands of a woman. It demonstrates a general with confidence in a woman who had risen to a high place in Israel, largely because of one quality, her abiding faith in God.

At the utterance of Deborah, the tribes under Barak's command rose up against their Canaanite oppressors led by Sisera. The armies met on the slopes of Mount Tabor and Sisera and his chariots were defeated. Sisera himself, however, succeeded in escaping the slaughter. He fled on foot from the battlefield to Kenite territory (the Kenite tribe was a nomadic community, but were well absorbed by Judah). When he reached the tent of Heber the Kenite, he went to Jael, Heber's wife, seeking a hiding place. Jael gave him a warm welcome, but after he had fallen asleep in her tent, battle-weary and drowsy, she stealthily crept up to him, took a tent-peg, grabbed a mallet, and drove a hole right through his temple. On that day Israel was protected by the hand of a woman exactly as prophesied by Deborah.

To celebrate this great victory, the ode of Deborah, one of the earliest martial songs in biblical history, was composed: "That warriors in Israel unbound their hair, that the people came forward with a will, for this bless Yahweh... Dead, dead were Israel's villages until you rose up, O Deborah; you rose up a mother in Israel... Blessed be Jael among women; among all women that dwell in tents may she be blessed... She struck Sisera, crushed his head, pierced his temple and shattered it..." (Judges 5:1-31). In the song, Deborah is called "a mother in Israel." She brought peace to the land for forty years. And so, we see in Jael a herald of the woman of Genesis 3:15, who will crush the head of her enemy, Satan. I am referring to Mary, the Woman of Israel, the Mother of all Nations and Queen of Peace, who will usher in the reign of her Son, the King of all Nations and the Prince of Peace.

Judith

The Book of Judith is the history of another victory won by the chosen people over its enemies, thanks to the intervention of another woman. Over a thousand years later, around 125 BC, Jael's story will be told afresh. Judith (her name means "the Jewess") would supplant Jael, but the message would be the same. Two sides are in conflict, that of the people of God and that of the pagan *nation*s. God's side seems doomed to extermination, but he intervenes anew to save his people through the hands of a woman.

An Assyrian general, Holofernes, the evil henchman of King Nebuchadnezzar of Babylonia, whose ambition was to lay the whole world at the feet of Nebuchadnezzar and to destroy all other religions, marched against Palestine and laid siege to the city of Bethulia. The city's water supply failed and the people of the city were in such despair that they decided to surrender if no help came within five days. But there lived in that city a young and pious widow named Judith. When she heard that the city would be given up, she called together the leaders and warned them that they were committing a great sin by not trusting in God. She urged them to do penance for this sin. She then went home, put ashes on her head as a sign of penance, and prayed to God for help, asking him to make her strong and brave so that she might save her people.

She then dressed herself in her finest clothes and with one of her maids she went to the enemy camp of the Assyrians and asked to be led to the general. When Holofernes saw her, he was so attracted by her beauty that he commanded that she be allowed to go and come as she wished. Each night Judith prayed that God would guide her in this dangerous work. On the fourth night the general had a dinner for his friends. Lusting for her, he also invited Judith. However, after the feast, the general, overcome with wine, fell into a deep sleep. Judith waited till everybody had left. She stood weeping and praying: "Strengthen me, O Lord, that I may act according to your will." Then taking out the sword of Holofernes, she cut off his head, and gave it to her maid to carry in a bag. They hurriedly left the camp and returned to Bethulia.

In the morning the people of Bethulia hung the head of Holofernes upon the city walls, took up arms and went against the Assyrian camp. When the Assyrians saw the headless body of their general, they were filled with terror and fled. The army of Israel then took courage and attacked and defeated their leaderless enemies. Judith had saved her people.

When Judith brought the head of Holofernes to Bethulia, the song of thanksgiving will take up the theme of Deborah's canticle: "May you be blessed, my daughter, by God Most High, beyond all women on earth; and may God be blessed, the Creator of heaven and earth, by whose guidance you cut off the head of the leader of our enemies…" (Judith 13:23-24). Joachim, the High Priest, and the elders of the Israelites also praised her: "You are the glory of Jerusalem! You are the great pride of Israel! You are the highest honour of our race. By doing all this with your own hand you have deserved well of Israel, and God has approved what you have done. May you be blessed by the Lord Almighty in all the days to come!" (Judith 15:9-11).

The evil Holofernes was decapitated by Judith, and so, once more the Old Testament gives us a prototype of Mary, the woman of Genesis 3:15, the greatest of all the women in the Bible, who was destined to crush the head of the most evil one of all, the ancient serpent. It is the woman "and her seed" who will crush the head of the serpent, as promised by God in the Garden of Eden. But wasn't "her seed," the Redeemer, foreshadowed several centuries earlier by David when he decapitated the head of the great giant Goliath with the Philistine's own sword? Old Testament Heralds of Mary (1 Samuel 17:49-51).

Esther

Finally, let us turn to Esther, the great Jewish Queen of Persia. The Hebrew name of the Queen of Persia was Haddassah, meaning "myrtle." Her Persian name, Esther, means "star." Indeed, the ancient writers' opinion of Esther's importance to the story in the Book of Esther becomes apparent, for in this short book of the Old Testament her name appears no less than fifty-five times. Only Sarah, whose name appears as Sarah thirty-five times and as Sarai sixteen times, comes close to this record.

The Book of Esther, like that of Judith, also tells of the deliverance of the nation by the intervention of a woman. The Jews were living in exile in Persia after Jerusalem was sacked by the Babylonians, but they had many enemies. At that time the singular beauty of Esther, a Jewess, attracted the Persian king, Ahasuerus (485-464 BC), and she was taken into his palace, succeeding Vashti as queen. The king, however, did not know that she was Jewish. The Book relates that Haman, a high official in the king's administration, akin to prime minister, resolved to wipe out all the members of the Jewish race throughout the empire of Persia. The date chosen by lot (pur) for this extermination was the 13th day of the 12th month, which is the Hebrew month of Adar. In fact, Haman has been described by modern Jewish writers as a typical Hitler, manifesting an intense hatred for the Jews.

Haman convinced the king of this necessity and the decree for the extermination was signed in the name of King Ahasuerus, sealed with his ring, and letters were sent by runners to every province of the realm, ordering the destruction, slaughter and annihilation of all Jews, young and old, women and children. It was to be on the one day, the 13th day of the 12th month. When Queen Esther's maids told her about it, she was totally overcome with grief. She then sent a message to her uncle Mordecai, a fellow Jew and Benjamite, who was also hated by Haman, and said to him: "Go and assemble all the Jews now in Susa and fast for me. Do not eat or drink, day or night, for three days. For my part, I and my maids would keep the same fast, after which I shall go to the king in spite of the law; and if I perish, I perish." In those days no one could approach the king's chambers without his invitation, not even the queen.

On the third day, when she had finished praying, she took off her mourning attire and dressed herself in her full splendour. Radiant as she was, she then appeared in the presence of the king, whose anger eventually turned into a milder spirit. Although Esther risked her life by appearing before him unannounced, he was so impressed by her beauty and her courage that he rescinded the order and Haman was hanged. Moreover, the Jews were allowed to avenge themselves on the guilty Persians. The king's command and decree came into force on the 13th day of the 12th month, Adar, and so, the day on which the enemies of the Jews had hoped to crush them produced the very opposite effect. It was the Jews who crushed their enemies through the intervention of a woman.

And so, as St. Augustine once said: "The New Testament lies hidden in the Old and the Old Testament is revealed in the New. Through the "Intervention" of the greatest of all women, Satan's head was crushed as prophesied by God in Genesis 3:15.

A Gustave Doré Illustration of Deborah (Judges 5:1-31)

Old Testament Heralds of Mary

Jael and the Slain Sisera (Judges 4:21)

Judith with the Head of Holofernes (Judith 13:8)

Her Majesty Mary, Queen of Peace

David Decapitates Goliath (1 Samuel 17:49-51)

Chapter 8

431 AD. The First Marian Dogma

Four centuries after the death of Our Lord, the First Marian dogma was defined. Its history began at the Annunciation and was proclaimed by Elizabeth, having been inspired by the Holy Spirit: "And how does this happen to me that the *mother of my Lord* shall come to me," asks Elizabeth (Luke 1:43). Apart from this passage in Luke, the biblical basis for this title, *"mother of my Lord,"* is found in Matthew 1:23: "Behold the virgin shall be with child and bear a son, and they shall call him Emmanuel — a name which means 'God is with us.'" It is also in Luke 1:35: "And so, the child will be holy, and will be called Son of God," and in Galatians 4:4: "But when the appointed time came, God sent his son, born of woman." In short, the Scriptures clearly testify that Mary is indeed the *Mother of God*.

This title *Mother of God* was not rejected by anyone until 428 AD. On April 10, 428 AD, Archbishop Nestorius, the newly elected patriarch of Constantinople, began to teach that Mary was indeed the Mother of Christ but not the Mother of God. He used the term Christokos (Mother of Christ) for Mary and not Theotokos (God bearer). The borderlines were clearly drawn when one of his priests, Anastasius, whom he took with him from Antioch, preached in December 428 AD: "Let no one call Mary 'Theotokos,' for Mary was but a woman, and it is impossible that God should be born from a woman." This teaching Nestorius publicly approved and he himself preached. However, the Church's earliest teaching, based on Scripture, was that Jesus was one person, fully human (Hebrews 2:14,17) and yet divine or "true God" (1 John 5:20). Now, since this one person was born of Mary, she is truly the mother of one divine person.

And so, the one Jesus was both God and man, and he was referred to in each of these roles separately as the "Son of God" and the "Son of Man" at different times and in different contexts. With this distinction, we can thus say that in one role he created Mary and in another he was procreated by her, that is to say, in his divine nature he produced her but in his human nature he was produced by her. She was the mother of the divinity of Jesus but the mother of the divine person, Jesus. He was the divine eternal person, the Word, who in time assumed a human nature of Mary, but remained the Word, uniting in himself his divine nature and his incarnate human nature.

But how can God have a mother, some critics ask, since that would imply that she is older than God? Sure, they say, she was only Christ's mother. However, as divine, the second Person of the Trinity had *no beginning*, but an eternal past, yet as human, he had a beginning *in time* in the womb of Mary. Now, that same Jesus claimed that he had existed before Abraham. "Before Abraham was I am" (John 8:58), and even before the world (John 17:5). Obviously, Mary did not exist before God. Jesus is the Son of God from all *eternity,* who also became the Son of Mary in *time* and for eternity. And so, whereas she gave him his flesh and blood, his divinity was given by the Father. The one Jesus was therefore both God and man.

On June 22, 431 AD, the third ecumenical Council was held at Ephesus, over which St. Cyril presided. Nestorius was deposed and excommunicated, his Christological doctrine was condemned. In the city of Ephesus the faithful waited anxiously outside the hall while the Council Fathers, one hundred and fifty to two hundred bishops, deliberated inside regarding the role of Mary, whether she could truly be accepted in faith as the Mother of God. The concern involved faith in Jesus as the Son of God, the Word made flesh, even more than it involved Mary, for Mary's role is always in relationship to Jesus. When it was announced to the people waiting outside that Mary must truly be believed to be the Mother of God (Theotokos), the joy of the people was expressed in cheers, and dancing ensued on the streets of Ephesus. The decision taken at Ephesus was explicitly promulgated as dogma in 451 AD by the

Council of Chalcedon.

The controversy did not surface again in Christianity until some time *after* the Reformation. But the three great pillars of the Reformation, Luther, Calvin and Zwingli, all accepted this doctrine wholeheartedly. Indeed, most Protestants have been surprised when told that although the founders of Protestantism rejected certain Catholic doctrines, they actually insisted on honouring Mary as *Mother of God*. For example, in 1539, Luther wrote in a treatise entitled *Of Councils and Churches*: "Hence this Council (of Ephesus) did not establish anything new in the faith, but defended the ancient faith against the new vagueness of Nestorius. Indeed, the article according to which Mary is *Mother of God* has been in the Church from the beginning and has not been newly produced by the Council but on the contrary is contained in the Gospel and in the Holy Scripture..." (Martin Luther's works, Weimar, 50:591, 22-592). Huldrych Zwingli, the Swiss Reformer, also wrote in 1524: "I have never thought, still less taught, or declared publicly, anything concerning the subject of the ever Virgin Mary, mother of our salvation, which could be considered dishonourable, impious, unworthy or evil... I hope this is sufficient to have made plain to pious and simple Christians my clear conviction on the matter of the *Mother of God*."

Timothy Ware, an Orthodox priest, once spoke of the similarity between the Roman Catholic Church and the Orthodox Church with respect to Mary as *Mother of God*. He said: "Orthodox, like Roman Catholics, venerate the *Mother of God* but in no sense do the members of either Church regard her as a fourth person of the Trinity nor do they assign to her the worship due to God alone... We honour Mary because she is the *Mother of God*. We do not venerate her in isolation but because of her relation to Christ. But the maternal rights exercised by Mary over her son are much more of a privilege than a right, and the authority which she has over Jesus is only an authority conceded to her out of his goodness, kindness, love and humility. As Son of God, begotten from all eternity, Jesus does not and cannot depend on any creature, not even his mother, but in his human nature he is the servant of his father and subject to the authority of his mother."

And so, according to St. Eiphanus of Salamis in Cyprus: "Let Mary be honoured, but let the Lord be worshipped." Indeed, in heaven Jesus obeys his own fourth commandment and honours her. Indeed, in heaven, the Son of God still calls her "Mother."

Chapter 9

649 AD. The Second Marian Dogma

In 649 AD, the Lateran Council defined the second Marian dogma—the Perpetual Virginity of the Blessed Virgin Mary. While hardly any Catholic challenges the doctrine of Mary's virginity and the miraculous virgin birth of Jesus since it is clearly detailed in Matthew 1:18-25, affirmed by Luke 1:27, stated by Mary herself (Luke 1:34), and acknowledged by the archangel Gabriel (Luke 1:35-37), there are those who still debate the doctrine of Mary's *perpetual* virginity out of an unfortunate lack of knowledge of the Bible, or a deliberate obstinacy in not wishing to acknowledge the truth in their prejudiced commitment to dishonour *"the Mother of the Lord."*

In calling Mary "ever virgin," Catholic and Orthodox tradition is saying that after conceiving Jesus in virginity, Mary always remained a virgin, abstaining from all conjugal relations. It also implies that the birth of Jesus left intact the virginity of his mother. On the other hand, when Protestants use the term the Virgin Mary, they mean that she was a virgin only *until* the birth of Jesus. They believe that she later had children, all those called "the brethren of the Lord" in the Bible.

Now, the Hebrew and Aramaic languages spoken by Christ and his disciples do not have two separate words for "brother," "cousin," or "near-relative." For example, in the original Hebrew translation, Lot is called "Abraham's brother" (Genesis 14:14). Yet we know that Lot was Abraham's nephew (Genesis 11:27). Indeed, the Jews used the word "brother" for any near-relative, without necessarily meaning "sibling." From the fourth century, almost all great religious teachers agreed with the statements of the Second Council of Constantinople (353 AD) regarding Mary's perpetual virginity. All these brilliant scholars knew that the Greek words for "brothers and sisters" were also used to refer to other close relatives—cousins, nephews, nieces, et cetera.

Moreover, in the Scriptures Mary is never called the mother of these "brothers of the Lord." There is also no mention of them in the episode of the three days' loss of Jesus at the age of twelve, yet it would have been unthinkable for a Jewish mother to leave her other children at home so that she might travel for this great feast in Jerusalem. Nor would Mary have been consigned to the care of John by Jesus on Calvary (John 19:27) if there were close siblings who could and should take care of her. All of this, and much more circumstantial evidence, confirm that the "brothers and sisters" of Jesus were kinsfolk but not siblings, thus indirectly supporting the ancient tradition of Mary's continued virginity after the birth of Jesus.

The womb that bore the God Incarnate was exclusively reserved for him alone. In fact, God also saw it fit to highlight his Son's divinity by a certain exclusivity in several aspects of his life. For instance, in manifesting his palm-strewn entrance into Jerusalem, Jesus chose to ride on a colt that *no one* had ever ridden (Luke 19:30). He was laid in a tomb that *no one* had been laid in before (John 19:41). And so, he chose the womb of a virgin who had never known man, and who would bear *no one* but himself. This sacred vessel, therefore, that bore the Messiah was to be reserved for him alone. How else could it have been! It was the Tabernacle of the Most High.

Theologians also believe that this was foretold in the Old Testament passage in Ezekiel 44:2-3: "This gate shall remain shut, for the Lord, the God of Israel, has entered it. The Prince himself is the only one who sits inside the gateway." It is noteworthy that this was the eastern gate about which Ezekiel spoke, and is the one that led directly to the sanctuary of the temple, for "the glory of the Lord entered the temple through the gate facing east" (Ezekiel 40:6). Significantly, this Eastern Golden Gate of Jerusalem is still closed to this day!

But the fundamentalists also argue their point on the verse: "And he knew her not *till* she brought forth her first-born son" (Matthew 1:25). They argue that the natural inference from "till" is that Joseph and Mary lived together afterwards as husband and wife in the usual sense, and had several children. But *"until"* or *"till"* in the Bible simply means that "something" did not happen up to a certain point. It certainly does not imply that the something did happen later, which is the modern sense of the term. In fact, if the modern sense of the word is forced on the Bible, some ridiculous meanings result. Consider this line, for example: "Michal, the daughter of Saul, had no children *until* the day of her death" (2 Samuel 6:23). Are we, therefore, to assume that she had children *after* her death? Then there was the burial of Moses. About the location of his grave, it was said that "no man knows *until* this present day" (Deuteronomy 34:6). But we do know that no one has known *since* that day either. These examples could be multiplied. In short, it should be clear that nothing at all can be proved from the use of the word *"till"* in Matthew 1:25. Recent translations give a better sense of the verse: "He had no relations with her at any time before she bore a son" (New American Bible) and: "He had not known her when she bore a son" (Knox translation).

They also ask, bringing up their second point, why then would Jesus be called first-born? Does this not mean that there must have been a "second born," etc? However, under the Mosaic Law, it was the "first-born" son that was to be sanctified (Exodus 34:20). To the first born came the birthright. And so, the first male child of a marriage was termed the "first-born" *even if* he turned out to be the only child of the marriage. This usage is aptly illustrated by a funerary inscription discovered in Egypt. The inscription refers to a woman who died during the birth of her "first-born"!

At the time of the Annunciation the Scripture says: "She was found to be with child through the Holy Spirit" (Matthew 1:18). "She has conceived what is in her by the Holy Spirit" (Matthew 1:20). "The Holy Spirit will come upon you," the angel answered, "and the power of the Most High will cover you with its shadow. And so, the child will be holy and will be called the son of God" (Luke 1:35). This daughter of the Father then became the bride of the Holy Spirit. For this bride therefore to have any intimate relationship with the foster-father of Jesus would be against the sixth commandment: "Thou shalt not commit adultery." And so, she was perpetually a virgin. It is not only theological sense. It is more basic than that. It is common sense.

But it also seems that today's Protestants and all those others who "protest" against Mary's perpetual virginity do not also know this history of Protestantism, for in this also the founders of the Protestant tradition strongly supported the perpetual virginity of Mary. This is what Luther had to say: "It is an article of faith that Mary is Mother of the Lord and still a virgin... Christ, we believe, came forth from a womb left perfectly intact" (*Works of Luther*, v.11, 319-320; v.6, 510). And on February 2, 1546, the feast of the Presentation of Christ in the Temple, he also said: "...A virgin before the conception and birth, she remained a virgin also at birth and after it." In fact, this was a constant belief of Luther throughout his whole life!

Calvin was no less supportive. He condemned those who would assert that Mary had other children besides Jesus. Helvidius had maintained at the end of the fourth century that the Virgin Mary, after the miraculous birth of Jesus, had several children of Joseph, namely, those who are referred to as the "brethren" and "sisters" of the Lord in the gospels. As far as Matt. 13:55 was concerned, Calvin strongly opposed Helvidius: "We have already said in another place that according to the custom of the Hebrews all relatives were called 'brethren.' Still Helvidius has shown himself to be ignorant of this by stating that Mary had many children just because in several places they are spoken of as 'brethren' of Christ."

Lastly, Calvin's stance is made even more clear in a sermon on Matt. 1:22-25, which was published in 1562: "There have been certain folk who have wished to suggest from this passage (Matthew 1:25) that the Virgin Mary had other children other than the Son of God and that Joseph had then dwelt with her later; but what folly this is! For the Gospel writer did not wish to record what happened afterwards: he simply wished to make clear Joseph's obedience and to show that Joseph had been well and truly assured that it was God who had sent his angel to Mary. He had therefore never dwelt with her nor had he shared her company... And besides this, Our Lord Jesus Christ is called the first-born. This is not because there was a second or a third, but because the Gospel writer is paying regard to the precedence. Scripture speaks thus of naming the first-born whether or not there was any question of the second. Thus we see the intention of the Holy Spirit. This is why to lend ourselves to foolish subtleties would be to abuse Holy Scripture, which is, as St. Paul says, "to be used for our edification" (Calvin, *Sermon on Matthew* 1:22-25, published in 1562).

The Swiss Reformer Zwingli was equally assertive: "I firmly believe that Mary, according to the words of the Gospel, was a pure Virgin and brought forth for us the Son of God and in childbirth and after childbirth was forever a pure, intact Virgin" (Zwingli, Opera, v.1, 424). And in January 1528, three years before Her Majesty appeared in the New World, Zwingli declared in Berne, Switzerland: "I spoke of this in the holy church in Zurich and in all my writings: I recognize Mary as ever Virgin and Holy." And so, present-day Protestants are certainly not "one" in their original theology and religious beliefs.

Chapter 10

1054. Disunity in the Church Christ Founded

In 1054, the Church was rent asunder by a division that still has serious repercussions today. It marked the beginning of the schism of the Roman Catholic and the Orthodox Churches. Disunity was introduced into the Church of Christ. This disunity was the culmination of differences in the cultural, linguistic, spiritual and political traditions that had grown between the western and eastern halves of Christendom. Then during the 16th century, Europe was rocked by a number of reforming movements that challenged the Catholic Church. These movements, collectively known as the Reformation, altered the face of Christianity. They gave birth to new churches known as Protestant, because of their "protest" against the Roman Catholic Church. More and more splinter groups or churches were formed, each claiming to be more pure and faithful to the Gospel of Jesus Christ than the other groups, and the Reformation split the Church into many fragments and divided bodies.

Martin Luther (1480—1546)

The most important reforming movement was begun by Martin Luther (1480—1546), a German Augustinian monk, who was a professor of biblical theology at Wittenberg University in Germany. On October 31, 1517, Luther posted his famous ninety-five theses on the door of Wittenberg church. The theses were forwarded to Rome. Luther's doctrines were thoroughly examined and a Papal Bull condemned forty-one of his propositions, indicted his writings, and threatened him with excommunication unless he retracted within sixty days. On December 10, 1520, Luther burnt the Bull and also declared that the priesthood and the episcopal office must be done away with. He denounced the authority of the Catholic Church and the Popes, and rejected the sacraments of the Church, except Baptism, the Eucharist, and Penance. He appealed to the cupidity of the princes in Europe by offering to make them heads of the Church in their own states if only they threw off the Pope. Indeed, his countrymen, the German princes, were among the first to rally themselves with Luther.

Luther was formally excommunicated from the Catholic Church at the Diet of Worms in 1521. However, much to the disgust of his friends, he eventually laid aside his religious habit and married the ex-Cistercian nun, Catherine Bora. After his marriage, Luther urged all monks, nuns, priests, and even the Archbishop of Mainz to follow his example. Having thus definitely set himself against the whole Roman position, he began to organize his followers into a new church. He died of a stroke on February 18, 1546, in his sixty-third year. But as Alan Schreck wrote in *The Compact History of the Catholic Church*: "It is enough to say that Lutheranism was the most Catholic form of Protestantism because Luther retained many aspects of Catholic belief and traditions, except those things that he felt were not in the Bible. Other streams of the Reformation were to depart even more radically from Catholicism."

Henry VIII and The Anglican Church

Meanwhile, in 1509, England's Henry VIII succeeded his father Henry VII on the throne of England. In the same year he married his deceased brother's widow, Catherine of Aragon, after obtaining the papal dispensation required for such a marriage. He publicly burned the writings of Luther and in 1521, he wrote a book against him, entitled *The Defence of the Seven Sacraments*, which won for him the title of Defender of the Faith from Pope Leo X (1513-1521), to whom the book was dedicated. Indeed, at one time England was referred to as the "Dowry of Our Lady," and it was England's St. Simon Stock who is said to have received the devotion of the Brown Scapular from the Blessed Virgin on July 16, 1251. However, it was this same king who tore the English Church from Rome and it was his English people who in less than a hundred years turned Protestant almost to the last man.

In 1527, he had a violent passion for Anne Boleyn, maid of honour to the Queen, and he was determined to marry her. He applied to Pope Clement VII (1523-1534) for a declaration that his marriage to Catherine of Aragon was null and void on the grounds that marriage with a deceased brother's wife was forbidden by Divine Law (Lev. 18:16), and consequently that the dispensation given by Pope Julius II (1503-1513) was worthless. This, of course, was not correct. When Pope Clement VII refused to grant him a divorce, Henry broke completely with the Holy See and in November, 1534, a subservient Parliament enacted the Act of Supremacy, namely, that "the king, his heirs and successors, should be taken and reputed the only heads of the Church of England."

Pope Paul III (1534-1549) excommunicated Henry in 1538, and when Henry died in 1547, the Court orators forbade the people to weep for him, "because such a pious king must have surely gone straight to heaven." The total number of men and women, priests, and monks, who were martyred in England for the Catholic faith from 1535 was over six hundred. Of course, this is only a very brief history of the origin of the Anglican Church in England, but as Fr. John Laux, instructor of religion and professor of psychology, Villa Madonna College, Kentucky, wrote in his book *Church History*: "What sinister power was it that made Protestants of a king and a nation who did not want to be Protestants at all, and brought hundreds of loyal Catholics to a cruel death? It was the demon of lust. All the world knows what happened to Anne Boleyn, for whose sake England was separated from the Holy See, and to the other wives of Henry."

Henry VIII was succeeded by Edward VI, the son of Henry and Jane Seymour, the third of his six wives. (No. He did not have eight wives!) Under Henry's son, the boy King Edward VI who was just ten years of age and a mere puppet in the hands of Archbishop Thomas Cranmer, the English Church became out-and-out Protestant. Lutheran and Calvinist professors were imported from the continent to teach theology at Oxford and Cambridge. The Mass was abolished as idolatrous, a new Creed was drawn up as the official Creed of the English Church, and the work of pulling down altars and destroying ornaments, pillaging churches, went merrily on. But when Edward died on July 6, 1553 at the young age of sixteen, men whom Henry VIII would have condemned to the flames for their heretical opinions were back in control of both Church and State. A Catholic restoration had taken place under Queen Mary I or Mary Tudor (1516-1558).

It is interesting that a "Mary" was the first female monarch of England. It is even more interesting that it was a "Mary" who restored Catholicism to that country. Mary was the daughter of Henry VIII and his first wife Catherine of Aragon. In fact, Catherine had six children of whom five died at birth, and the first to survive was the girl, Mary. The new Queen was known to be very attached to the old religion. She showed great moderation at first. The bishops who had been removed under Edward VI, her half brother, were restored, and those who had supplanted them were in turn deprived of office. Anti-papal legislation was repealed, and many men who had been prominent in promoting the new religion were reconciled to the faith. The reformers from the continent were given passports to leave England, but no compulsion was used against English people who had changed their faith.

On Mary's death in 1558, Elizabeth, the daughter of Henry VIII and Anne Boleyn was proclaimed Queen. At her coronation she took the oath to uphold the Catholic faith but her ministers had little difficulty in persuading her "to put down a religion which proclaimed her a bastard, and to support the reformed doctrines which alone could give stability to her throne." With a majority of only three votes, her first Parliament in 1559 passed an Act of Supremacy, which declared the Queen supreme governor in spiritual as well as in temporal matters of England. The altars were again destroyed and the Mass proscribed. In 1570, Pope Pius V excommunicated Elizabeth and violent persecution of Catholics then set in, and great numbers of the clergy were fined, imprisoned, or put to death.

It was during the reign of Henry VIII and around this European period of disunity and division in the Church, with the loss of millions of the Catholic faithful to the Protestant and Anglican fold, that the Blessed Virgin Mary appeared in the New World in 1531. Another Queen Mary this time, Her Majesty, the Queen of Heaven and Earth brought Christianity and Catholicism to the New World.

Chapter 11

1531. Her Majesty Appears in the New World

It was Satan's empire and the Woman of Genesis 3:15 came to Mexico to do battle with him. Luther had divided her son's Church since 1517 and Henry VIII's passion for Anne Boleyn around 1527 led him to ask the Pope to annul his marriage to Catherine of Aragon. It was the beginning of the Anglican Church.

Christopher Columbus had already discovered the New World in 1492. The year was now 1531, ten years after the Spanish conquest of Tenochtitlan (now Mexico City). It was very early on Saturday morning, December 9, at that time the feast of the Immaculate Conception. A humble 57-year-old Aztec, whose new Christian name was Juan Diego, was on his way to Mass on that great feast day of Mary. As he drew near to the little hill of Tepeyac, day was beginning to dawn. Much to his amazement, he heard singing on the hill. It was the singing of many birds, and their songs were extremely soft and melodious. He looked towards the hill top, towards the easterly direction from which the sun was rising, and from where the heavenly singing was coming. Suddenly the singing stopped. Then he heard someone affectionately calling to him from afar: "Juanito, Juan Diegoito," using the diminutive of his name. He ventured in the direction of the voice and when he reached the top of the hill, he saw a brilliant white cloud surrounded by the arc of a rainbow, formed by rays of dazzling light streaming from the cloud.

A young lady of exquisite beauty, seemingly about 14 years old, then appeared in front of the cloud. The sun was not yet above the horizon, but when Juan saw her, her clothes were shining as bright as the sun with golden beams that rayed around her from head to foot. Indeed, so gloriously bright was she that her radiance seemed to turn rocks into pendants of jewels, cactus leaves into emeralds, and their trunks and their thorns shone like gold. It was the first "visitation" of Her Majesty to the New World. It was the beginning of the greatest mass conversion in Mexico from paganism to Christianity.

She came from the east, and arrived early in the morning when it was beginning to dawn. She appeared as bright as the sun. But isn't the sun a star? She appeared, therefore, as the Morning Star! But it was also a star from the east which announced her Son's birth: "Where is he that is born King of the Jews? For we have seen his star in the east, and have come to worship him" (Matthew 2:2). And so, Solomon's Song of Songs 6:9 was depicted by this apparition: "Who is she that comes forth as the morning star, fair as the moon, bright as the sun, terrible as an army set in battle array." It is the standard of the Legion of Mary. Indeed, she came forth to declare war on Satan and bring about the conversion of his Aztec empire. Juan Diego was her personal Aztec convert and ambassador.

She beckoned him to approach her and when he reached the spot where she was, he was filled with wonder as her perfect grandeur surpassed all imagination. It was on a hill in Tepeyac where the Aztecs had once built a temple to the pagan mother-goddess Tonantzin. Juan Diego instinctively prostrated himself before her. It was then that she identified herself: "Know for certain, my dearest and youngest son, that I am the perfect and perpetual Virgin Mary, mother of the true God, through whom everything lives, the Lord of all things, who is master of creation and of heaven and earth. I ardently desire a temple be built here for me where I will show and offer all my love, my compassion, my help and my protection to the people. I am your merciful mother, the mother of all who live united in this land, and of all mankind, of all those who love me, of those who cry to me, of those who seek me, of those who have confidence in me. Here I will hear their weeping and their sorrow, and will remedy and alleviate their sufferings, their necessities and their misfortunes. Therefore, in order that my intentions be made known, you must go to the house of the bishop of Mexico City and tell him that I sent you and that it is my desire to have a temple built here."

"I am the perfect and perpetual Virgin Mary, Mother of the true God," she said. She thus confirmed in a single sentence the second Marian dogma, the Perpetual Virginity of Mary, proclaimed at the Lateran Council in 649 AD, and the first Marian dogma of the Council of Ephesus in 431 AD, which defined her as "Mother of God." In Guadalupe, however, she added "true," because the Aztecs worshiped false gods. "I am your merciful mother," she added, "mother of all who live united in this land," acknowledging the title given to her by St. Augustine in the 4th century AD, "Mother of Unity": "Father may they all be one as we are one" (John 17:21), her son lamented during the Last Supper.

Understandably so, Bishop Juan de Zumarraga did not believe Juan Diego's message and very politely dismissed him. At the end of the day Juan returned to the little hilltop where the "Mother of the true God" was waiting for him at the very spot where she had appeared the first time. "I beg you, my lady, my queen, my little one," he respectfully pleaded, "to entrust one of the nobles to bear your kind breath, your kind word; someone who is held in esteem, someone who is known, respected and honoured, in order that he might be believed, because I am really just a man of no importance. The place in which you sent me is a place where I am unaccustomed going or spending any time. My youngest daughter, my lady, my little one, please forgive me..."

The perfect and perpetual Virgin listened to his plea with great sympathy and understanding, but implored him to go again to see the bishop on the morrow and to tell him: "It is I, personally, the ever Virgin Mary; I, who am the Mother of God, who sends you." Juan obeyed and returned to the bishop. This time the bishop was more impressed, but he told him that the lady must provide some proof that she was really the Mother of God. A reasonable reaction, in my opinion!

Juan relayed the message of the bishop. She then told Juan Diego to climb up the hill and that there he would find flowers in bloom which he should pluck and bring back to her. Juan climbed the hill with great alacrity and renewed vigour, and on reaching the hill-crest his eyes opened in wonderment. There on the hill was a brilliant profusion of flowers. They were Castilian roses of exquisite fragrance, fresh and glittering with dewdrops. Not only were they in bloom out of season, but it would have been impossible for any flowers to grow in such a stony terrain which could only yield thistles and cactus plants.

Spreading out his tilma like an apron, he filled it with the colourful blooms and with great joy he descended to where the Lady was waiting for him. She then gave a feminine touch to the miraculous bouquet and carefully rearranged the flowers with her own hands, saying as she did so: "My youngest and dearest son, these flowers are the proof, the sign that you are to take to the bishop... You will be my ambassador, fully worthy of my confidence. Tell him everything. Tell him once again all that you have seen and heard here..."

Juan Diego returned to the bishop's house, opened his folded tilma and exposed the bouquet of roses, arranged à la Maria. They were Spanish Castilian roses for the Spanish bishop. But they were not just ordinary roses. Indeed, they were mystical roses from the Mystical Rose herself! But after the roses cascaded to the floor, another and greater shock was in store for Bishop Zumarraga. There upon the tilma was a full portrait of the Mother of God as Juan Diego had seen her. All the people in the room fell to their knees. Full of awe, the bishop, weeping and sorrowful, begged her forgiveness for not having immediately complied with her wishes. It was Tuesday, December 12, 1531. Two weeks later, a triumphant procession of Aztecs, followed by Franciscan and Dominican missionaries, carried the sacred image to a small make-shift chapel on Tepeyac hill, singing exultantly: "The Virgin is one of us! Our Sovereign Lady is one of us!" They learnt this from Juan.

The image of Our Lady of Guadalupe on the tilma of Juan Diego remains one of the greatest Marian miracles in history. To the Aztec Indians, the image was much more than a mere portrait. It was a pictograph which they were able to read and understand. The Lady stood in front of the sun and this signified to them that she was greater than the dreaded sun-god Huitzilopochtli. Her foot rested on the crescent moon which signified one of their foremost deities, Coyolxauhqui, the goddess of the moon. This was a sign

1531. Her Majesty Appears in the New World

that God had given her power over all of nature. The blue-green hue of her mantle was the colour worn by Aztec royalty; therefore she was a Queen.

The stars strewn across her mantle told them that she was greater than the stars of heaven, which they also worshipped as gods. Yet she could not be a god since her hands were joined in prayer, her head bowed in reverence, clearly to One greater than herself. The black cross on the gold brooch on her neck was identical to the cross on the banners and helmets of the Spanish conquerors, telling them that her religion was that of their conquerors. The sash around her waist with tassels signified that she was pregnant, and her right foot stood on a dark quarter moon.

This miraculous image is there in the Basilica of Our Lady of Guadalupe in Mexico for all to see, skeptics as well as believers. Scientists too have seen and have remained silent, being unable to offer any scientific explanation for its existence. The image is a painting on a tilma made of fibers from the maguey cactus which is known to disintegrate after 20 years, yet this image is as new as ever for over 460 years. For more than a century the image hung above an altar with no protection whatsoever. It was also exposed to the smoke from thousands of votive candles placed under it and in spite of this it shows no damage over the years. On November 14, 1921, a bomb which was concealed in a bouquet of flowers placed under the sacred image exploded during Mass. The force of the explosion twisted a heavy metal Cross on the altar into a semi-circular shape, but the sacred and beautiful image of Our Lady of Guadalupe was miraculously untouched.

The hypothesis that the sacred image is simply a painting was discredited in 1946 when a microscopic examination surprisingly revealed that there were no brush strokes. Further studies revealed other inexplicable qualities. For example, the colours used for the image are of unknown origin for they are neither animal, vegetable nor mineral dyes as known on this earth. Then, in May 1979, two American scientists, Professor Phillip Callahan of the University of Florida and Professor Joddy Smith of Pensacola, Florida, took infra-red photographs to study the image: "I am interested in doing what William James said a hundred years ago—to bring together religion and science. These infra-red photographs showed that the image was made without any underdrawing sketch, an essential first step for portraits made during that era," said Professor Smith.

In recent years over twenty scientists have looked at the eyes of the image under high magnification. Dr. Enrique Graue, Director of the Opthalmology Hospital, Nuestra Señora de la Luz, in Mexico City, had this to say: "I was dumbfounded. The eyes displayed depth and curvature and reflected light exactly like living eyes. In the eyes of the image were reflected twelve people who were present in the courtyard on the day Juan Diego opened his cloak, and the amazing fact is that the same figures appeared in both eyes at precisely the positions expected by the law of optics and twin-eyed physiology."

Under high magnification the image also shows no detectable signs of cracking—an inexplicable occurrence after 450 years of existence. "It may seem strange for a scientist to say this," concluded Professor Callahan, "but studying the image was the most moving experience of my life. Just getting that close, I got the same strange feeling that others did, who worked on the Shroud of Turin... I believe in logical explanations up to a point, but there is no logical explanation for life. You can break life down into atoms but what comes after that? Even Einstein said God!"

She appeared as the woman clothed with the sun, and her right foot was seen standing on a dark quarter-moon. It depicted the right foot that will crush the serpent's head. She was pregnant. This was certainly the Woman of the Apocalypse: "Then the sanctuary of God in heaven opened and ark of the covenant could be seen inside it... Now a great sign appeared in heaven: a woman, adorned with the sun, standing on the moon, and with the twelve stars on her head for a crown. She was pregnant, and in labour, crying aloud in the pangs of childbirth" (Rev. 11:19; 12:1-2). That Woman of the Apocalypse is also the Woman of Genesis 3:15, the Coredemptrix.

Her Majesty appeared in Guadalupe on a Saturday, the day of the week dedicated to her. It was December 9, 1531, at that time the feast of the Immaculate Conception. It was her first confirmatory hint that she was indeed the "Immaculate Conception." It was

1531. Her Majesty Appears in the New World

to become the third Marian dogma three hundred years later.

Our Lady of Guadalupe

The hand of Da Vinci (1503)   The Hand of God (1531)

The site of the apparition on Tepeyec Hill

A statue of Our Lady of Gaudalue weeping blood

Chapter 12

1571. The Battle of Lepanto

Forty years after the apparition of Her Majesty in Guadalupe, a major battle took place. After more than seven hundred years of struggle, Spain had finally driven out its Muslim rulers, and in 1453 had again become an independent kingdom. In the east, however, there was a resurgence of Islamic power, and a thirst for conquest in the rapidly expanding Turkish (Ottoman) Empire had taken place. Indeed, the capture of Constantinople by the Turks in 1453 had encouraged their desire to conquer and enslave all of Christendom. Their army invaded the Balkan Peninsula and subjugated all of the eastern Mediterranean countries. By the middle of the 16th century their navy had captured Cyprus and was menacing Venice.

The Turkish plan was to build the greatest navy the world had seen to that time, and then use it to conquer all the European countries bordering on the Mediterranean Sea. From there they would push upward until they had all Europe in their power. Faced with this threat, Pope Pius V (1566-1572) realized that he had to take drastic action. By skillful diplomacy he persuaded the Spanish and Italian powers to set aside their own rivalries and unite with the Papal squadron to form the Holy League to oppose the advance of the Muslims.

While all this was taking place, Don Fray Alonso de Montufar, the second Archbishop of Mexico, like his predecessor Bishop Zumarraga, was an enthusiastic champion of Our Lady of Guadalupe. Being very alert to the impending crisis in Europe, he had a small reproduction of the sacred image on Juan Diego's tilma made, touched to the original, and sent it as a present to King Philip of Spain in 1570. It is said that Archbishop Montufar expressed the hope that when the battle was imminent, the king would place the copy of the sacred image in a suitable location in the Christian navy. King Philip complied and had it mounted in the cabin of Admiral Giovanni Andrea Doria in anticipation of the battle of Lepanto near Greece.

The naval forces of the Holy League assembled. There were two large squadrons, one from Spain, the other from Venice. The smaller squadrons from the Papal States were joined to the Genoese (Italian) forces under Admiral Doria. The supreme command was given to Don Juan of Austria, half brother of King Philip of Spain, however, the Christian forces were greatly outnumbered by the Turkish fleet. Their ships were lined up just inside the entrance to the Gulf of Lepanto (now the Gulf of Corinth in Greece) and stretched almost from shore to shore in the form of a crescent. Ali Pasha, the supreme commander of the Turkish fleet, was in the centre.

The Christian allies, on the other hand, had formed into three squadrons; in the centre the Spanish ships, to the left the Venetians, and to the right the squadron commanded by Andrea Doria. From the human point of view, the outcome was inevitable, and so, Pope Pius V called upon every Catholic in Europe to invoke the aid of the Mother of God under the title of *Help of Christians,* and to storm heaven unceasingly with rosaries. The faithful duly responded and the battle got underway. It was a battle which would determine the fate and faith of Europe.

At a critical moment when it seemed that the Christian forces would lose, a tremendous wind arose and blew the Turkish navy into total disarray. It would be many days afterwards before word reached Rome of the outcome of the battle. However, the Pope was mysteriously informed of the result because at the very moment when the victory was gained, he suddenly interrupted a conversation and exclaimed: "Let us give thanks to God. The victory is ours." The Turks lost 230 galleys; the Christians 16. Some 1,500 Christians who had been chained to the oars in the Turkish galleys were freed. It was the last sea battle fought with oar-propelled vessels. The victory of Lepanto brought to an end the Muslim seapower, never more to be a threat to the Christian world.

Those words of the Pope were taken down and sealed, and a

1571. The Battle of Lepanto

fortnight later a messenger arrived in Rome announcing the glad tidings of the victory which took place exactly at the moment when the Pope announced the outcome of the battle on October 7, 1571. The Pope then proclaimed that day a feast day in honour of *Our Lady of Victories*. The victory however was attributed to the storming of heaven with rosaries and the following year it was renamed the feast of *Our Lady of the Rosary*. The word "rosary" is from the Latin "rosarium," meaning "a garden of roses." But *Our Lady of Guadalupe's* image was in the cabin of Admiral Doria. She had performed the miracle of the "garden of roses" in Guadalupe, Mexico 40 years previously in 1531!

Chapter 13

1830. The Medal of the Immaculate Conception

The first of the apparitions of the Blessed Virgin in modern times took place in France in the 19th century. On a midsummer's night on July 18, 1830, significantly, the eve of the feast of St. Vincent de Paul, the Blessed Virgin came to a humble and narrow back street in Paris called the Rue du Bac. It was in the chapel of the Mother House of the Sisters of Charity, founded by St. Vincent de Paul, that she appeared to a nun, Sr. Catherine Labouré.

Catherine was awakened from sleep and led to the chapel by an angel alleged to be St. Michael. As she entered the chapel all the lights were suddenly and inexplicably turned on. She then saw the Virgin descend the altar steps and seat herself in a chair close by. Catherine rushed to her and knelt, resting her hands on the Virgin's lap. It felt solid! Her Majesty then began to specify the sorrows and dangers to come in France and the world. She spoke in broken sentences, in halting phrases, fighting back the tears that glistened her eyes.

On November 27, 1830, Her Majesty appeared once more in the convent. This time Catherine saw the Virgin standing on a globe with her right foot on the head of a green and yellow serpent. Her eyes were lifted to heaven and in her hands, which were raised to the level of her heart, she held a globe surmounted by a Cross. She said to Catherine: "The globe which you see represents the whole world, especially France, and each person in particular." All at once the globe disappeared and she lowered her hands. Each finger was then seen to be covered with three rings set with precious stones, from which sprang rays of such brilliance that her feet and robe were then no longer visible. "Behold," she said, "the symbol of the graces which I bestow on those who ask for them."

Then she added: "The gems from which rays do not fall are the graces for which souls forget to ask."

An oval frame then appeared around the image, and forming a semi-circle inside the frame were the words written in gold: "O Mary, conceived without sin, pray for us who have recourse to thee." She then requested: "Have a medal coined upon this model. Those who wear it around their necks will receive great graces." The frame then appeared to turn around and Catherine saw a large **M** surmounted by a Cross and beneath were two hearts, one with a crown of thorns and the other pierced by a sword. Around the edge of the frame were twelve equally-spaced stars.

Now, because the other side of the frame was surrounded by the words: "O Mary conceived without sin...," Catherine asked Her Majesty what should be written on this side of the medal. "The **M** and two hearts say enough," was the Queen's gentle response; a response which, in my opinion, has not been given enough emphasis and publicity. Indeed, it says more than enough. In fact, all the mysteries of Mary are found in the symbols on the *Medal of the Immaculate Conception*, as it was originally called, but because of the miraculous favours which many people experienced in those early days of its distribution, it was popularly called the Miraculous Medal. However, by so calling it, we obscure the true theological significance and message of the medal. It is the *Medal of the Immaculate Conception*!

The Virgin standing on the globe with her foot on the serpent's head signified the new Eve who will crush the serpent's head as promised by God in Genesis 3:15: "*I will put enmity between you and the woman, between your seed and her seed; (s)he will crush your head.*" In that threat God was referring to the second Eve who will give birth to the second Adam, the Redeemer of mankind.

The rays emanating from the rings on her fingers signified that she is also the *Mediatrix of Graces*. Grace, as Augustine of Hippo put it, is a supernatural gift of God the Father bestowed upon us through the merits of Jesus Christ for our salvation, and all grace came to mankind through the suffering and resurrection of Christ. But as St. Pius X added: "It cannot be denied that the dispensing of these gifts, graces, belong by strict and proper right to Christ for they are the exclusive fruit of his death. Nevertheless, by this union in sorrow and suffering which existed between Him and his mother, who at the foot of the Cross of Redemption died a martyr's death without dying, it has been allowed the august Virgin to be the most powerful *Mediatrix* between Jesus and man," and the dispensatrix of graces.

"O Mary conceived without sin" was this time the *written* confirmation of her *Immaculate Conception*, which she had *inferred* when she first appeared in Guadalupe on December 9, 1531, at that time the feast of the *Immaculate Conception*. See how she unfolds it all to us! Now, *Immaculate Conception* means that from the very first moment of her own conception, through the anticipated merits of her divine Son, she was preserved by special grace from the stain of original sin. This immaculate Queen was the singular exception to the universal law, for how could God abide in a womb which was once under the dominion of Satan, even for a moment. The law was therefore not made for her.

"Pray for us who have recourse to thee" signified that she is our *Advocate* with the son, and pleads to him on our behalf. Indeed, her first public manifestation of such a role was during the wedding feast in Cana (John 2:1-11). In the Old Testament, the Queen Mother brought the petition needs of the people of Israel to the throne of her son the king (1 Kings 2:19). In like manner, the Church teaches that Mary is the New Testament Queen Mother and Advocate in the kingdom of her son, and brings the petitions of her children to the throne of Christ the King.

The **M** surmounted by a Cross, all in one unit, signified the *Redeemer* on the Cross united to the *Coredemptrix* beneath the Cross. St. Therese of Lisieux once said that there can be no great love on earth without great sorrow. Indeed, the two hearts side by side beneath the **M** were not only symbols of their love but also of their sorrows. One was seen with a crown of thorns, the other was pierced by a sword.

The twelve stars signified that she was the Woman of the Apocalypse, the Woman of the Revelation 11:19, 12:1 "The temple of God in heaven opened and the ark of the covenant could be seen inside it... Then a great sign appeared in heaven, a woman clothed with the sun, standing on the moon and with twelve stars on her head for a crown." The twelve stars represented the twelve tribes of Israel and the twelve apostles, for she is the Woman of Israel and the Queen of the apostles, a title bestowed upon her in the Litany of Loreto. Obviously, John was not seeing the ancient *Ark of the Covenant* of Mosaic times. That has since been lost somewhere on earth. He was given a vision of the living *Ark of the Covenant*, Mary, the womb of the Mediator of the new Covenant, and the Tabernacle of the Most High. The Medal of the Immaculate Conception is therefore inextricably linked to the proposed dogma of the *Coredemptrix, Mediatrix,* and *Advocate*. And so, the mother of the second Person of the Blessed Trinity has herself a trinity of gifts and titles.

France was in turmoil after 1830, as prophesied by Our Lady to Catherine, and by September 1870, the Third French Republic had taken over after the fall of Louis Napoleon in September 1870. Divided inwardly, France was forced to fight an outward enemy in the vicious revolution which exploded on March 18, 1871, and which called itself the *Commune* of Paris. The men of the *Commune* were the dregs, not only of France but of Italy, Germany, Russia and America. Paris had become the rendezvous of all wickedness. While many historians hold that these men were not Communists, as we know the word today, there can be little doubt that Karl Marx and other anarchists had tremendous influence over this mob and that the spirit of communism permeated the *Commune*. Catherine Labouré was thus the first saint in modern times to be caught up in a Communist rebellion. As Fr. Joseph Dirvin in his biography of the saint, *Saint Catherine Labouré of the Miraculous Medal*, wrote: "Before the terrible weeks were over, the churches of Paris would be desecrated, profanation of things sacred would be commonplace, and the clergy would be arrested by the dozens."

Around that time Sr. Catherine had a dream. She dreamt that the Blessed Virgin came to the convent and said: "Tell Sr. Dufès (the Mother Superior) that she would have to leave, but that I would guard her house, and she will return on May 31." They did leave but not before Catherine, at that time 65 years old, removed the crown from Our Lady's statue in the chapel, promising that she

1830. The Medal of the Immaculate Conception

would return to crown her before the month of May was gone. The *Commune* was eventually defeated and Sr. Dufès and her Sisters arrived in Paris on May 30, and on May 31 Catherine Labouré carried out the little crowning ceremony she had promised the Mother of God: "I told you, my good Mother, that I should return to crown you on the 31st of May," she said with great satisfaction and love. It was a prophetic prophecy of the importance of the day May 31 in subsequent Marian history (see chapter 23).

On February 11, 1836, a canonical inquiry into Catherine's apparitions was conducted and the findings of the inquiry completely validated Catherine. The court extolled her character and virtue, and placed whole-hearted credence in her visions. Overjoyed at the findings of the court, Archbishop de Quélen gave free rein to his life-long devotion to *the Immaculate Conception* of the Blessed Virgin. In a series of pastoral letters he promoted this devotion to his people, and consecrated himself and his diocese to *the Immaculate Conception*. Indeed, through his efforts, the invocation "Queen conceived without sin" was inserted in the Litany of Loreto, and in 1854, Pope Pius IX declared belief in Mary's *Immaculate Conception* a dogma of the Catholic faith.

When her body was exhumed in 1933, 57 years after her death, a gasp of astonishment ran through the crowd. Catherine's body was as fresh and serene as the day she was buried. Her skin had not darkened in the least. Her eyes were as intensely blue as ever, and her arms and legs were as subtle as if she were merely asleep. Her preserved remains can be seen today in the chapel in the Rue du Bac in Paris.

Catherine had fulfilled her mission as best as she could. Hundreds of millions of medals had been stamped and diffused since the Virgin designed it and showed it to her. "Have a medal coined upon this model," she said. "Those who wear it around their necks will receive great graces." It was the promise of *the Immaculate Conception*.

The chapel in the Rue du Bac

The incorrupt body of St. Catherine Labouré

A depiction of Catherine's vision of Mary

The Medal of the Immaculate Conception

Chapter 14

Coredemptrix, Mediatrix, Advocate

The symbols of Her Majesty as Coredemptrix, Mediatrix and Advocate are imprinted in the Medal of the Immaculate Conception (Miraculous Medal). Its history began in Eden. When, in the fullness of time, God created Adam out of the dust of the earth and placed him in the garden of Eden, he then created Eve out of his rib and gave her to him as "a companion" (Genesis 2:18). Our first mother, the first Eve ("Mother of the living"), then brought death to her children and the world by her sin of disobedience and by wanting to be "like God." She, and soon afterwards the first Adam, fell prey to "the father of lies," the ancient serpent, once Lucifer, now Satan, who deceived them (Genesis 3:4-5).

It was then that God made his first promise to mankind when he said to Satan: "Because you have done this, I will put enmity between you and the woman; between your seed and her seed; (s)he will crush your head..." (Genesis 3:15). God was referring to a new Eve and a new Adam. It was to be Mary and Jesus in time to come. She was to defeat him through her seed, the second Adam. Eventually, in the fullness of time the new Eve was born. She was to be the mother of the man, the new Adam, who was to restore life and the friendship of God with mankind. She was to be the new "Mother of the living," the Mother of Mankind.

St. Thomas Aquinas, in his *Summa Theologica,* theologized that when man rebelled against God, God's justice required that adequate reparation be made; justice meaning "giving to everyone his due." But since God is infinite, an infinite insult was made to him when man rebelled against him, and if the reparation was to be adequate, that is, if justice were to be satisfied, such an insult required infinite reparation. Justice also required that the reparation be made by man, but man is a finite being and incapable of making infinite reparation. Left to himself, therefore, man would forever be separated from God. The only solution to the impasse was that the infinite God should become man, and as man offer reparation to God. Since the person offering the reparation would himself be infinite, the reparation would equal the crime and man would once more be united in friendship with God. And so, in his loving mercy, God sent his son to make reparation for the sin of man: "God so loved the world that he sent his only begotten son..." (John 3:16).

COREDEMPTRIX

Now, the first Adam and the first Eve were immaculate at birth. Sin had not entered the world as yet. The second Eve, too, in anticipation of merits of her son, by a special privilege of God, was preserved from the stain of original sin and was immaculate at birth. She was the Immaculate Conception. She was to be the helpmate and *"companion"* of the Redeemer, who was the "sinless One." The spiritual history of man was about to start all over again, this time not in Eden, but in Nazareth!

The first Adam gave birth to the first Eve. The second Eve gave birth to the second Adam. Indeed, she gave him the very instrument of redemption, his human body "Sacrifices and offerings you have not desired, but a body you have prepared for me" (Heb. 10:5-7). No human father was involved and scientifically speaking, therefore, his DNA was totally Marian! In the words of the late Mother Theresa of Calcutta: "Of course, Mary is the Coredemptrix. She gave Jesus his body, and it is his body which saved us."

The first Eve was proud. The second Eve was humble. The first Eve was disobedient. The second Eve was obedient. The first Eve said yes to Satan and sin. The second Eve said yes to Gabriel and God. It was a fruit which hung from a tree in the garden of Eden which was the instrument which Satan used to bring death to the world. It was the "fruit of her womb" (Luke 1:42) who hung from a tree on Calvary and restored life to mankind. The first Eve brought death to the world. The second Eve brought life. The Eden tragedy was reversed on Calvary.

In sum, it was a man and a woman who had sinned and, therefore, it had to be a man and a woman to restore what was lost by sin. It is as logical as that! Anyone therefore who leaves the "woman" out of that redemptive act is only preaching half Genesis 3:15, half the gospel, half the truth—and half-truth is no truth! It was Jesus **and** Mary.

Redemption had to come from suffering. As Eve gave the fruit to Adam as the instrument for the fall of humanity, Mary gave a body to Jesus as the instrument for the redemption of humanity, the body in which he would live and suffer and die for us. And so, by virtue of giving flesh to the "Word made flesh" (John 1:14), who in turn redeemed humanity, the Virgin of Nazareth uniquely merits the title Coredemptrix. But the climax of Mary's role as Coredemptrix was at the foot of the Cross where the total suffering of the mother's heart, "pierced with a sword," was obediently united with the suffering of the son's heart in the fulfilment of the Father's plan of redemption (cf. Gal. 4:4).

As Rev. Cyril Papali, O.D.C., in his book *Mother of God, Mary in Scripture and Tradition,* also said: "Hers was the most spiritual and the most pure, the most selfless, the most intense, incomprehensible suffering ever known. One solitary creature suffering with God and for God, suffering for all mankind and from them. That was the price of being the Coredemptrix. That is the meaning of being the second Eve." When therefore the Church calls Mary the "Coredemptrix," she means that Mary uniquely participated in the redemption of humanity with her son, although in a completely subordinate and dependent manner. As Mark Miravalle, Professor of Theology and Mariology at Steubenville University, Ohio, wrote: "Mary participated in Jesus' reconciliation of the human family with God like no other created person. Mary's unique participation in the redemption was scripturally foreshadowed in the prophecy of Simeon in the temple when he said to her: 'A sword would pierce your own heart, too'" (Luke 2: 35).

Miravalle clearly explained that the term "Coredemptrix" if properly translated means "the Woman *with* the Redeemer." Undoubtedly, God could have redeemed us on his own, but he willed otherwise. It would not have been perfect. The important point, however, is that Mary could never have redeemed us on her own.

Her role was secondary and subordinate. She was the Coredemptrix, and "Co" comes from the Latin *"cum"* which means "with" and certainly does not mean "co-equal," but "co-operating with." I wish to make this abundantly clear because it is of major theological and ecumenical importance. The co-pilot, for example, is not equal but is subordinate to the pilot. Indeed, Mary always knew her co-operative role: "I am the *handmaid* of the Lord. Let it be done to me according to your word" (Luke 1:38). But it was her "Immaculate Conception" which properly prepared her for and made her worthy of the intimate and unique role she had to play with the Redeemer in the work of salvation. And so, the title Coredemptrix should never be interpreted as Mary having an equal role in the salvation of the world with Jesus. Indeed, it was *never* at any time in Church history meant to be so interpreted.

We were redeemed on Calvary with the blood of the son and the tears of the mother. Redemption came from this suffering. It was a suffering which stemmed from "love." Indeed, the mother of the Redeemer was predestined to suffer with her son. Simeon only confirmed what she already understood before she gave her *fiat* to Gabriel: "And a sword would pierce thine own heart" (Luke 2:35).

This is not new doctrine. The earliest Christian writers and Fathers of the Church referred to Marian co-redemption with great profundity. For example, the fourth century Church Father, St. Jerome, said: "Death through Eve, life from Mary." The seventh century Church writer, Modestus of Jerusalem, stated that through Mary, we "are redeemed from the tyranny of the devil." St. John Damascene (eighth century) greeted her: "Hail thou, through whom we are redeemed from the curse," and the twelfth century Marian lover St. Bernard of Clairvaux (1090–1153) preached that "through her, man was redeemed." He added: "One man and one woman harmed us grievously. Thanks to God, all things are restored by one man and one woman, and that with interest. It is true that Christ would have been adequate, since all our sufficiency comes from him, but it was not good for us that it should be a man alone. It was more appropriate that both sexes should take part in our reparation, since both had wrought our ruin. But her *cooperation* means much more than this. It implies the true dependence of the whole work of redemption on her free will because God himself willed it to be *conditioned* by her consent. Redemption in its entirety is her *cooperative* work also and for that reason alone she deserves to be called Coredemptrix."

Indeed, it is against this rich Christian foundation that twentieth century Popes and saints have used the title Coredemptrix for Mary's unique role in human redemption. Pope Benedict XV (1940-1922) in his 1918 apostolic letter wrote: "To such extent that she (Mary) suffered and almost died with her suffering and dying son, and to such extent that she surrendered her maternal rights over her son for man's salvation, …we may rightly say that she together with Christ redeemed the human race."

As Miravalle researched: "In a Papal Audience in 1933, Pope Pius XI (1922—1939) marked a Marian milestone when for the first time in Church history a Pope had personally and explicitly attributed the title 'Coredemptrix' to Mary (The author wishes to add here that her *role* as such was always recognized by the Church.) It was the single word 'Coredemptrix' which was used for the first time." Pope Pius XI said: "In the very nature of things, the Redeemer could not help but associate his mother in his work and therefore we invoke her under the title of Coredemptrix. She has given us the Savior; she raised him for the work of redemption unto the cross, sharing in the suffering and death by which Jesus accomplished the redemption of all men. And it was upon the cross, in the last moments of his life, that the Redeemer proclaimed her our mother and the mother of all. 'Behold your son,' he said of St. John, who represented all of us; and those other words, spoken to the Apostle were addressed to us too: 'Behold your mother.'"

Pius XII referred to Mary as Coredemptrix no less than six times in various papal documents. In another Papal statement, 1935, he addressed Mary in these words: "O Mother of piety and mercy, who, when thy most beloved son was accomplishing the redemption of the human race on the altar of the Cross, did stand there suffering with him, as a Coredemptrix … Day by day preserve and increase in us the precious fruit of his redemption and your compassion as his mother."

In his homily on the feast of the Immaculate Conception in the cathedral in Krakow before he became Pope John Paul II, Karol Cardinal Wojtyla summarized this Marian truth: "In order to be Coredemptrix, she was first the Immaculate Conception" (December 8, 1973). But her Majesty herself made this connection during her apparitions in Amsterdam as the Lady or Mother of all Nations: "Tell the Theologians," she said to Ida Peerdeman, "that this is why the Lady of all Nations has been compelled to come now, in these present times, for she is the Immaculate Conception, and as a consequence of this, the Coredemptrix, Mediatrix and Advocate (see chapter 23)."

Then as Pope, John Paul II used the term Coredemptrix for Mary on five occasions during his pontificate. In a papal statement in 1985, for example, he specifically used the title "Coredemptrix" in developing the understanding of Mary's spiritual crucifixion at the foot of the Cross: "Crucified spiritually with her crucified son, she contemplated with heroic love the death of her God, she 'lovingly consented to the immolation of this Victim which she herself had brought fourth' (*Lumen Gentium*, No. 58) ... As she was in a special way close to the Cross of her son, she also had to have a privileged experience of his resurrection. In fact, Mary's role as Coredemptrix did not cease with the glorification of her son."

MEDIATRIX

A mediator is someone who is able to stand between two groups or at least has a special "in" with both sides so that she or he can hope to bring the two sides together. As M. Basil Pennington wrote in his book *Mary Today*, when God wanted to partake of our humanity, he looked for a free "yes" from us. It was Mary who stood there in our name and said that yes. Indeed, the medieval fantasy of a man like Bernard of Clairvaux, who depicts the whole human race gathered around Mary encouraging her to say that yes, waiting with bated breath until she does say it, is not altogether fanciful. Mary was our spokesperson before the Divine. Thus Mary, in a very real and special sense, is our mediatrix.

When God did become man and the Son of God embraced our

humanity, we then had *the* mediator—one who belonged totally to both sides and brought them together in deepest harmony and union. It was *this* mediator's first "yes" to the Father that truly reconciled humanity with the divine. Mary's was the second "yes."

Thirty years later the mother and her son were invited to a wedding banquet. The wine ran out. "They have no wine," she said to her son, pleading on behalf of the bride and groom in Cana. It was then that he changed water, not merely into wine, but the *best* wine. It was the first documented manifestation of her role as mediatrix with the one mediator between God and man. As Jesus said: "I am the Way, the Truth and the Life. No one can come to the Father except through me" (John 14:6). And as St. Paul says: "There is one God, and there is one mediator between God and man, the man Christ Jesus, who gave himself as a ransom for all" (1 Tim. 2:5-6). This, of course, is a teaching that the Catholic Church fully acknowledges. However, as Miravalle said, the text of Paul's Letter to Timothy, while excluding any other parallel mediation, does not exclude subordinate mediation.

It is at Cana, therefore, that we see the first public manifestation of both the divinity of Christ, the one mediator, and the motherly intercession of Mary for the needs of her children. Mary, then, is mediatrix with the mediator. At the moment that he expressed that "yes" *in its fullness* on Calvary hill, the one chosen by God to stand at his side and be a total "yes" with his "yes" was Mary. "There stood by the cross of Jesus his mother" (John 19:25).

And so, in his encyclical *Redemptoris Mater*, Pope John Paul II professed Mary as the "mediatrix," who in her position as mother has the right to intercede for mankind, and in the General Audience of Wednesday, September 24, 1997, he also said: "Having entered the Father's eternal kingdom she can more effectively exercise in the Spirit the role of maternal intercession entrusted to her by divine Providence... As maternal mediatrix, Mary presents our desires and petitions to Christ, and transmits the divine gifts to us, interceding continually on our behalf."

MEDIATRIX OF ALL GRACES

Now, grace flows from the Father to the Son and when the Church says that the mother of Jesus is Mediatrix of all Graces, she means that all favours and graces granted from the Father to the Son reach us through Mary. It is a privilege given to her by the son. Indeed, didn't Her Majesty herself not give this hint during her apparition in Paris when she showed the image of the Medal of the Immaculate Conception in the Rue du Bac to Catherine Labouré in 1830? "These are the graces I bestow upon those who ask for them," she said to Catherine, referring to the rays emanating from the rings on her fingers. Mary's role as Dispensatrix or Mediatrix of the graces of the redemption follows appropriately from her role as Coredemptrix because of her special participation in meriting the graces of redemption. Indeed, Mary also mediated all graces to humanity by giving birth to Jesus and by bringing the source and author of all graces to the world.

St. Bernard of Clairvaux, who has been rightly called the "Doctor of Mary's Mediation," once wrote: "It is the will of him who wanted us to have everything through Mary ... God has placed in Mary the plenitude of every good, in order to have us understand that if there is any trace of hope in us, any trace of grace, any trace of salvation, it flows from her... God could have dispensed his graces according to his good pleasure without making use of this channel (Mary), but it was his wish to provide this means whereby grace would reach you." And so, to put it another way, in appreciation of his mother's *companionship* and *cooperation* from the crib to the Cross, the godliness of the God-Man, and manliness of the Man-God extended to his mother the privilege to distribute his graces to whomsoever requests them.

Pope Pius VII (1800–1823) referred to Mary as the "Dispensatrix of all Graces." Pope Pius IX (1846–1878), the Marian Pope who defined Mary's Immaculate Conception, wrote: "God has committed to Mary the treasury of all good things, in order that everyone may know that through her is obtained every hope, every grace, and all salvation." Pope Leo XIII (1878–1903) referred to Mary as the "treasurer of our peace with God and dispensatrix of heavenly graces."

Pope Benedict XV (1914—1922) strongly encouraged the spread of the doctrine of Mediatrix of all Graces by granting a special feast of "Mediatrix of all Graces" to any Bishop who desired to celebrate it in his diocese. It was Cardinal Desirée Mercier of Belgium who was the first to receive, through his intercession and petitioning to Pope Benedict XV, the Mass and Office of Mediatrix of all Graces. Pope Pius XII (1939–1958) also had his say: "And since," as St. Bernard declared, "it is the will of God that we obtain all favours through Mary, let everyone hasten to have recourse to Mary... She teaches us all virtues; she gives us her son and with all the help we need, for 'God wished us to have everything through Mary.'"

Finally, in 1989, in a Papal address, John Paul II referred to Mary as the Mediatrix of Graces: "Enlightened by the fullness of Christ's light, Mary, Mediatrix of Graces, reflects him in order to give him to all her children." And so, in the light of the fact that the doctrine of Mary as Mediatrix of all Graces has been universally taught throughout the Church by Popes of the last two hundred years, and in virtue of this universal teaching of the Church, the doctrine of Mediatrix of all Graces already possesses the nature of a defined doctrine of faith. In other words, Mary as Mediatrix of all Graces represents essential Catholic teaching through the order of the ordinary Magisterium.

ADVOCATE

The Church also teaches that Mary intercedes to God the Father through the Son and by the Holy Spirit on behalf of humanity as our Advocate, especially in times of danger and difficulty. As Mark Miravalle also wrote in his book *Mary Coredemptrix, Mediatrix, Advocate*, we can see an authentic foreshadowing of the role of the mother of Jesus as Advocate in the Old Testament role of the Queen Mother, the role and office held by the mothers of the great Davidic kings of Israel.

In the kingdom of Israel, the mother of the king held the exalted office of the Queen Mother. At times she even sat enthroned at the right side of the king. Indeed, the office and authority of the Queen Mother made her the strongest *advocate* to the king for the people of the kingdom, as exemplified in 1 Kings 2:19-20: "And the king rose to meet her, and bowed down to her; then he sat on his throne, and had a seat brought for the king's mother; and she sat on his right. Then she said: 'I have one small request to make of you; do not refuse me.' And the king said to her, 'Make your request, my mother; for I will not refuse you.' "

This Old Testament role of the Queen Mother as Advocate prophetically foreshadows the role of the great Queen Mother of the New Testament, for as the Mother of Christ, the King of all Nations, she is automatically Queen and Mother in the kingdom of God and Mother of all nations on earth. But this title of "Advocate" is ancient Church doctrine. Between 1000 and 1100 AD the *Salve Regina* (Hail, Holy Queen) was composed, and it was the first Christian prayer recited in the New World by Columbus and his men on the island of San Salvador: "Hail, Holy Queen, Mother of Mercy… turn then, most gracious Advocate, thine eyes of mercy toward us…" And so, Her Majesty is not only Advocate but she is also the Queen of Heaven or more precisely the Queen Mother of Heaven — and Earth.

MARY is her name and one can argue a case for using it as a mnemonic where **M** is for Mediatrix, **A** for Advocate, **R** for Redemptrix (Co) and **Y** for the "Yes" she said to Gabriel and God when, as a consequence of her Immaculate Conception, she became Coredemptrix, Mediatrix and Advocate.

Chapter 15

1846. Her Majesty Weeps in La Salette

Of all the Marian apparitions of the last two centuries, the apparition at La Salette is certainly not the best known, as the fame of Guadalupe, Lourdes and Fatima has overshadowed it. Commenting on it, however, Giovanni Ricciardi wrote in the magazine *Thirty Days*: "The La Salette apparition is unique, not only in terms of the message Our Lady gave to the two French shepherds, but also because of the very special human circumstances of the visionaries and the endless polemics over the 'secret' the Virgin left with them that became the object of a whole series of Vatican interventions in the years that followed. It is a complex affair..."

This complex affair began on a September day in 1846 when the Blessed Virgin appeared to two children, Melanie Calvat and Maximin Giraud, in the French village of La Salette in the Alpine mountains, and expressed her sorrow that people had drifted away from prayer and the sacraments and that the world was degenerating. She also criticized the irreverence and impiety of some of the priests and warned of impending disasters if mankind continued on the path of godlessness. It was on a Saturday, the eve of the feast of Our Lady of Sorrows (celebrated at that time on September 20) that she appeared to the children, weeping copiously.

The two youngsters, aged 15 and 11, had not been given any kind of education, religious or otherwise, and what struck people most was that neither of them had much of a memory, but when they had to relate the message of the apparition, they were able to repeat it word for word. Moreover, at no time did they contradict each other, even when they were questioned individually.

Describing the appearance of the weeping Madonna, whom they saw on September 19, Melanie wrote: "Her face was majestic and imposing. She compelled a respectful fear but at the same time as Her Majesty compelled respect, it was mingled with love and she drew me to her. Her gaze was soft and penetrating... The holy Virgin was all beauty and all love, and in her finery as in her person, everything radiated the majesty, the splendour, the magnificence of a Queen beyond compare. Her voice was soft, enchanting, ravishing and warming to the heart. It soothed and softened. The clothing of the most holy Virgin was silver-white and quite brilliant, and the crown of roses which she wore upon her head was so beautiful that it defies imagination. It formed a most beautiful diadem which shone brighter than the earth's sun."

Melanie continued: "She had a most pretty Cross hanging around her neck. It was Our Lord on the Cross. At one end of the Cross there was a hammer and at the other end, a pair of pincers. The Christ was flesh-coloured and at times he appeared to be dead. His head was bent forward and his body seemed to give way as if about to fall, had he not been held back by the nails which held him to the Cross. At other times, he appeared to be alive. His head was then erect, his eyes open, and he seemed to be on the Cross on his own accord. At times, too, he appeared to speak and he seemed to show that he was on the Cross for our sake, out of love for us, to draw us to his love.

"The Holy Virgin, was crying nearly the whole time that she was speaking to me. Her tears flowed gently, one by one, down to her knees, then like sparks of light they disappeared. These tears of our sweet mother, far from lessening her air of majesty, of a Queen, seemed on the contrary to embellish her, to make her more beautiful, more powerful, more filled with love, more maternal, more ravishing. Is it possible to see a mother cry, and such a mother, without doing anything possible to comfort her and change her grief into joy?"

What a moving, eloquent and beautiful description of Her Majesty! Now, with respect to her diadem, the word "rosary" is derived from the Latin *rosarium,* meaning a crown of roses or sometimes, a garden of roses. In short, the colourful crown of roses on her head and which is depicted in drawings of the Virgin of La Salette with the colours red, yellow and white, was in fact the first of her apparitions with a "rosary." It was represented by the crown of roses on her head which "shone brighter than the sun." It signified the spiritual power of her rosary. Indeed, her first miracle in the new world was the garden of roses which blossomed on Tepeyac hill on a winter's day in Guadulape, Mexico on Saturday 9 September 1531.

But Melanie's messages, their prophetic language, the heart-rending appeal to the clergy, and the announcements of fearful punishments were found to be very severe and accounted for the clear hostility of the French Church hierarchy against her. Indeed, she would say later on in one of her letters to a Mr. Schmid. "There are people who believe it is their duty to see that Almighty God does not say things that are too severe or too shocking when he lowers himself to talk to his creatures. They allow the Good Lord to complain about farmers working on Sunday, blasphemy or the omission of Mass... but they do not allow him to complain about the clergy..."

After five years of opposition in certain clerical quarters and after careful examination of the facts, the Church eventually authorized the cult of Our Lady of La Salette. That decree of the Church's approval of the event as supernatural was dated September 19, 1851, the fifth anniversary of the apparition. It stated: "We judge that the apparition of the Blessed Virgin to two shepherds on September 19, 1846 on a mountain in the Alps in the parish of La Salette... shows all the signs of the truth and the faithful have grounds for believing it indubitable and certain."

Melanie Calvat died on December 15, 1904. She had lived a long life of sorrow, frustrations, disbelief in her messages, and humiliations. Yet she persevered. What is probably little known is that at certain times, particularly on Fridays and during Lent, she experienced the stigmata of Christ and bled profusely, but in her humility she begged that the pain remain just as violent but that the outward signs should disappear. These mysterious wounds, however, reopened a number of times and some of her last letters carried the stains to prove it. This was confirmed by Abbé Combe, her spiritual director, who was also her parish priest for the last years of her life.

Fourteen years after her death, permission was given for the disinterment of her virginal corpse. The ceremony took place at 3:00 a.m. on December 19, 1918. The body was found to be intact. After Mass, the precious remains were removed to a small room adjoining the garden before being placed in a magnificent tomb in the middle of the church which was dedicated to the Immaculate Conception. Indeed, it was appropriate for her incorrupt earthly remains to rest in the bosom of the Church of the Immaculate Conception.

On the occasion of the 150th anniversary of the Mother of Sorrows' appearance at La Salette, Pope John Paul II issued this address from the Vatican on May 6, 1996: "This year the diocese of Grenoble, the Missionaries of La Salette and many faithful throughout the world will celebrate the one hundred and fiftieth anniversary of the apparition of the Blessed Virgin on this peak of the Alps in which her message has been unceasingly heralded... In this place, Mary, a mother filled with love, manifested her sadness in the face of the moral evil of humanity. Her tears help us understand the painful gravity of sin, the denial of God, as well as the passionate fidelity that her son, the Redeemer, maintains towards her children, despite a love wounded and rejected.

"The message of La Salette was given to two young shepherds at a time of great suffering. People were scourged by famine, subjected to many injustices, indifference and hostility towards the Gospel message worsened. As she appeared bearing on her breast the likeness of her crucified son, Our Lady showed herself associated with the work of salvation, experiencing compassion for the trials of her children, suffering when they strayed from the Church of Christ as they forgot or rejected the presence of God in their lives, the blessedness of his name.

"The wide diffusion of the event of La Salette bears convincing attestation that the message of Mary is not contained within the suffering expressed by her tears. The Virgin begs us to regain our spiritual composure. She invites us to penance, to perseverance in prayer, and especially to fidelity in the observance of Sunday. Through the witness of the two children, she asks us that her message be made known to all her people... Mary is as present in the Church today as she was on the day of the Cross, on the day of the

Resurrection and the day of Pentecost. She will never abandon the people created in the image and the likeness of God. May she lead all the **nations** of the earth to her son."

Her copious tears shed in La Salette in 1846 would however turn to blood later on in the twentieth century.

The Basilica of La Salette

The two young children of La Salette

Our Lady as she looked in La Salette

The Virgin weeps in La Salette

Chapter 16

1854. The Third Marian Dogma

Let us put it this way. Just as we inherit through genetic transference the bodily and other characteristics of our parents, in like manner, at the spiritual level, our souls have inherited the original sin of our first parents. It is the Church's teaching that the stain of this original sin is removed through baptism, which brings sanctifying grace to the soul, thus making it spiritually alive again, capable of entering heaven and also making the recipient a member of the Church.

Now, it is true that Paul in Romans 3:23 states that "all have sinned," however, if this is taken with absolute literalness we would then also have to include the man Jesus Christ, which is absurd. Jesus was by nature sinless and did not need redemption. The Immaculate Conception, however, does not refer to the conception of Jesus but means that Mary, whose own conception was brought about the normal way, was nonetheless conceived in the womb of her mother without the stain of original sin. She was, as it were, baptized in the womb. This is teaching of the Church.

However, this is not to deny the fact that Mary, too, required a Saviour, for like the other descendants of Adam, by her nature she was subject to the necessity of contracting original sin. But by a special privilege of God, she was preserved from the stain of original sin and certain of its consequences. She was redeemed therefore by the grace of Christ, but in a special way—by anticipation. Hers then was a "preventive" redemption rather than "curative."

In receiving this very special kind of baptism at her conception, Mary was the only exception to the universal law. In the scientific sense, one may say that, as in the case of a vaccine, she was immunized against original sin. The Church also believes that by the grace of God, Mary, like her son, remained free of personal sin her whole life long. Is this teaching scriptural? In fact, there is also no direct statement in the scriptures which say that the God-man was conceived immaculate, and so, although there are also no direct references to the doctrine of Mary's immaculate conception, there is certainly nothing in scripture which denies it. There are, however, a number of indirect scriptural references to support it.

As Mary was uniquely predestined to be the bride of the Holy Spirit (Luke 1:35), to most theologians she obviously had to have a sinless body to bear the God Incarnate, Jesus. Consider also the fall of our first parents. God said to the serpent in the Garden of Eden after the Fall, "I will put enmity between you and the woman, and between your seed and her seed. She will crush your head" (Genesis 3:15). It is therefore through the offspring that she would crush the head of the serpent. This could not be a reference to the first Eve and her offspring Cain. Christian tradition refers to the woman's offspring as Christ for who else but Christ, by the redemptive act of his sacrifice on Calvary, would crush the head of the serpent? If therefore the offspring of the woman is Christ, the "woman" of Genesis 3:15 must be Mary, referred to as "the second Eve."

But the prophesized victory of "crushing" the head and power of Satan would not have been a meaningful victory if the conquering Redeemer had assumed his body from a woman who had once been subject to his adversary. His would only have been a pyrrhic victory if his suffering and subsequent glorified body, the very instrument of the victorious redemption (1Cor. 11:24), had been conceived from a mother who had been contaminated or "conquered" by his enemy through sin, even for a moment.

And so, as the Franciscan St. Bonaventure once said: "It was becoming that the Blessed Virgin Mary by whom the devil was to be conquered should never, *even for a moment,* have been under his dominion." In other words, the perfect bride is not one who had given herself to another man—*even for a moment.* As St. Augustine also said as early as the fourth century: "The honour of Christ forbids the least hesitation on this subject of possible sin by his mother."

The primary theological reason for Mary's immaculate conception given in the encyclical *Ineffabilis Deus* by Pope Pius IX states that she was predestined to be the Theotokos (God-bearer) by the Persons of the Trinity. Other scriptural texts which have been used to support the dogma are found in Luke 1:42: "...and she (Elizabeth) exclaimed with a loud cry: 'Blessed are you among women, and blessed is the fruit of your womb,' and he (Gabriel) came to her and said, 'Hail, full of grace, the Lord is with you.'"

Every law has its exception and it is a maxim that the exception proves and confirms the law. Of this exemption of Mary from the law of spiritual death, the Old Testament Queen Esther is a most interesting illustration. Esther is described in scripture as being exceedingly fair and of incredible beauty. King Ahasuerus of Persia loved her more than all the women and made her his queen, as related in chapter 7 of the Book of Esther. When she approached the king unannounced, contrary to the law, and revealed her Jewishness to him, he said to her: "What is the matter, Esther? Fear not. You shall not die. This law is not made for you, but for all others." And she who was exempted from the law became the instrument through which her nation was saved. Indeed, she was a prefigure of Mary.

In fact, Mary is the most wonderful exemption from the common law in so many other ways. No creature ever was before or will be again the *Mother of God*. She is the mother without man's cooperation. She is the Mother of God and man at the same time. She is a mother while remaining a virgin. Her child is born whilst her virginal integrity is preserved. She nourishes God at her breasts. She commands him by her words and he is subject to her. In all these instances, and so many others, she is the exemption to the law.

God chose his own mother and made the most perfect of women that could be made. He made her sinless and immaculate. That is what St. Bonaventure meant when he wrote: "Mary is that being which God cannot make greater. He can make a greater earth and a greater heaven but not a greater mother." She is the Immaculate Conception, the immaculate preservation, the immunity, the exemption from original sin, all phrases which bear the same significance. But wasn't the first Eve immaculate at birth? Sin had not entered the world as yet. The second Eve was therefore born with the same favourable handicap.

In the 14th and 15th centuries, the great universities and almost all the great religious orders had become bulwarks for the defence of the Immaculate Conception. In the year 1497, the University of Paris unanimously published a statute to the effect that henceforward no one should be admitted as a member of the university who did not swear that he would, to the utmost, assert and defend the position that the Blessed Virgin was preserved and exempted from original sin. Toulouse in France followed the example, and in Italy (Bologna and Naples), in Germany (Cologne, Mayance and Vienna), in Belgium (Lauvin), in England before the Reformation (Oxford and Cambridge), in Spain (Salamanca, Toledo, Seville and Valencia), in Portugal (Coimbra and Evora), and in South America (Mexico and Lima), all their great universities and seats of theological learning bound their members by oath to defend the Immaculate Conception. Such was the religious and Marian fervour in those times.

But it was the Franciscan theologian John Duns Scotus (1266-1308) who was chiefly responsible for introducing the notion of "preservative" redemption into the explicit consciousness of the Church. This was a major breakthrough in helping pave the way for its dogmatic definition. Defenders of the privilege also produced an enormous literature on the subject and between 1600 and 1800, the Jesuits alone brought out three hundred works on the Immaculate Conception. Ruling princes supported the doctrine, and the royal house of Spain sent several delegations to Rome to request the definition of the dogma. Indeed, in 1648, King Juan of Portugal consecrated and dedicated his country to Mary under the title of the Immaculate Conception, and since then no king or queen of Portugal ever wore a crown. It was reserved for the Immaculate Conception!

But Marian theology and devotion deteriorated during the age of the Enlightenment and the revolution which followed it. The revival came from an unexpected source—the apparition of the "Miraculous Medal" (the Medal of the Immaculate Conception) in the Rue du Bac, Paris, in 1830. The final stage of development of the dogma of the Immaculate Conception was thus effected to the accompaniment of a spreading movement of the prayer: "O Mary conceived without sin, pray for us who have recourse to thee."

Pope Pius IX took note of the increasing demand during the pontificate of his immediate predecessor Gregory XVI and the early years of his own for a dogmatic definition of the Marian privilege. It had come from bishops, the secular clergy, religious orders, sovereign rulers and the faithful. That he might proceed with great prudence, he established a special congregation of cardinals and also selected priests, both secular and regular, well-trained in the theological sciences, bidding them to consider the matter and report to him. Of twenty theologians whom the Pope consulted in 1848, seventeen gave a favourable reply. To a preliminary meeting of the Congregation of Cardinals, he put two questions: "Should he define the privilege? How?" To the first, they answered affirmatively, and to the second they advised consultation of the bishops. Of 603 bishops consulted, 546 favoured the definition, 4 opposed and the remainder were undecided either as to its opportuness or timing.

And so, on December 8 of that memorable year 1854, during the celebration of a solemn Mass by Pope Pius IX, surrounded by 152 bishops, 53 cardinals, more than 200 prelates, a vast body of clergy from many countries and some 30 or 40 thousand people who crowded the vast Basilica of St. Peter's in Rome, the Cardinal Dean of the Sacred College advanced to the Pontifical throne, accompanied by an archbishop of the Greek Rite, an archbishop of the Armenian Rite and by 12 of the senior archbishops of the western Church, and addressed the Pope with these words: "For a long time, most blessed Father, has the Catholic Church most ardently wished and entreated with all her desires, that, in your supreme and infallible judgment, you define the Immaculate Conception of the most Holy Virgin Mary, Mother of God, for the increase of her praise, glory and veneration. In the name of the Sacred College of Cardinals, bishops of the Catholic world, and of all the faithful, we humbly and earnestly entreat of you that on this solemnity of the conception of the Most Blessed Virgin, our common vows may be fulfilled..."

To these words the Pontiff answered: "We declare, pronounce, and define that the doctrine which holds that the most blessed Virgin Mary, in the first instant of her conception, by a singular grace and privilege granted by Almighty God, in view of the merits of Jesus Christ, the Saviour, was preserved from all stain of original sin, and is a doctrine revealed by God and therefore to be believed firmly and constantly by all the faithful."

In the Papal Bull, *Ineffabilis Deus*, defining the Immaculate Conception as a dogma of faith, Pope Pius IX began by saying: "… In order that what had been lost in the first Adam would be gloriously restored to the second Adam, from the very beginning and before time began, the eternal Father chose and prepared for his only begotten Son a Mother in whom the Son of God would become incarnate and from whom, in the blessed fullness of time he would be born into this world. Above all creatures did God so love her that truly in her was the Father well pleased with singular delight. Therefore, far above all the angels and all the saints so wondrously did God endow her with the abundance of all heavenly gifts (graces) poured from the treasury of his divinity that this Mother, ever absolutely free of all stain of sin, would possess that fullness of holy innocence and sanctity…, which, outside of God, no mind can succeed in comprehending fully. Hence the words of our predecessor Alexander VII (1655-1667) … 'Ancient indeed is that devotion of the faithful based on the belief that her soul, in the first instant of its creation and in the first instant of the soul's infusion into the body, was, by a special grace of God, in view of the merits of Jesus Christ, her Son and the Redeemer of the human race, preserved free from all stain of original sin. And in this sense have the faithful ever solemnized and celebrated the feast of the conception.'"

The Papal Bull ended by saying: "… all our hope do we repose in the most Blessed Virgin, in the all fair and immaculate one who has crushed the poisonous head of the most Cruel serpent and brought salvation to the world… In her, who, with her only begotten son, is the most powerful Mediatrix and Conciliatrix in the whole world… And since she has been appointed by God to be the Queen of heaven and earth, and even stand at the right hand of her only begotten Son, Jesus Christ, she presents our petitions in a most efficacious manner. What she asks, she obtains. Her pleas can never be unheard."

Chapter 17

1858. "I Am The Immaculate Conception"

Following the apparitions of the Blessed Virgin to Catherine Labouré in 1830 and during the reign of Pius IX, an event of momentous importance in Church history took place. It was the definition of the dogma of the Immaculate Conception in 1854. Four years later on February 11, the Blessed Virgin appeared in the little town of Lourdes. Her Majesty chose the humble grotto of Massabielle near the river Gave to appear to a fourteen-year-old peasant girl, Bernadette Soubirous, on the Thursday before the Mardi Gras. It was to be the first of eighteen apparitions which would end on July 16, 1858.

Bernadette was in the grotto collecting wood. A gust of wind was suddenly heard but not a leaf moved. Her attention was drawn to the cleft of the rock of Massabielle, from which hung the flexible and shaking branches of a wild rose bush. In fact, this spot was very reminiscent of the cleft in the rock fashioned into the sepulcher where Jesus was buried. The mystic Maria Valtorta described it in her diary *The Poem of the Man-God*: "Eventually they rolled the heavy sepulchral stone into its lodging. Some long branches of a ruffled rose-bush hanging from the top of the grotto towards the ground seems to be knocking at the stone door. They seem to be weeping tears of blood as they shed their red petals, and their corollas lie along the dark stone."

Bernadette then saw a golden-coloured cloud which preceded a light. It was a light "more brilliant than the sun." In the midst of this supernatural light a young lady appeared in an instant. She seemed to come out of the depth of the niche cut into the rock. She was dressed in a white garment that also shone brilliantly, with a long white veil, which, covering her head, came down over the shoulders. Her garment was gathered at the waist by a blue cincture, fastened with one bow. Her feet, resting on a carpet of grass and twigs, were bare, but on each one there was a golden rose. This was the panorama which Bernadette experienced and never forgot up to the day she died.

J. B. Estrade, a government official, had faithfully recorded the actual words of Bernadette during her investigation by the French authorities in 1858: "Without thinking what I was doing, I took my rosary in my hands and went on my knees. The lady made a sign of approval with her head and took into her hands a rosary which hung on her right arm (in La Salette she wore a crown of roses). When I attempted to begin the rosary and tried to lift my hand to my forehead, my arm remained paralyzed, and it was only after the lady had signed herself that I could do the same. The Lady left me to pray all alone. She passed the beads of her rosary between her fingers but she said nothing; only at the end of each decade did she say the *'Gloria'* with me." This last detail, which Bernadette in her simplicity could not have invented, reveals a deep theological truth. The *Gloria,* which is a hymn of praise to the Trinity is indeed the only part of the rosary which is suitable to the Virgin. The *Our Father* is certainly not for one who had no need to pray for her daily bread. As for the *Hail Mary,* the angel's greeting, this could only be recited by Bernadette, as the apparition had no need to greet her own self.

A call to penance was given on Friday, February 27. Three times Bernadette heard the word from the Lady's lips and it was followed by her order: " You will kiss the ground for sinners." This message was not only for herself. Bernadette then invited the crowd of about eight hundred to follow her example by bending down and kissing the filthy ground of Massabielle. According to W.B. Sandhurst in his book *We Saw Her,* "Most of them did so gladly, but some, particularly newcomers, were deeply shocked. They never grasped the meaning."

On March 25, 1858, the sixteenth apparition, Bernadette asked the Lady her name. She had previously done so on three occasions, but this time Her Majesty, who until then had kept her hands joined together, that day opened her arms and lowered them as she appeared on the Medal of the Immaculate Conception, thus causing her rosary to slip down towards her wrists. Then she joined her hands again, brought them above her breasts, raised her eyes to heaven in an expression of reverential gratitude, and said: *"I am the Immaculate Conception."* It was the most important sentence in creation history ever uttered by a woman about herself. Then she smiled, spoke no more, and disappeared smiling. It was something to smile about!

It was in this cleft in the rock in Massabielle that the Lady with the lovely face and sweet sounding voice made that historic announcement. The scene immediately brings to mind the words of the Song of Songs 2:13-14: "Arise my love, my beautiful one, and come! O my dove in the cleft of the rock, in the secret recesses of the cleft, let me see you, let me hear your voice, for your voice is sweet, and you are lovely."

Now, she never said that she was "Our Lady of Lourdes." Neither did she say: "I am the result of an Immaculate Conception," nor "I am she who was conceived immaculately." She said: *"I am the Immaculate Conception."* As W. R. Ainsworth once said: "To those who have difficulty with this form of expression, it may well be said that it runs in the family as it was her son who said: *'I am the resurrection and the life'*" (John 11:25). It was an identity which she had *hinted* in Guadalupe in 1531 when she appeared on the feast of the Immaculate Conception, and which she *wrote* on her Medal of the Immaculate Conception in the Rue du Bac, Paris, in 1830. But it was in Lourdes that she *spoke* to Bernadette the words which to this day reverberate throughout its hills and valleys: "I am the Immaculate Conception." It was on March 25, 1858. It was the feast of the Annunciation of the Lord when she accepted the invitation of Ambassador Gabriel to be the Mother of the Redeemer. But to be the Mother of the Redeemer she had first to be the Immaculate Conception!

On Monday July 16, 1858, significantly, the feast of Our Lady of Mount Carmel, the Blessed Virgin appeared to Bernadette for the last time. It was her eighteenth apparition to the little French girl. There was no spoken message. It was a silent farewell. Bernadette, when twenty-two years old, then disappeared into a life of silence and prayer on July 9, 1864, and she donned her nun's habit as Sr. Marie-Bernard of the Sisters of Charity of Nevers. On April 16, 1879, at the age of thirty-five, Bernadette died after a long painful illness. Thirty years later, in 1909, as part of the procedure to canonize her, Pope Pius X instituted an enquiry into her "reputation of holiness." During the course of the enquiry on September 9, 1909, Bernadette's body was exhumed in the presence of the Bishop of Nevers, the Mother Superior of the convent, the civil authorities, and two forensic medical experts. Bernadette's body appeared to be intact!

In 1923, Pope Pius XI ordered a final examination of her body before declaring her "Blessed." On April 18, 1925, forty-six years after her death, Bernadette's body was exhumed once more. This time the autopsy revealed the perfect condition of her internal organs. The surgeon, Dr. Comte, noted, in particular, the astonishingly well-preserved state of her liver, which is the organ most subject to decay. She was canonized in 1933 by Pope Pius XI. Over a hundred years after her death, Bernadette, looking beautiful and as if asleep, lies incorrupt in a glass casket behind the altar rail in the chapel of St. Gildard's convent in Nevers. Thrice I visited the chapel and beheld this miracle which defies all scientific explanation. But the Virgin's apparitions in Lourdes were not to be the last of her apparitions in France during the nineteenth century.

1858. "I Am The Immaculate Conception"

I am the Immaculate Conception

John Paul II in Lourdes

The incorrupt body of St. Bernadette

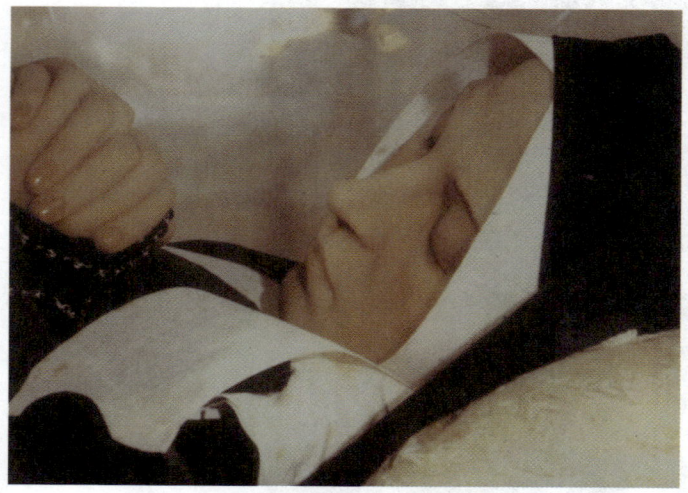
A close up of Bernadette

Chapter 18

Lourdes and Our Lady of Mount Carmel

The Immaculate Conception first appeared to Bernadette Soubirous in Lourdes on March 25, 1858, the feast of the Annunciation. She chose the date for her last apparition in Lourdes. It was on July 16, 1858, significantly the feast of Our Lady of Mount Carmel. There was a reason for this and it highlights the importance of this feast day in Marian history.

Now, the Israelites, in spite of Yahweh's favours and miracles, were still seduced by Baal and other pagan gods. They continued to break the covenant and it was the Prophet Elijah who admonished them in a most dramatic way. The pagans believed that Baal was the master of the earth and agriculture, who controlled the weather and also had the power to allow women to have children. He was called the son of Dagon (the god of agriculture). In Hebrew, Dagon means "grain." The Canaanite religion was chiefly a fertility cult and its practice included ritual prostitution, both male and female, and sometimes child sacrifice. Throughout the centuries this ritual, which included music, magic and sexual orgies, offered a seductive challenge to the Israelites and it is documented that in the later years of his reign (965-926 BC), even the great King Solomon departed from fidelity to Yahweh.

Following the death of Solomon, the reign of King Jeroboam in Israel (931-910 BC) and Rehodoam in Judah (931-913 BC) put Israel deeper and deeper into apostasy. The House of Jeroboam in Israel was succeeded by the House of Omri and King Omri's son, Ahab (874-853 BC), like his predecessors in office, tolerated the practice of Baalism in Israel. However, he angered the God of Israel more than all the other kings of Israel before him as Baal worship came closer to becoming the religion of Israel. Yahweh, however, eventually moved to put an end to this apostasy and duplicity and he called on Elijah to summon Ahab and his people back to single-hearted devotion to Him.

So said, the most severe drought and famine befell the land. The drought slowly began to ravage the land over which Baal was supposedly the almighty lord, and which he alone supposedly could keep rich and fertile. After some three years, during which time the drought had taken its toll, Yahweh told Elijah that it was time to call the people to repentance and to single-hearted devotion to him.

Ahab agreed to a test of strength between Yahweh and Baal, and issued a proclamation summoning all citizens of Israel to the mountain of Carmel, which towered over the plain of Jezreel where they lived. Then Elijah said to the people: "I, I alone am left the prophet of the Lord, but Baal's prophets are four hundred and fifty men. Let two bulls be given to us and let them choose one bull for themselves and cut it in pieces and lay it on the wood (of their altar), but put no fire to it. I will prepare the other bull and lay it on the wood (of my altar) and put no fire to it. You will call on the name of your god and I will call on the name of the Lord and the god who answers by fire—he is God indeed."

The prophets of Baal took the bull which was given to them and laid it on the altar, calling on the name of Baal from morning until noon, saying: "O Baal, answer us," but there was no voice and no one answered. Elijah then put the wood in order, cut his bull in pieces and laid it on the wood. Then, after pouring four jars of water (to make the miracle more impressive) over the holocaust and the crowd, he called upon the Lord, saying: "O Lord, God of Abraham, Isaac and Israel, let it be known this day that you are God in Israel and that I am your servant. Answer me, O Lord, that these people may know that you, O Lord, are God, that you have turned their hearts back."

Then fire fell from heaven and consumed the burnt offering, even though it was soaked in water, and when all the Israelites saw it, they fell on their faces and said: "Yahweh is God! Yahweh is God!" Following this, at the command of Elijah, the awe-struck people seized the false prophets of Baal and brought them down to the river Kishon where they were slaughtered. And so, Mount

Carmel was the mount of God's intervention through the Prophet Elijah in the 8th century BC. It was the mountain where hearts were turned and the Israelites returned to their one God. It was the mount of the renewal of the covenant.

Following the massacre of the prophets of Baal, Elijah now foresaw that the three-year drought would end and he climbed towards the top of Carmel and sat with his face bowed between his knees, waiting. Seven times he sent a servant round the hill to look out over the Mediterranean Sea. It was not until the seventh time that the servant reported seeing a tiny cloud rising above the horizon in the shape of a foot. It was to be the bearer of the rain which would deliver the parched land. And so, Yahweh ended the great drought, thereby demonstrating that it was he who controlled rain, fertility and the powers of nature, and not the pagan god, Baal.

For centuries many commentators on the holy Scriptures have seen in this cloud a prototype of the Holy Virgin who bore in her womb the Redeemer of the world, the Mediator of the new Covenant, he who would bring the water of life to our arid souls. It was a foot-shaped cloud. It was the symbol of the woman who was to arise immaculate from the sea of humankind to crush Satan beneath her heel as she brought forth the Saviour of the world (Gen. 3:15). It was because of this belief that a sanctuary dedicated to the Virgin was built on Mount Carmel.

After many centuries of changes and enlargement of the chapel, it was ruined by the Moslems in 1291, and in 1766, Giambattista, with a great desire to rebuild the chapel, supervised the construction of the larger Carmelite monastery over the site of the first chapel ever built in honour of the Blessed Virgin Mary. And so, it can be said that the Order of the Carmelites was founded by Elijah with the Blessed Virgin Mary as its patroness. It was respected preeminently as the first Marian Order. It is apparently for this reason that the Virgin has a special predilection for Carmel and has sometimes appeared as *Our Lady of Mount Carmel*.

After the Crusaders suffered a severe defeat at the hands of the Moslems, the Holy Land was overrun by the Saracens and groups of Carmelites started leaving Mount Carmel for Europe. In 1242, Sir Richard de Grey of England brought some "Brothers of Our

Lady of Mount Carmel," as they were then called, to his estate of Aylesford in Kent. There they founded a religious house and in 1247 the Brothers elected a Prior General with authority over the Carmelites everywhere.

Tradition has it that, facing many serious difficulties, Simon Stock, the Prior General, had begged the Virgin, as patroness of the Order, to grant some privilege to the Brothers who bore her name. One day he was devoutly reciting the Flos Carmeli (Flower of Carmel) prayer when the Blessed Virgin responded to his fervent plea and appeared to him, holding in her hand a brown scapular. She then said: "Dear son, take the scapular of your Order as the badge of my brotherhood and a special grace for you and all Carmelites. Whoever dies in this garment will not suffer everlasting fire. It is a token of salvation. It safeguards in danger. It pledges us to peace and the covenant." This was on July 16, 1251, now celebrated as the feast of Our Lady of Mount Carmel.

The brown scapular is the continuation of the most ancient gesture of consecration known to man. Elijah, the founder of the Order of Carmel, consecrated his successor Elisha by throwing a cloak over his shoulders, and when Elijah was taken away from this earth, his mantle fell upon Elisha to give him the "spirit of Elijah" (2 Kings 2:14-15). Likewise, the scapular, the symbol of the religious habit, is Mary's consecration cloak. Simply, it is the Woman of Carmel putting her cloak over her children to protect those who wear her habit faithfully and live with the spirituality it denotes. The choice of the colour brown, the colour of humility and of the earth from which we are made, appears to have been Mary's preference.

Carmel is Mary's mount because it is the mount of the Order dedicated to her, and it is also the mount of the renewal of the Covenant by the great Prophet Elijah and the Virgin is the living Ark of the New Covenant. Her ancestors, it is said, also helped carry the ancient Ark of the Covenant. It was all in God's divine plan.

Lourdes and Our Lady of Mount Carmel

Stella Maris Monastery on Mount Carmel

Our Lady of Mount Carmel

Chapter 19

1871. Pontmain and the Franco-Prussian War

"There will be a series of wars until the last war," the Virgin of La Salette, among other prophecies, had told the two little shepherds in 1846. Now, prior to 1870, Prussia was an independent power which, from a small duchy in the sixteenth century, rose to dominate the whole of central Europe and became one of the most powerful empires of recent European history. In 1861, King William I (1797-1888) had appointed Otto von Bismarck to head the Ministry of Foreign Policy and obtain the submission of Parliament. Indeed, Bismarck, at the very beginning of his ministry, informed the Diet that "the question of the day was not to be decided by speeches and majority votes, but by blood and iron."

He then built up the Prussian economy, the military and its financial power. From 1868 onwards, he set about to accomplish the unification of Germany, if necessary, in a war of all the German states against France, while Emperor Napoleon III sought through military preparedness and alliances to defeat Prussia and recover part of the Rhine frontier. Bismarck eventually provoked a conflict with France, and on July 19, 1870, the French were foolishly taunted to declare war on Prussia. To Bismarck's great satisfaction, the south German states, regarding France as the aggressor, at once came to his support. It was the beginning of "a series of wars," as predicted by the Virgin. The Prussian army was superior to the French in almost every respect and the Germans won a decisive victory at the battle of Sedan on September 1-2, 1870. Napoleon III was taken prisoner.

This unification of Germany ended centuries of disunity and division and is regarded as one of the most significant events of the 19th century. German unity had been brought about by bringing all the separate states within Prussian control, for Prussia was greater in area and population than all the rest of the German Empire together, and the Prussian capital Berlin was also the imperial capital. The German Empire was, therefore, in reality a Prussian empire. It led to a complete change in the European "balance of power."

The France of 1870-71 was a country that bothered little at that time with matters of the spirit and the churches were empty. However, Pontmain, a village of about 500 people, was a fortunate exception to the rule of religious indifference. Pontmain's people were farmers and devout believers. In July 1870, when the Franco-Prussian War had begun, thirty-eight young men from Pontmain had been conscripted and were serving in the defense of their homeland. Their families and friends were desperate with fear and concern for them and for the nation.

On January 17, 1871, the Prussians were closing in on Laval, the capital of the region in which tiny Pontmain was situated. On that morning, even as the Prussian General Schmidt was leading his soldiers closer and closer, the parish priest of Pontmain, Abbé Michel Guérin, was offering prayers of hope: "Let us add penance to our prayers," he said, "and then we may take courage. . . God will have pity on us; his mercy will surely come to us *through Mary.*"

It was no more than eleven hours later that his words began to be fulfilled for Pontmain. It was a wintry day. About six o'clock in the evening and twenty feet above the roof tops, two children saw a beautiful lady with her hands stretched out in a gesture of welcome. She wore a blue dress studded with golden stars. This star-studded tunic without a belt fell straight down to her feet and barely covered her gold-ribboned slippers. She also wore a black veil which hid her hair and her ears, and at the back reached down to her waist. On her head was a plain crown widening towards the top. It was without decoration except for a red band almost midway around it. This is what the children, Eugene and Joseph Barbedette, saw. A little later two other children, Francoise Richer and Jeanne-Marie Lebossé, also witnessed the apparition.

Around the upper half of her body were three white stars disposed in the shape of a triangle, one above her head and the other two to the right and left of her waist line. An oval frame of the same blue colour as her dress surrounded the vision. Inside the frame four candles stood on horizontal ledges, two at heart level and the other two around knee height. Then from beneath the oval frame the children saw a little star move from candle to candle, lighting them on the way before it rested in a position directly above the frame.

Little by little, the villagers gathered and they, too, saw the three stars but not the Virgin.

The parish priest invited the crowd to say the rosary and the Virgin's expression showed how attentive she was to the prayer. As the rosary was completed, Abbé Guérin began to recite the *Magnificat*. The old man's heart was full of emotion. Devotion to the Mother of God had been a passion all of his life. Soon, under her feet, a scroll unrolled, on which, one by one, gold letters slowly appeared. They were spelt out excitedly in a loud voice by the children and in the end the sentence read: "But pray my children. God will answer you in a short while. My son will respond to your prayers."

As the people rejoiced over this news, the Virgin smiled gloriously in response. A small red Cross then appeared over the Lady's heart and the vision grew larger in size as the prayers were being said. How significant! The stars on her gown seemed to multiply so fast that she seemed clothed in gold rather than navy blue. After a momentary silence the priest suggested that they sing the hymn "Mother of Hope." At the end of the hymn the banner bearing the inscription vanished and a large blood-red crucifix was then seen in front of the vision bearing the body of Christ of the same colour. She held it in both hands, slightly tilted towards the children, and at the top of the Cross was an inscription in large red letters against a white background: **JESUS CHRIST**. She showed it to the children with a look of such deep sorrow that the children's faces suddenly became sad as they saw the sorrowful expression of the beautiful Lady. The Blessed Virgin kept looking at the Cross of her son.

Indeed, all his life Joseph Barbedette remembered that moment as it made a deep impression on him. He wrote in his diary:

"Her face was marked with a profound sorrow... The trembling of her lips at the corner of her mouth showed a deep feeling...Yet, no tears ran down her face... A few months later, I saw my own mother overwhelmed with grief when my father died. One knows how such a sight can affect the heart of a child. Nevertheless, I remembered thinking that my mother's sorrow was nothing in comparison with that of the Blessed Virgin. It was truly the Mother of Jesus at the foot of her son's Cross."

The crowd prayed fervently and started to sing the hymn *Ave Maris Stella*. The blood-red crucifix then disappeared and the Virgin extended her hands again towards the people, and smiled ever so sweetly. At the same time, two small white crosses appeared on her shoulders. Once more her face lit up with joy and then the vision slowly vanished. It was almost 9 o'clock in the evening.

On the day after the vision, January 18, 1871, the relentless advance of the German troops which had reached the gates of Laval suddenly stopped and following instructions from higher authorities, General Schmidt and his German troops unexpectedly withdrew without fighting and abandoned the country. Ten days later, on January 28, Paris surrendered, the armistice was signed, the war was over, and the thirty eight soldiers who had been conscripted from the parish of Pontmain all returned home unscathed. In gratitude, the prayers which the Virgin requested continued to grow in fervour and crowds from many miles around the village flocked to Pontmain. Many conversions followed and the parish church was no longer big enough to house the faithful. A huge basilica now stands in its place, and there some two hundred thousand pilgrims go each year to pray to "Our Lady of Hope," the lady who came to save a little village which prayed and had hope in her. The Basilica was later called the Basilica of Our Lady of Hope.

As for the children, they were thoroughly examined by three doctors, who ruled out any question of hallucination and other neurotic factors to explain their testimony. After an extensive enquiry, on February 2, 1872, Mgr. Wicart, Bishop of Laval, came to this decision: "We judge that the Immaculate Virgin Mary, Mother of God, truly appeared on the 17th January, 1871 to Eugene Barbedette, Joseph Barbedette, Francoise Richer and Jeanne-Marie Lebossé in the hamlet of Pontmain."

And so, once more Her Majesty appeared at a time of war, impending or actual, either to warn or to console, while asking for prayer and penance. These wartime apparitions will continue into the twentieth century. The Franco-Prussian War of 1870-71 eventually led to the World War I of 1914-18.

Our Lady of Hope in Pontmain

The Basilica in Pontmain

Chapter 20

1917. Our Lady of the Rosary of Fatima

On August 20, 1914, Pope Pius X died and on September 3, Giacomo della Chiesa was elected Pope. He chose the name Benedict XV. World War I had just begun on August 20, 1914, and in his first statement as Pope, on September 8, 1914 (the feast of the Nativity of the Blessed Virgin Mary), Benedict XV mourned the bloodshed, and pleaded for a quick end to the war. He denounced the war as a crime against religion, humanity and civilization, waged as it was by Catholic countries. He blamed both sides equally for allowing it to happen and to continue. In his first encyclical *Ad Beatissimi*, issued on November 1, 1914, he also criticized the warring Christian peoples. "Who could realize," he said, "that they are brethren, children of the same Father in heaven?" His encyclical closed with a call for prayer to Christ and to the Blessed Virgin Mary, "who bore the Prince of Peace."

On May 31, 1915, at the height of the war, he sent a letter addressed to all the bishops of the world: "Let us raise our prayers more ardently and fervently than ever towards him in whose hands are the destiny of the nations and let us confidently implore the Sorrowful and Immaculate Heart of Mary, the very sweet mother of Jesus and our mother, that by her powerful intercession, she may obtain from her divine Son the prompt ending of the war and the return of peace and tranquility."

The Angel and the Eucharist

In the spring of 1916, while World War I was raging across Europe, an angel, believed to be Michael the Archangel, appeared to three little children, Lucia, Jacinta and Francisco, in the Cova da

Iria, about two miles from Fatima. He said: "I am the Angel of Peace. Pray with me." Then, kneeling on the ground, he bowed until his head touched the ground and asked them to pray with him: "My God, I believe, I adore, I hope and I love you. I ask pardon for those who do not believe, do not adore, do not hope, do not love you." Then raising his head, he said: "The Hearts of Jesus and Mary are attentive to the voice of your supplications." He then disappeared.

The second apparition of the angel took place two months later in the summer of 1916. Once more, he spoke of the Hearts: "Pray, pray, very much! The Hearts of Jesus and Mary have designs of mercy on you. Offer prayers and sacrifices constantly to the Most High." In the autumn of the same year, the angel appeared for the third and final time. He was holding a chalice, and a Sacred Host was suspended above it. Most significantly, and in confirmation of the transubstantiation as taught by the Orthodox and Catholic Churches, drops of blood fell into the chalice from the Host.

Leaving the chalice and the Host, both miraculously suspended in the air, he then prostrated himself before the Sacred Presence and recited this prayer: "Most Holy Trinity, Father, Son and Holy Spirit, I adore you profoundly and I offer you the most precious Body, Blood, Soul and Divinity of Jesus Christ, present in all the tabernacles of the world, in reparation for the outrages, sacrileges and indifference with which He Himself is offended. Through the infinite merits of His most Sacred Heart and the Immaculate Heart of Mary, I beg of you the conversion of poor sinners." He then gave the Host to Lucia and the chalice to Francisco and Jacinta from which to drink.

On May 5, 1917, in a letter to his Secretary of State, Cardinal Gasparri, Benedict XV wrote: "Our earnestly pleading voice, invoking the end of this vast conflict, the suicide of civilized Europe, was then and has remained ever since unheard... Since all graces which the Author of all good deigns to grant to the poor children of Adam, by a loving design of his divine providence, are dispensed through the hands of the Most Holy Virgin, we wish that the petition of her most afflicted children, more than ever in this terrible hour, may turn with lively confidence to the august Mother of God."

He then directed that the invocation "*Queen of Peace*, pray for us" be added permanently to the Litany of Loreto, and made his ultimate appeal to her: "To Mary, then, who is the Mother of Mercy and omnipotent by grace, let this loving and devout appeal go up from every corner of the earth, from noble temples and tiniest chapels, from royal palaces and mansions of the rich as from the poorest hut, from every place where a faithful soul finds shelter, from blood-drenched plains and seas. Let it bear to her the anguished cry of mothers and wives, the wailing of innocent little ones, the sighs of every generous heart; let her most tender and benign solicitude be moved and the peace we ask for be obtained for our agitated world."

Enter Her Majesty

Eight days later, on Sunday May 13, 1917, Her Majesty responded to the prayers of the Pope and the rest of the Catholic world, and appeared in Fatima, Portugal. May 13 was in those days the feast of Our Lady of the Blessed Sacrament or Our Lady of the Eucharist. It was not an accidental choice of date. It was a glorious spring day in Fatima when she appeared to the three children, Lucia, Jacinta and Francisco. Atop a small holm oak tree about three feet tall, they saw a ball of light, within which stood a Lady clad in white. To quote Lucia's own words: "We beheld a Lady all dressed in white. She was more brilliant than the sun and radiated a light more clear and intense than a crystal glass filled with sparkling water, the rays of the burning sun shining through it."

She wore a white mantle falling to her feet, edged in burnished gold. A prominent star shone from the hem of her robe, while from her hand hung an exquisite rosary of white pearls. The children were within two yards of her. "Do not be afraid," she said. Her voice was ever so musical and gentle. It was the assurance she herself had heard when the Archangel Gabriel first greeted her in Nazareth (Luke 1:30). Calmly awed by her regal appearance, Lucia politely asked: "Where does Your Excellency come from?" "I come from heaven," the Lady replied. "I want you to come here on the 13th of each month until October when I will tell you who I am and what I want."

"Your Excellency," Lucia said. And how appropriate! She then spoke to them about personal matters and of their own salvation. But in her last words to them on that day, she stressed the immense crisis which had brought her from heaven, and implored: *"Say the rosary to obtain peace for the world and the end of the war."* Then, rising from the top of the little holm oak tree, she slipped away into the sky toward to east. Significantly, on the very day that Her Majesty came to the children in the Cova da Iria in Fatima, a young Vatican diplomat named Eugenio Pacelli was consecrated Archbishop in the Sistine Chapel where the College of Cardinals meets to elect Popes. One day he would take the name Pope Pius XII and he would define the fourth Marian dogma of the bodily Assumption of the Blessed Virgin Mary.

On June 13, the Lady came back to the Cova da Iria. She then showed them a vision of her Immaculate Heart, encircled by piercing thorns representing the sorrows she suffered and the sins that wounded her. It is therefore a vision of her Sorrowful and Immaculate Heart. She then said to Lucia: "God wishes you to remain in the world for some time because he wants you to establish in the world devotion to my Immaculate Heart, for the Heart of Jesus wants my Immaculate Heart to be venerated by His side. I promise salvation to those who embrace it and their souls will be loved by God as the flowers placed by myself adorn His throne." Soon after saying this, she departed into the east as before. The upper leaves in the oak tree remained for several minutes stretched and bending towards the east, as if bidding her farewell. And so, nature also responds to and salutes Her Majesty!

On July 13, after showing the children a vision of hell, the Lady said to Lucia: "You have seen hell where the souls of poor sinners go. To save them God wishes to establish in the world devotion to my Immaculate Heart. If people do what I ask, many souls will be saved and there will be peace. The war (World War I) is going to end soon, but if people will not stop offending God, another and more terrible war will begin during the reign of Pius XI. . . To prevent this, I shall come to ask for the consecration of Russia to my Immaculate Heart and the Communion of Reparation on the five first Saturdays. If my requests are granted, Russia will be converted and there will be peace. If not, she will scatter her errors throughout the world, provoking wars and the persecution of the Church. The good will be martyred, the Holy Father will have much to suffer and various nations will be annihilated. In the end my Immaculate Heart will triumph, the Holy Father will consecrate Russia to me, Russia will be converted and a certain period of peace will be granted to the world." Now, it is important to note that at that time Russia was a very Christian country, mainly Orthodox, nor did the uneducated children ever hear of that country before. In fact, they thought that "Russia" was the name of a woman!

Russia did indeed scatter her errors, wars and persecutions throughout the world. However, Mary's warning and her promise resounded down through years and all over the world millions of people did pray the rosary as she had asked, and pleaded for a rescue from heaven. Perhaps none prayed more devoutly and passionately than the victims of Communist rule in Eastern Europe and Russia, where, although the Fatima prophecy was never allowed to be publicly mentioned, it was very widely known.

On August 13, among other things, she said to the children: "I want you to continue praying the rosary every day. In the last month [October], I will perform a miracle so that all may believe." The following month, on September 13, she also spoke very briefly: "Continue to say the rosary to bring about the end of the war. In October, Our Lord will come also, as well as Our Lady of Sorrows and Our Lady of Mount Carmel. St. Joseph will appear with the Child Jesus to bless the world. God is pleased with your sacrifices."

The Miracle of the Sun

It was now October 13. Expectations were high. The Cova da Iria was crowded with 70,000 curious spectators. There were also, of course, many skeptics. The ground was quite muddy from the heavy downpour of rain that day. Indeed, there were umbrellas in abundance. According to Dr. Joseph Garrett, Professor of Natural

Sciences at Coimbra University, as quoted in Francis Johnston's book (*Fatima: The Great Sign*): "A little after one o'clock the children arrived at the site. It must have been about half past one when there rose up on the precise spot where the children were, *a column of smoke*, a delicate and slender bluish column which went straight up above their heads and then evaporated. The phenomenon lasted for some seconds and was perfectly visible to the naked eye. It was repeated yet a second and a third time." This was Her Majesty's calling card, as it were. It was one of her Marian symbols—*the column of smoke* (Song of Songs 3:6; 8:5).

It was soon after that the children suddenly saw the usual flash from the east. To quote Lucia's own words: "We saw the flash of light, and then Our Lady appeared on the holm oak. She said: 'I want to tell you that a chapel is to be built here in my honour." And then, as promised on May 13, she disclosed who she was: *"I am the Lady of the Rosary.* Continue to pray the rosary every day. The war is going to end, and the soldiers will soon return to their homes."

Now, I wish to emphasize that she never called herself "Our Lady of Fatima." That terminology, as far as I am concerned, is solely geographic. She said: *"I am the Lady of the Rosary,"* and by calling her "Our Lady of Fatima," we obscure her true message. My personal choice of name is the *Lady of the Rosary of Fatima*!

The Queen of the Universe then opened her hands, and it seemed to Lucia that light rose straight up from them to the very zenith of the grey skies. The clouds then parted, the sun appeared in the blue window thus opened, and the three children saw a tableau of the Holy Family with St. Joseph holding the Child Jesus in one arm. He then raised the other arm three times to bless the crowd with the sign of the Cross. Our Lord appeared in his glorified manhood and blessed the world as St. Joseph had done. Finally, Lucia saw the Blessed Virgin Mary wearing the brown robe of *Our Lady of Mount Carmel*, holding the brown scapular in her hand and her infant son on her knee, after which the sun began to dance, whirl violently, while flinging off brilliant streamers of coloured lights before it began to hurl itself to earth. It was the greatest miraculous spectacle in Marian history.

Two days later, on October 15, 1917, the *Diario de Noticias*

(Daily News) which commanded the largest circulation in Portugal at the time, had a headline which read: *The Miracle of Fatima. More than fifty thousand people gather at the place of the apparitions.* The article continued as follows: "A wave of emotion seemed to take hold of those many thousands of believers and curious alike. As a great number of people had their umbrellas open, the little ones asked the people to shut them. Then an extraordinary thing happened. According to the testimony of thousands and thousands present there, the sun appeared like a dull silver plate spinning round in a circular movement as if it were moved by electricity, according to the expression used by knowledgeable people who witnessed the fact. Then thousands of people, swayed by emotion and who knows, even dazzled by the light of the sun that had appeared for the first time that day, fell to the ground, weeping and raising their hands, joined instinctively in prayer. On their faces expression of ecstatic rapture could be observed. Their simple hearts prayed and wept in the presence of this strange sensation, which for them at the moment was miraculous. According to what we heard, there were people who seemed to see the sun leave its supposed orbit, break through the clouds and descend to the horizon, many crying out in fear that the giant orb would precipitate itself to the earth on top of them, and imploring the protection of the Holy Virgin."

Dr. Garrett also wrote the following testimony in December 1917: "The sun had broken through the thick layer of clouds that hid it and shone clearly and intensely... It was a remarkable fact that one could fix one's eyes on the brazier of heat and light without any pain in the eyes or blinding of the retina... The sun's disc did not remain immobile for it spun round on itself in a mad whirl, when suddenly a clamour was heard from all the people. The whirling sun seemed to loosen itself from the firmament and advanced threateningly upon the earth as if to crush us with its huge fiery weight. The sensation during those moments was terrible."

After ten minutes the sun retreated to its celestial abode. The spectators were rescued, as it were, from apparent annihilation! October 13, 1917 was an unforgettable experience for those 70,000 people. The poet Alfonso Lopes Vieira saw the miracle of the sun from his own house. Other distant witnesses of this event absolutely destroyed any theory of mass suggestion or hallucination generated by emotion and expectation among the crowd as an explanation of what was seen in the sky.

At that time science knew little about nuclear fission and fusion of atoms. An atom with its central nucleus is the smallest possible piece of an element. However, it was not until 1938 that the German physicist Otto Hahn discovered a new radioactive process: nuclear fission, with the power to release unprecedented amounts of energy. Nuclear fission is the splitting of the nucleus of an atom with the release of a huge amount of heat energy. This is the principle of the atom bomb. Nuclear fusion, on the other hand, is the joining together of two atoms of the lightest element, hydrogen, to form helium, which is the second lightest element by atomic weight. However, a high temperature is needed before hydrogen is affected by nuclear reactions.

Now, the sun is a gigantic ball of hydrogen nearly 1 million miles in diameter and in its core there is a furnace of about 15,000,000°C, which continually converts hydrogen into helium by fusion. In other words, the sun is a gigantic nuclear reactor, a continuously exploding hydrogen bomb. It must be difficult to appreciate what a temperature of 15,000,000°C means. Water, for example, boils at about 100°C, and the temperature in an electric stove is less than 3,000°C. The surface of the sun is about 6,000°C but its center is 15,000,000°C. Indeed, if the solar surface was as hot as its core, the earth would be vaporized within a few minutes.

This nuclear fusion reaction in the sun has resulted in continuous explosions over the past 5 billion years (the estimated age of the sun). It is these continuous nuclear explosions which illuminate the planets and sustain life on earth. In fact, the idea of a hydrogen bomb is to produce an extremely rapid conversion of hydrogen into helium, that is, to do exactly what the sun does, but to do it quickly. This is achieved by including a device causing an extremely high temperature in the bomb. This scale of temperature occurs during the explosion of an uranium or plutonium bomb. It is about 150,000,000°C, which is about ten times greater than the temperature at the center or core of the sun! The miracle of the sun on October 13, 1917, performed by the Woman of the Apocalypse (Rev. 11:19;12:1), should now assume its true apocalyptic significance. It appears therefore that Satan is using the principle of the nuclear reactor, the sun, not to sustain life on earth but to destroy it.

Three days after the miracle, on October 16, the Russian Bolshevic Central Committee authorized Vladimir Lenin's return from exile in Switzerland to Petrograd and a few days later he slipped back into Russia disguised with a grey wig, large spectacles and with his beard shaved off. On November 8, 1917, the Communist government was formally established under the name of the Soviet of Peoples' Commissars. Lenin was President, Trotsky was Commissar for Foreign Affairs, and Stalin, the Commissar for Nationalities. Then on November 13, 1917, six months after the Blessed Virgin Mary had warned in Fatima, the Kremlin fell to the communists in Moscow!

Our Lady of the Eucharist

Jacinta, Francisco, Lucia

Pope John Paul II greets Sr. Lucia

Chapter 21

Why Did Mary Choose Fatima?

The history of the village called Fatima dates back to the time when the Mohammedans capitulated and left Spain and the Iberian Peninsula. Their last holdings were in Portugal, which they had occupied for centuries. Legend has it that among the last persons preparing to leave was a maiden named Fatima, the daughter of the last Muslim chief. She was in love with a Christian and was attracted to his faith. When her countrymen finally left Portugal, Fatima became a Christian, married, and to this day the village where the couple settled bears her name.

Fatima is also the name of the daughter of the Prophet Muhammad and after her death he wrote: "You shall be the most blessed woman in Paradise, after Mary." In a variant of the text, Fatima is made to say: "I surpass all the women, except Mary." In fact, the Koran has many passages on the Blessed Virgin and acknowledges her Immaculate Conception and also her virgin birth. However, Jesus is seen in the Koran as a Prophet, but not as great as Muhammad. Muhammad is seen as the ultimate and greatest Prophet of God, and the central doctrine of the Muslims is expressed in their frequent declaration, "There is no God but Allah, and Muhammad is His Prophet."

Islam denies the divinity of Jesus and also teaches that he was not put to death on the Cross. The Koran also condemns the dogma of the Trinity. It is, therefore, of more than passing interest that not only did the Blessed Virgin choose to appear in a village with the name of Fatima, but that her apparitions there were preceded by the proclamation of the divinity of Jesus and the adoration of the Holy Trinity by the "Angel of Peace."

In his address at the International Congress, preparatory to the closing of the Holy Year at Fatima in October 1951, the much revered Bishop Fulton Sheen asked the question: "Why should Our Lady be known by the same name as a descendant of Muhammad, albeit a convert?" The Bishop, expressing his personal interpretation, answered his own question: " It is because Our Lady came for the conversion, not merely of the hammer and the sickle, but also of the carriers of the crescent and the star!" In the October Revolution of that year (1917), the Bolshevik Party seized power in Russia, promising the great lie, as history has since shown, of "peace, land, and bread," and in March 1918, the Party changed its name to the Russian Communist Party. Its manifesto was that of Karl Marx, who had rejected the idea of a God, deciding that religion was merely the "opiate of the people." His arrogant colleague Zinoviev also declared: "We shall vanquish God in his highest heaven!"

The Thirteenth of the Month

In the light of the seriousness of the Fatima secrets, why did Mary choose the thirteenth day of the month for her six apparitions in Fatima? Abbé André Richard, D.D., one of the greatest experts on the Fatima message, was also asked: "What is the meaning of the star on Our Lady's robe when she appeared in Fatima? He answered: "Read the Book of Esther."

The Book of Esther tells the story of the great and courageous Jewish Queen Esther, one of the wives of King Ahasuerus of Persia, who was unaware of Esther's Jewish ethnicity. The Jews were in that land in exile from their homeland Israel after the Babylonians' victory over them. However, the treacherous anti-semitic Haman had persuaded the king to annihilate them and a date was chosen by lot for their destruction. It was the thirteenth of the month (Adar 13). It was then that the noble Mordecai, himself Jewish, entreated Queen Esther to intervene for the Jews. "I shall go to the king in spite of the law; and if I perish, I perish," she said. The king acceded to Esther's plea and through her courageous *intercession*, her people were saved from mass annihilation on the thirteenth day (see chapter 7).

In Fatima another courageous woman and "intercessor" appeared on May 13, 1917, wearing a star on the hem of her dress.

She came to save the world from the continuing carnage of World War I and to warn of the impending peril which the world was facing. Esther means "Star." And so, Queen of Heaven came *in the spirit of Esther* to save her children from mass annihilation. All the statues of Our Lady of Fatima have a golden crown on her head, but she never wore a crown when she appeared in Fatima. She did however wear a golden star just above the hem of her gown. Her "crown" was therefore subtly represented by the star!

She came calling for conversion and reparation for our souls' sake. She also came promoting adoration of the Holy Trinity and Jesus in the Blessed Sacrament. She came proclaiming the divinity of her son and calling for devotion to His Sacred and Her Immaculate Heart. She pleaded for the daily recitation of the rosary, the wearing of the scapular and the communion of reparation on the five first Saturdays. These were the weapons to be used against the spirits of darkness in these end times.

The Rosary and the Scapular

The only remaining survivor of the three children of Fatima, Lucia, now Sister Mary of the Immaculate Heart in the Carmelite cloister in Coimbra, Portugal, was once asked why Our Lady held the scapular in her hand in the final apparition of Fatima. She answered: "Because Our Lady wants everyone to wear the scapular... The reason for this is that the scapular is our sign of consecration to the Immaculate Heart of Mary." Asked if the scapular is as necessary in the fulfillment of the requests of Our Lady of Fatima as is the rosary, Lucia replied: "The scapular and the rosary are inseparable."

One may also well ask why did Her Majesty choose Portugal for this important manifestation? It is because Portugal since its foundation was called "La Terra de Santa Maria" and was officially consecrated to the Immaculate Virgin under the title of "the Immaculate Conception" in 1646 by King John IV, the restorer of national independence, and on October 20 of that year, as a sign of his love and recognition, he laid down his royal crown at the feet of Our Lady of the Immaculate Conception. With all his nation reunited, he proclaimed her patroness of his kingdom. This consecration proceeded by two centuries the Marian Dogma of the Immaculate Conception by Pope Pius IX. After that ceremony, no king of Portugal ever wore a crown. It was reserved for Her Majesty, the Queen of Heaven and Patroness of Portugal.

Francisco and Jacinta

In December 1918, Francisco fell ill with Spanish influenza, which was ravishing the country. Shortly after, Jacinta fell victim to the same dreaded disease, which was to claim 20 million lives around the world. He died on April 4, 1919 after begging everyone's pardon for anything that he may have done to offend them. He expired peacefully and his body was buried in quicklime as was the custom. When it was finally exhumed in 1952 for translation to the new Basilica of the Rosary in Fatima, only his bones were found but clutched in the remains of his fingers was his fifteen decade rosary. Jacinta died on February 20, 1920. She had been heard lamenting the lost souls who were in hell and pleading with God to accept the pain and penance for hardened sinners.

Great numbers came to pay their respect in the Church of the Angels and everyone noticed an unearthly fragrance emanating from Jacinta's body. In 1935, her body was transferred to lie beside the mortal remains of Francisco. When the coffin was opened on that occasion, everyone was astonished to find that the body was well preserved, despite the quicklime in which it had been buried. Jacinta's body was then transported to the new Basilica of the Rosary, still in a remarkable state of preservation.

On May 13, 1938, in an impressive ceremony, 500,000 pilgrims poured into the Cova da Iria when the solemn consecration of Portugal to the Immaculate Heart of Mary was renewed. It is highly significant that the sole diocese in Spain which had been similarly consecrated, that of Seville, was the only one left unscathed by the Spanish Civil War (1936—1939), which claimed 2 million casualties.

Chapter 22

The Meaning of Devotion to the Immaculate Heart

When I was a very young boy I could not help noticing the large painting in my mother's room of Jesus as the Sacred Heart with his heart in flames and with such anatomical prominence. At that time I found it to be somewhat unreal and awesome. However, its significance eventually came with time—a long time.

Symbolically, the heart is the organ of love. This tireless pump, about the size of a clenched fist, and weighing only slightly more than half a pound, unceasingly beats more than 2.5 billion times in seventy years. Now, just as the physical heart is an "untiring" organ, incessantly beating during life, the heart of Jesus as an object of devotion is a reflection of his untiring and indefatigable love for men. It is his physical heart which during his mortal life did beat in his breast and still beats in his glorified body in heaven. In fact, it is the word which has been used most often in the Bible. It occurs about seven hundred times, even more than the word "God" or "Lord." The first time that it is mentioned is in Genesis 6:5-6: "The Lord saw that the wickedness of man was great on the earth. . . It grieved him to his heart." The last time is in the Book of Revelation 2:23: "It is I who search the heart and loins and give each of you what your behaviour deserves."

The cult of devotion to the heart of Jesus was spread by St. Margaret Mary Alacoque after she received visions of Our Lord as the "Sacred Heart" in 1671 in her convent in Paray le Monial, France. Indeed, the devotion to the Immaculate Heart of Mary must be seen as a logical sequence to the devotion to the Sacred Heart of Jesus. The first message the nun received was on December 27, 1673. Significantly, it was the feast of St. John the Evangelist, often referred to as the "apostle of love" and "the beloved disciple." It was then that Jesus first spoke of his great love: "My divine heart is so inflamed with love for men, and for you in particular, that it is unable any longer to contain within itself the flames of its burning love. It needs to spread them abroad through you and so manifest itself to them, in order to enrich them with the precious treasures which this heart contains—graces of holiness and salvation which are necessary to withdraw them from the abyss of perdition. I have chosen you, in spite of your unworthiness and lack of knowledge, for the accomplishment of this great design so that it may better appear that it has been done by myself."

Thereupon he asked her for her heart, which she then implored him to take, and in a mystical transaction of which only God is capable, he took it from her breast and planted it into his own heart, then, withdrawing it as a burning flame in the form of a heart, he replaced it in her breast. Dr. Christian Barnard should have acknowledged this as the first documented heart transplant! To the doubting Thomases of the world this may sound impossible, but there was visible proof that this mystical transaction had taken place for there was a closed wound in Margaret's side which opened on the first Friday of each month. Indeed, this extraordinary physical evidence left no doubt as to the authenticity of her revelations. Of relevant interest also is that many historians believe that the Crucifixion took place on the "first Friday" of the month of April.

The "Great Revelation," as it is called, was the occasion in June,1675 when Jesus appeared in all his splendour and said to St. Margaret Mary: "Behold this heart which has so much love for men that it spared nothing, even to exhausting and consuming itself, in order to give them testimony of its love. If only they would give me some return for my love I would think but little of all that I have done for them and would wish, were it possible, to suffer still more. But in return I mostly receive only ingratitude through their irreverence and sacrileges, and through the coldness and scorn that they have for me in the sacrament of Love." Then he added: "But what gives me most sorrow is that there are hearts consecrated to me who treat me so. Do you at least console me by making up for the ingratitude as far as you can. Therefore, I ask of you that the first Friday after the octave of Corpus Christi be set apart for a special feast in honour of my heart, by communicating on that day, and by making solemn reparation to it by a solemn act in order to make amends for the indignities which it has received during the time it has been exposed on the altars. I promise you that my heart shall expand itself in abundance the influence of its divine love upon those who shall so honour it, and cause it to be honoured."

But she did give birth to him. There was no human father in that conception. It is to Mary, therefore, that we owe the heart of Jesus, and so, thanks to her consent, he took upon himself a human heart. But at the same time it is to Jesus that we owe the heart of Mary! And so, in a sense, the two hearts are one heart and they are one in their love. The credible St. Bridget of Sweden (died 1373) had a great devotion to the heart of Mary, and Jesus himself spoke to her about the loving identity and oneness of their two hearts: "The heart of my mother," he said to her, "was like mine. Therefore, I confirm that we worked together for the salvation of mankind; I, by the sufferings endured in my body; she, by the sorrows of the love in her heart."

The earliest written justification of devotion to the Immaculate Heart of Mary is found in the Gospel of St. Luke: "But Mary kept all these words, pondering them in her heart." (Luke 2:19). The heart of Mary, like the heart of Jesus, symbolizes her love. But the heart that loves also feels the pain of our sins, and so, the sins of mankind which wound the Sacred Heart of Jesus also wound the Immaculate Heart of his mother.

Several events gave added impulse to the popularity of the devotion to the heart of Mary. A major one was the apparition of the Blessed Virgin to St. Catherine Labouré in the Rue du Bac, Paris on November 27, 1830. It was the occasion when the Blessed Virgin showed Catherine a vision of a medal, bearing on one side a representation of herself with the inscription: "O Mary, conceived without sin, pray for us who have recourse to thee," and on the other side a large M surmounted by a Cross, beneath which were two hearts close to each other; one surrounded with a crown of thorns and the other pierced by a sword. It was an image of the

Sacred Heart of Jesus and the Sorrowful and Immaculate Heart of Mary.

Shortly afterwards in 1832, Abbé M. des Genettes was assigned as pastor to the Church of Notre-Dame des Victoires (Our Lady of Victories) in Paris. After four years of frustration he became completely discouraged by the lamentable lack of devotion of his parishioners. Then on December 3, 1836, while he was celebrating the Mass he thought he heard an inner voice which said twice: "Consecrate your parish to the most holy and Immaculate Heart of Mary." He hesitated a long time in disbelief. Finally he obeyed the call and established a confraternity to honour the Immaculate Heart of Mary in a special way so as to obtain the conversion of sinners through her intercession. Within a short period sinners began returning to Jesus Christ in great numbers, and the parish was completely transformed and revitalized. It was the talk of Paris!

Then in 1916, the great Fatima apparitions of 1917 were heralded by the apparitions of the Angel of Fatima, who, preparing the little visionaries for the visit of "the Immaculate Heart," taught them about devotion to the two Hearts: "The Hearts of Jesus and Mary are attentative to the voice of your supplications," he said. During his second apparition, he said to them: "The Hearts of Jesus and Mary have designs of mercy on you…" Then at the angel's third apparition, the children were taught to pray thus: "Most Holy Trinity, Father, Son and Holy Spirit, I adore you profoundly. I offer you the most precious Body, Blood, Soul and Divinity of Our Lord Jesus Christ, present in all the tabernacles of the world, in reparation for the outrages, sacrileges and indifference by which he is offended. Through the infinite merits of His Sacred Heart and the Immaculate Heart of Mary, I beg the conversion of poor sinners."

The following year, the first apparition of Our Lady of the Rosary of Fatima was on May 13, 1917. It was during her second apparition to the children on June 13, 1917 that Her Majesty explicitly announced the devotion to her heart when she said to Lucia: "Jesus wishes to make use of you to make me known and loved. He wants to establish in the world devotion to my Immaculate Heart. I promise salvation to those who embrace it, and those souls would be loved by God like flowers placed by me to adorn his throne."

(Interestingly, more recently in an apparition elsewhere, Her Majesty has said that every day she places flowers before the throne of God.)

Now, as Our Lady spoke these words, she opened her hands and in front of the palm of her right hand, she held a heart encircled by piercing thorns. The children understood that this was meant to be her Immaculate Heart outraged by the sins of mankind. As she stood in this position with her hands outstretched she communicated with the children through the rays of an immense light in which they saw themselves immersed in God. "I think that the main purpose of this light was to infuse us with a special knowledge and love for the Immaculate Heart of Mary," wrote Sr. Lucia. In describing the apparition, Lucia also said that the thorns in her heart were the only part of the apparition not made of light. The thorns were burnt-out brown, and natural looking. Of what significant is this? In his book *Fatima Today. The Third Millinneum*, Fr. Richard Fox answers this question: "Our Lady was all light, as were her adornments; but that which represented the sins of mankind was not luminous."

Indeed, as Our Lady promised in 1917, Lucia was left on earth to spread devotion to the Immaculate Heart of Mary and is still alive today at 93 while her two cousins died in 1919-20. In fact, Sr. Lucia once wrote that little Jacinta had told her before going to hospital sometime before she died: "It would not be long now before I go to heaven. You will remain here to make it known that God wishes to establish in the world devotion to the Immaculate Heart of Mary. Tell everybody that God grants his graces through the Immaculate Heart of Mary, and that the Heart of Jesus wants the Immaculate Heart of Mary to be venerated at his side. Tell them also to pray to the Immaculate Heart of Mary for *peace* and that it has been entrusted to her. If I could only put into the hearts of all the fire that is burning within my own heart, and which makes me love the Hearts of Jesus and Mary so very much."

Now, on December 10, 1925, the Blessed Virgin appeared to Sr. Lucia in her convent at Pontevedra, Spain. The Child Jesus was by her side and they were elevated on a cloud of light. In one hand Our Lady held her heart surrounded by sharp thorns. The Child

Jesus spoke first: "Have pity on the heart of your Most Holy Mother. It is covered with the thorns with which ungrateful men pierce it at every moment, and there is no one to remove them with an act of reparation." It was then that Our Lady spoke: "My daughter, look at my heart surrounded with thorns with which ungrateful men pierce it at every moment by their blasphemies and ingratitude. You, at least, try to console me, and say that I promise to assist at the hour of death, with the graces necessary for salvation, all those who, on the first Saturday of five consecutive months, go to confession and receive Holy Communion, recite five decades of the rosary and keep me company for a quarter of an hour while meditating on the mysteries of the rosary, *with the intention of making reparation to me.*"

Four years later, on June 13, 1929, Our Lady spoke to Lucia once more. It was on that occasion that Lucia saw a vision of the mystery of the Most Holy Trinity and beneath the right arm of the Cross was Our Lady. In her palm was her Immaculate Heart with a crown of thorns and flames. Our Lady then said to her: "The moment is coming in which God asks the Holy Father, *in union with all the Bishops of the world,* to make the consecration of Russia to my Immaculate Heart, promising to save it by this means. There are so many souls whom the justice of God condemns for sins committed against me that I have come to ask for reparation; sacrifice yourself for this intention and pray."

It was the next year, during the night of May 29-30, 1930, that Our Lord informed Sr. Lucia of the reasons for the five First Saturdays rather than some other number like nine First Fridays or seven for the Seven Sorrows. He said to her: "My daughter, there are five kinds of offenses and blasphemies uttered against the Immaculate Heart of Mary—blasphemies against her Immaculate Conception, blasphemies against her virginity, blasphemies against her divine maternity and at the same time the refusal to recognize her as the Mother of mankind, blasphemies of those who openly seek to foster in the hearts of children indifference or contempt or even hatred for this Immaculate Mother, and the offenses of those who directly outrage her in her holy images. Here then, my daughter, is the reason why the Immaculate Heart of Mary has inspired me to ask this small reparation, the effect of which will be that I will show compassion by forgiving those souls who have had the misfortune to offend her. As for you, strive without ceasing by your prayers and sacrifices to move me to compassion towards these poor souls."

"The misfortune to offend her." These are serious words. They remind me of the revelation of the 16th-century Franciscan nun, the Venerable Maria de Jesus of Agreda in Spain, whose vision of the fall of the angels is documented in chapter 1. In her chapter on the ascension of Our Lord, which she relates in detail, she says that before he ascended into heaven he spoke these words to his disciples: "...I now tell you that he who knows my mother, knows me; he who hears her, hears me; and whosoever honours her, honours me." I would think therefore that the corollary should also be clearly understood, namely, "he who dishonours my mother, dishonours me; he who offends her, offends me." This is a chastening warning to all those who dishonour Her Majesty.

Some years ago, Cardinal Cerejeira, the Cardinal Patriarch of Lisbon, summarized Fatima quite appropriately when he said: "It is the manifestation of the Immaculate Heart of Mary in the world of today in order to save it." Fatima indeed is the revelation of the Immaculate Heart of Mary just as Paray le Monial in France was the site of the revelation of the Sacred Heart of Jesus. But the message of Fatima did foretell the ending to the saga: "In the end my Immaculate Heart will triumph." This indeed is the heart of the matter.

The Sacred Heart appears to St. Margaret Mary

The incorrupt body of St. Margaret Mary

John Paul II in Beauraing

Sr. Lucia's vision of the Immaculate Heart of Mary

Sr. Lucia's vision of the Trinity

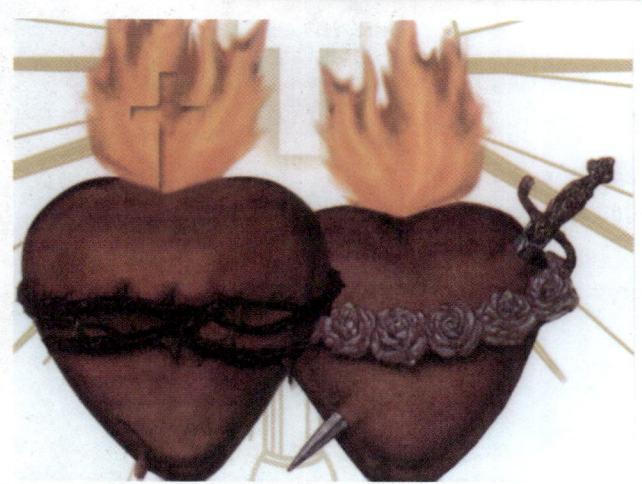

The Sacred Heart and the Immaculate Heart

Chapter 23

1945. Amsterdam.
The Mother of all Nations

As a consequence of World War I, by 1932 five million unemployed Germans looked to Hitler's Nazi party to solve their problems. Britain was also in deep industrial depression and in October of that year, hunger marchers, protesting unemployment, fought pitched street battles with the police. In America, some fourteen million were also jobless. Unemployed executives and skilled workers begged on street corners and the smash hit song was: "Buddy, can you spare a dime?" It was "the worst of times."

This was the world scene when on November 29, 1932, five little children in Beauraing testified that they saw the Blessed Virgin Mary. On December 2, 1932, she identified herself for the first time by nodding her head affirmatively when asked if she was "the Immaculate Virgin." Notably, as in Lourdes, she wore a rosary with a gold chain on her right arm. On December 29, some eight thousand people were present for the apparition which took place at 7:00 pm. It was on that occasion that she appeared with a brilliant heart of gold near the centre of her chest and surrounded by little golden rays. It was meant to be the Immaculate Heart of Mary. Indeed, she showed her heart of gold on five different occasions in Beauraing.

There was a total of thirty-three apparitions in Beauraing from November 29, 1932 to January 3, 1933. In her last apparition on January 3, 1933, she said: "I will convert sinners." "I am the Mother of God, the Queen of Heaven. Pray always." Her last words to the children were: "Do you love my son? Do you love me? Then sacrifice yourself for me. Farewell." And so, the substance of the message of Beauraing, which was delivered in very few words, can be reduced to four elements: prayer, sacrifice, the conversion of sinners and devotion to the Immaculate Heart of Mary. Notably, these were also the essential messages of Fatima in 1917.

Twelve days after her last apparition in Beauraing, she appeared in another Belgium hamlet, Banneux, fifty miles to the north of Beauraing. She was dressed in a garment similar to her Lourdes "outfit." A white rosary also hung from her right arm. Then on Wednesday, January 18, 1933, she identified herself: "I am the Virgin of the Poor." The world was still in economic depression. She therefore came to Banneux as the "Virgin of the Poor" to console them during the height of the great world economic depression which was a prelude to the emergence of Hitler's Third *Reich*. Less than two weeks later, on January 30, 1933, Adolf Hitler became chancellor of Germany. On the ides of March (March 15), Hitler established the third *Reich*. World War II started on September 3, 1939 and May 10, 1940 Germany invaded Belgium. Two weeks later its troops surrendered to the Germans.

Now, Her Majesty appeared in Fatima on May 13, 1917 towards the end of World War I. On March 25, 1945, the feast of the Annunciation, once more towards the end, this time of World War II, she appeared to a humble pious lady, Ida Peerdeman, in Amsterdam, Holland. The series of fifty-six mystical apparitions ended on May 31, 1959. The messages of the years 1945-1950 are of a general character with images, warnings and prophecies that clearly reflect the spiritual and political turbulence of the second half of the twentieth century. After the proclamation in 1950 of the dogma of her bodily Assumption into heaven, Her Majesty appeared standing on the globe and identified herself as "*the Lady or Mother of all Nations.*" The messages then took a new turn and gradually the plan was unfolded through which the *Lady of all Nations* wants to save the world.

On June 17, 1996, less than one month after the long-awaited approval by her bishop, Ida Peerdeman died at the age of 90. Her mission was accomplished. An Order of nuns called the Sisters of the Family of Mary Co-Redemptrix, who received papal recognition on March 25, 1995, has been in charge of the chapel in Ida's home in Amsterdam since July 31, 1996. They promote the worldwide devotion of the *Lady, Mary, Mother of all Nations*. His Ex-

1945. Amsterdam. The Mother of all Nations

cellency Mgr. Bomers, the Bishop of Haarlem, Amsterdam, personally presided over Ida's funeral service, a tribute to his high regard for this exceptional woman. He began his homily with the words: "We have gathered together here as people who have loved, admired, and esteemed Ida Peerdeman… I am certainly without a doubt that she was absolutely sincere and truthful about her experiences. Her entire life was dedicated to venerating Mary under the title of *'Mother of all Nations.'*"

One year later, Cardinal Alfons Maria Stickler, on the occasion of the First International Day of Prayer in honour of the *Mother of all Nations*, held in Amsterdam on May 13, 1997, said: "On the occasion of this time of grace, I would like to express my personal conviction concerning the messages which began in Amsterdam in 1945. I see them as a valuable gift. While reading the messages of Amsterdam, which were entrusted to a woman without any theological education, I was impressed from the very beginning by their simplicity and profundity."

Bishop Paul Maria Hnilica, the longest surviving bishop in the Roman Catholic Church, also had this to say on that occasion: "Before I begin speaking about the theme of this conference, I would like to thank the Bishop of this diocese, His Excellency Mgr. Bomers and his Auxiliary Bishop, His Excellency Mgr. Punt, for approving in an official decree the veneration of Mary under the title *Mother of all Nations*. As far as the contents of the messages from Amsterdam and the supernatural origin are concerned, they have stated that everyone is free to form their opinion. I personally, along with others such as Cardinal Stickler, do not hesitate to confess openly that I am convinced about the authenticity of the messages."

He continued: "I have a deep esteem for the prophetic contents of the messages and their unique contributions to the understanding of the vocation of Mary as *Coredemptrix, Mediatrix* and *Advocate*. These three titles are uniquely united for the first time in the messages of Amsterdam. Mary revealed herself in Amsterdam to a very simple woman named Ida Peerdeman. I personally was acquainted with the visionary who died last year. What especially struck me about her was h simplicity and humility, and amid many sufferings, she lived an unbroken obedience to the Church.

Ida Peerdeman, through her faithfulness, through the suffering of not being understood and the calumny which she endured for fifty years, contributed to our being able to be here today to honour the *Mother of all Nations*. Pope John Paul II, who knows from personal experience the value of suffering, has called on the Mother of God several times during his Pontificate as 'Coredemptrix of the human race.' Indeed, there has never been a negative decision of any kind from Rome regarding Amsterdam."

Speaking on the same occasion, Fr. Paul Maria Sigl made this comment: "In order to carry out with conviction what is requested in the message, one has to be certain that it comes from God and that the prophet is a prophet of God. The Lord does not expect vain credulity from us—rather he warns us to beware of false prophets. But when the authenticity is proven, we must open ourselves thankfully to the messages, obey like children and fulfill everything exactly as God through Mary gives us to understand. Only seldom in the history of Marian apparitions does one find such fascinating proofs of the authenticity of the messages as here in Amsterdam. Let us cite only one example. On the night between 18—19 February, 1958, the Mother of God announced to the visionary that in the beginning of October [hence in eight months], Pope Pius XII, who at that time was completely healthy, would die. She said: 'This Holy Father Pope Pius XII will at the beginning of October of this year be taken up to dwell with us. *The Mother of all Nations, the Coredemptrix, Mediatrix and Advocate* will lead him to everlasting bliss.' Pope Pius XII died on October 9 at Castelgandolfo."

In fact, not only did she predict the passing away of Pope Pius XII, as Fr. Sigl said, but, five years later, after receiving Communion on May 31, 1963, Ida heard a voice say: "Do not tell anyone before it has happened." Then she heard: "Montini." Pope John XXIII died three days later on June 3, 1963, and Cardinal Giovanni Montini was elected Pope on June 21, 1963. He took the name Paul VI. Pope Paul VI died fifteen years later on August 6, 1978. Ida was praying that the Holy Spirit would enlighten the minds of the cardinals in their choice of a new Pope when she heard the voice again: "He who comes from afar would be Peter's successor." This was repeated on October 16, 1978. That night Ida heard over the radio that the Polish Cardinal Wojtila had been elected Pope in the name of Pope John Paul II. The following year, 1979, once more on May 31 Ida heard: "The Netherlands will be revived through her whom I have sent. Implore the Spirit of Truth. The Holy Father will proclaim her Coredemptrix, Mediatrix and Advocate."

March 25, 1945

When the apparitions of the *Lady, Mary, Mother of all Nations* began in Amsterdam on the feast of the Annunciation, March 25, 1945, Ida said that she was in conversation with her sisters and her spiritual director, Fr. J. Frehe, at her home. To quote her testimony: "I felt drawn to the adjoining room. I suddenly saw a light and said to myself: 'Where is this light coming from? What a curious light?' The wall then disappeared before my eyes. There was instead one sea of light in an empty space, and out of it I suddenly saw a figure moving forward, a female figure.

"She was clad in white and wore a sash. She stood with her arms lowered and the palms of her hands turned outwards towards me. I thought it must be the Blessed Virgin and that it could not be anyone else. I then said: 'Are you Mary?' She answered: 'They will call me the Lady, Mother.' As she said it, there was a smile on her face. [By that time her sisters had joined her in the room.] I repeated what she said loudly and with that I heard Fr. Frehe say: 'Lady? Well, I never heard that before. The Lady!' The Lady lifted up three, then four, and finally five fingers. While doing this she said: 'The three represent March, the four, April, and the five is for the fifth of May.'" Immediately afterwards she showed Ida the rosary, and said: "It is thanks to this. Persevere [in saying it]." Then Ida saw a large crowd of soldiers, many of whom were soldiers of the Allies. The Lady said: "Now, these will soon return to their homes." After that she withdrew very slowly and only then did the light disappear and Ida saw everything around her in the room as it always had been.

As she had hinted with her five fingers, World War II ended in Holland on May 5, 1945. It was at that time the feast of St. Pope

Pius V. Significantly, it was this Pope who rallied Christendom in Europe to storm heaven with rosaries before the battle of Lepanto. The Islamic fleet vastly outnumbered the Christian fleet but was defeated. The victory was attributed to the rosary. The date was October 7, 1571, and to this day October 7 is celebrated as the feast of the Most Holy Rosary of the Blessed Virgin Mary.

Over the years the Lady appeared to Ida many times, always in the same way, bringing her messages which were recited very slowly and which her sister accurately recorded. Five years after the first apparition, on November 1, 1950, the dogma of the Assumption of the Blessed Virgin Mary was proclaimed by Pope Pius XII. It was only after this, on November 16, 1950, that her new title of *Lady or Mother of all Nations* was mentioned for the first time. This title is closely linked to the new dogma which she requested. She said to Ida: "Now the moment has come for you to speak about Mary as *Coredemptrix, Mediatrix and Advocate under the title of the Lady of all Nations.*" She later added: "It may be asked why this title is not mentioned in the messages of the first five years. It is because the dogma of the Assumption had to come first. All the dogmas which had preceded it concerned the life and the departure from this life of the Lady. The last and greatest Marian dogma will follow it."

The visionary
Ida Peerdeman

1945. Amsterdam. The Mother of all Nations

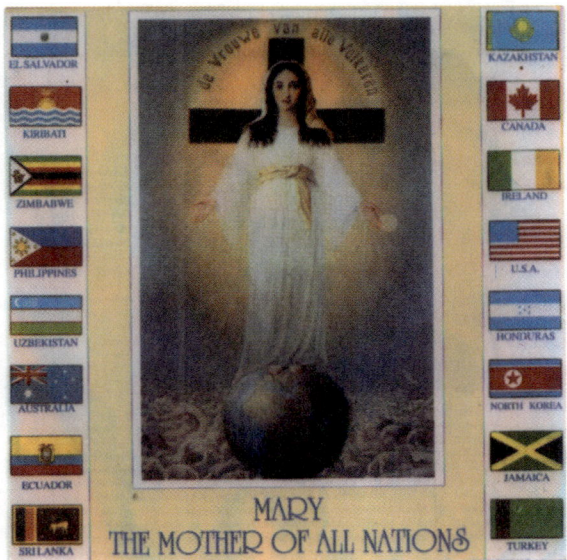

The Mother of all Nations

Visiting the tomb of Ida Peerdeman in Amsterdam

Chapter 24

The Political Prophecies of the Lady

I was so impressed with the many political prophecies and visions given to Ida by the Blessed Virgin that I researched in detail these prophecies. Many of them have already "come to pass." They were given so many years in advance that it is impossible that the visionary, simple and uneducated as she was, could have invented or surmised these events of history. I will now elaborate on only a few examples of what Ida saw and heard as it would take several chapters to document them all.

About the Korean War

"I see in the Far East, the sun and the moon. The moon is its half-phase. The red flag waves over China. Here are Mohammedans. Here are all the Orient . . ." (October 7, 1945).

"'The fighting in Korea is an omen and the beginning of great misery,' the Lady said. Then I see demarkations being marked out. Next I see someone leaning his head on his hand in deep thought. I take him to be Stalin. I suddenly hear beside me: 'I have warned you against that danger.'" (August 15, 1950).

"I see Chinese marching. I see them cross a line. 'The Eastern nations have been roused by an ideology which does not believe in the Son,' said the Lady. The Lady points out America and moves a disapproving finger to and fro, as she says: 'Do not push your politics too far'" (December 10, 1950).

The Chinese Communists, led by Mao Tse-tung, overthrew the Chiang Kai-shek nationalistic government in a civil war, and in October, 1949, Mao proclaimed the People's Republic of China, which soon converted to a Communist state ("The red flag waved over China"). Indeed, the Eastern nations are predominantly non-Christian and Islamic, and an Islamic symbol is the crescent moon ("the moon is in its half-phase"). After World War II ended in 1945, Korea was then divided into two spheres of influence on the 38th parallel. Its industrial North was occupied by the Soviet Union and the agricultural South by the United States. However, on June 25, 1950, the North Koreans, with the foreknowledge and approval of Stalin, invaded the South at the 38th parallel. When MacArthur's troops appeared north of the 38th parallel on the Chinese border, the Chinese reaction was strong and immediate. On November 27, 1950, 300,000 Chinese troops ("I see Chinese marching") attacked the American troops and joined the North Koreans, inflicting a severe defeat on the United States, and recaptured the capital of Seoul. It was not until the end of January 1951 that the US Forces slowed down the joint Chinese and North Korean offensive. Estimates suggested that the war was "the beginning of great misery" and was fought at a cost of 3 million casualties in all, civilians included. "Do not push your politics too far," the Lady said of America!

Warnings about Formosa (Taiwan)

"Next I see the outline of an island. It seems to be Formosa (Taiwan). A smaller island lies further down. Now I hear the words: 'America be forewarned'" (August 15, 1950).

When the Communists, led by Mao Tse-tung, overthrew the Kuomintang (KMT) regime in 1949, driving Chiang Kai-chek and his followers over to the island of Formosa (Taiwan), where they set up a government, it was backed by vast contributions from the United States, who regarded it as the Government of the Republic of China. The US government was so deeply committed to the support of the KMT regime that their President announced in 1975 that the United States would protect not merely the island itself, but the offshore islands of Quemoy and Matsu within sight of the mainland, which were thought to be essential to its defence. However, China considers Taiwan and its neighbouring islands to be part of mainland China, and this is an ever-present source of tension. If China decides to invade Taiwan and the neighboring islands, the United States may feel obligated to come to their defence ("America, be forewarned," the Lady said).

The United States - Russian Cold War

"The Lady said: 'Europe must be on her guard. Warn the peoples of Europe . . . The East against the West . . . Be on your guard, Europe'" (February 7, 1946).

"She also said: 'Now, a great conflict is coming. America, Russia . . . It is drawing near'" (February 14, 1950).

"'Germany must start to restore its unity.' The Lady shows Ida a heavy line across Germany. She adds: 'Europe is divided into two'" (December 10, 1950).

At the end of World War I, Winston Churchill drew attention in 1946 to the increasing division in Europe by an "Iron Curtain" ("Europe is divided into two"). The Western powers then signed a treaty setting up a new alliance, the North Atlantic Treaty Organization (NATO), in April, 1949 ("the West against the East"). It was explicitly a defensive alliance, which provided for the defense of any member attacked. In August, 1961, after some two years of drawn-out diplomacy, the East Germans suddenly erected a wall to cut off the Soviet sector of Berlin from the Western ("a heavy line across Germany"). World history was also dominated by a prolonged and bitter Soviet-American antagonism. The result was a world seemingly divided into two camps, one led by Russia and the other by the United States.

On Israel

"'And Israel would rise again.' The Lady said this after showing me the Exodus from Egypt and the image of Cain and Abel" (April 21, 1945).

"Now I see a round dome. It seems to be situated in Jerusalem and I hear: 'In and around Jerusalem heavy battles would be waged.' All at once I see Cairo clearly and the sight fills me with a strange sensation. I see various Eastern tribes—Persians, Arabs, and so on" (December 26, 1947).

This prophecy came to pass three years later. After the end of World War II, there was the Jewish decision to establish a national state in Palestine by force. Its catalysts had been the Nazi revolution and persecution of the Jews by the Third Reich in Germany. However, this was a non-starter for the Arabs. After fierce fighting with the Arab countries, led by Egypt, Syria, Lebanon, Saudi Arabia, Iraq and Jordan, the Arab alliance was defeated and on May 14, 1948, the state of Israel was proclaimed after heavy fighting around Jerusalem and around the holy Mosque of Omar with its round golden top ("now I see a round dome"). In 1949, the Israeli government moved to Jerusalem, a Jewish national capital again for the first time in almost 2,000 years, with the exception of a few months in 135 AD.

Something on the Moon

"Then I see all of a sudden two lines, each with an arrow at the end. And on one it said: 'Russia' and on the other 'America.' Then I see the Lady and the moon before me. I say: 'There is something getting on that moon' " (February 7, 1946).

Eleven years later, on October 4, 1957, the USSR launched the first satellite, Sputnik. The Soviet Union roared ahead in the space race, a frantic competition between Russia and the United States ("each with an arrow at the end"). In 1961, the Soviets put Yuri Gagarin in orbit, the first man in outer space. On September 13, 1959, Luna 2 (USSR) crashed on the moon, the first man-made object to land there. On July 20, 1969, American astronaut Neil Armstrong was the first man to land on the moon.

The Fall of Communism

"I see the sickle and hammer, but the hammer breaks away from the sickle, and they both drop into a whirlpool" (December 26, 1947). . . 'In Russia a great upheaval would take place, . . .' the Lady said" (December 31, 1951).

Russia became a communist state in October, 1917, and, to the surprise of the world, " a great upheaval took place." The Communist Party suddenly collapsed on August 22, 1992 during the Mikhail Gorbachev and Boris Yeltsin era.

The War In Yugoslavia

"Then suddenly I see the Balkans. There is a war. 'They are fighting again,' the Lady of all Nations says. 'My child, there will be a fierce struggle. We have not seen the end of this struggle yet . . . I warn for the Balkans'" (August 27, 1977).

"They are fighting *again*," she said. Indeed, the history of Yugoslavia and the Balkans is one of a series of wars which began centuries ago. Suddenly in 1992, war started once more in Yugoslavia. It was a 'fierce' war of so-called religious and ethnic cleansing. It was a war among Catholics, Orthodox and Muslims.

Economic Disasters

"The Lady said: 'Economic disasters will come . . .' I see America and Europe lying side by side. After this I see

written: *'Economic warfare, boycotting, currency crises, catastrophes'"* (March 28, 1948).

"'I have said disasters will come, catastrophes of nature,' the Lady said" (August 15, 1951).

"'Economic and material disasters will strike the world. I have said disaster will come, disasters of nature . . . the material world is rushing into economic ruin (November 15, 1951) . . . It would be known that I am the Lady of All Nations when the great powers crumble and political and economic conflicts break out."

The frequency of natural disasters has been increasing exponentially and over the past decade many countries in the world have also suffered from downturns in the economy. Another threat to global economic stability has begun as a result of the terrorists' attack on the World Trade Centre in the United States on September 11, 2001.

Germ Warfare

"Now I see something like a cigar or a torpedo flying past me so rapidly that I can scarcely discern it. Its colour seems to be that of aluminum. All of a sudden I see it burst open. I feel with my hand and experience a number of indefinable sensations. The first is a total loss of sensation. I live and yet I do not live! Then I see faces before me, swollen faces, covered with dreadful ulcers, as it were, a kind of leprosy. Then tiny little black things are floating around me. I cannot distinguish them with my eyes and it is as if I were made to look at them through something (a microscope), and now I see slides of extraordinary brilliance, and upon them those little things enlarge. I do not know how I am to interpret this. "'Bacilli?' I asked. Then the Lady says: 'It is hellish!' I feel my face swelling and it is swollen when I touch it, all bloated and quite stiff. I can no

longer move. Then I hear the Lady again, saying: 'Just think! This is what they are preparing!' And then very softly, she added: 'These Russians, but the others as well.' Finally the Lady says: 'Nations be warned. It is diabolical and that is what they are in the process of inventing'" (December 26, 1947).

This vision was seen in 1947 and therefore *after* World War II. Germ weapons are small, cheap, easy to hide, simple to dispense and horribly effective. They are the poor man's atom bomb and the present threat. The vision describes missiles with warheads laden with "bacilli" (germs), causing ulcers. Germs causing ulcers include anthrax and smallpox!

In October 2001, the United States had its first experience of germ warfare with anthrax bacilli in several of its cities. Notably, the cutaneous type of anthrax infection can cause swelling of the face and ulcers of the head and neck. In fact, the anthrax bacilli spread by missiles or bacteria-laden aerosols, if sprayed around a city of, say, one million could kill over 30,000 people within a week! The nerve gas VX and certain other nerve gases can also be extremely lethal. And so, another one of the Lady's prophecies is coming to pass.

A strange war to come

"I see the Lady standing before me . . . Then she refers to a new, yet strange war in the distant future, which will cause terrible havoc . . . Then the Lady says: 'I predict another great catastrophe for the world.' This she says very sadly and she kept shaking her head. Then the Lady points to the east. I see a great number of stars in the air 'That is where it is coming from,' she says" (August 29, 1924).

And so, it is going to be "a strange war," which will cause "terrible havoc." In other words, it will be a different kind of war from that of World War II. It will start in the east. Far East or Middle East? September 11, 2001 probably saw the beginning of a "strange war," a war waged by terrorists, said to be trained in the East by Afghanistan. It began with the total destruction of the Twin Towers of the World Trade Center in New York by a fire which came from the sky through jet liners laden with fuel.

Comets and Meteors

"There are meteors. Watch out for them. There will be calamities; there will be cataclysms..." (March 20, 1953).

Comets are merely snowballs in orbit made mostly of ice and dirt (dirty snowballs). There are millions of them roaming about the sun. Fortunately, the earth's gravity is insufficient to drag passing comets to us, but every now and then, by chance, a comet would make a close pass by the earth. It is only a matter of time, but sooner or later, a large comet may indeed strike the earth with consequences that we can be quite sure will be catastrophic. Indeed, sixty-five million years ago, a comet came out of space, hit the earth, and extinguished much of the life on this planet, including the dinosaurs.

The world was transfixed when, significantly, on March 25, 1993, the feast of the Annunciation, a small band of comet and asteroid hunters found some twenty small, bright objects that no one had ever seen before, all orbiting Jupiter. They were first discovered by Eugene Shoemaker and David Levy. It soon became clear that each of them was about to crash into Jupiter, one by one, each behind the other. The first explosion occurred on July 16, 1994. It was on the feast of Our Lady of Mount Carmel. The impacts ended on July 22, the feast of St. Mary Magdalene. The size of the cometary fragments is estimated to have been a few hundred meters to perhaps a kilometer across, plummeting into Jupiter at sixty kilometers a second. Every impact left a dark blemish about the size of our earth.

Meteors and meteorites are pieces of other worlds and are composed of rock, iron or carbon. Every year about 1,500 meteorites strike the surface of the earth. Really large meteorites, however, are estimated to strike the earth about once every 10,000 years, and when they do, they sink deep into the crust and then explode with the force of an atom bomb. Indeed, some of the many impact craters on the moon are made by meteorites, but most are made by comets.

The Siberian Asteroid

> *"Next I see Asia. Then I see the Lady extend her hands over a certain part of it—it seems to me to be the Ukraine—as if to protect it. Then upward to the left, in Russia, I see a glaring light, a blinding light. It is as if it explodes from the ground upward. It is a horrible sight. 'And then you no longer see anything,' says the Lady, and I am blinded by that light. Then I see a scorched plain. It is a ghastly sight, just as if death had gone over it" (December 10, 1950).*

On June 30, 1908, something fell out of the sky in Siberia and, at an altitude of eight kilometers, exploded and devastated 850 square miles of Siberian forest. No impact crater was ever found but the blast was more powerful than that of the highest yield nuclear weapon in current arsenals. It had the force of 1,000 Hiroshima bombs. This explosion in Tunguska was caused by an asteroid exploding in the air near the ground. The Soviet Academy of Sciences eventually conducted a thorough survey several years later, apparently reluctant to travel to a site so swampy and remote. The explosion, the Academy reported, was caused by a comet, probably several kilometers in diameter and weighing one million tons, about a millionth of the weight of most comets. Earth was lucky! However, there is still debate as to whether the asteroid was a comet or a meteorite. It seems therefore that the Lady of all Nations showed Ida a scene that occurred in 1908 but which probably can occur again on earth.

Chapter 25

1950. The Fourth Marian Dogma

On November 1, 1950, Pope Pius XII defined the fourth Marian dogma, the bodily Assumption of the Blessed Virgin Mary. Now, Scripture does not speak of Mary as having died or not having died. However, in the early days of the Church there was strong belief in the Assumption, and the Fathers of the Church in the East and West preached homilies commemorating the Assumption with a directness which leaves no doubt as to their faith. But it is necessary to keep in mind what the Assumption is not. Some people think that Catholics believe that Mary "ascended" into heaven. This is not correct. Christ, by his own power, ascended into heaven. However, Mary was assumed or taken up into heaven by God. She did not do it under her own power.

In the homily of Theoteknos (he ruled between 560 and 650 AD) of Livias (on the left bank of the Jordan), he speaks of the feast of the Assumption: "If the God-bearing body of Saint Mary has known death, it has not, nevertheless, suffered corruption; it has been preserved from corruption and kept free from stain and it has been raised to heaven with her pure, spotless soul by the holy angels and powers." "It was fitting," he says later, "that the most holy body of Mary, the God-bearing body, the receptacle of God, divinised, incorruptible, illuminated by divine grace and full of glory... should be entrusted to the earth for a little while and raised up to heaven in glory, with her soul pleasing to God."

About 50 years later, the feast was introduced in Rome and was mentioned in the papal decree of Pope Sergius I (687-701 AD), who ordered a procession for the feast. The Orthodox Church also celebrates the feast. According to the teaching on Mary in the Coptic Orthodox Church, the Lord did not permit the body in which he himself had dwelt and from which he had formed his own humanity to become a prey to corruption. St. Mary was a human being;

she died but her body was assumed into heaven. In fact, by the 8th century the Assumption was fully accepted in the East. However, while the Orthodox Church also professes the doctrine of the bodily Assumption of Mary, it has not defined it as a dogma.

In the West, the feast of the Assumption of the Blessed Virgin Mary is commemorated on August 15. In the Coptic Church it is celebrated on August 22. The Ethiopian Orthodox Church, often referred to as the daughter of the Coptic Church, received the faith from Alexandria, and with it a great love for Mary. In fact, the Ethiopian hymnology to Mary is very numerous and rich, and they celebrate her Assumption not once a year, but monthly!

Between 1949 and 1950, numerous petitions for the doctrine to be made dogma arrived in Rome. They came from 113 cardinals, 18 patriarchs, 2,505 archbishops, 32,000 priests, 50,000 religious women, and 8,000,000 lay people. On May 1, 1946, the Pope had sent to the bishops of the world the Encyclical *Deiparae Virgins,* putting this question to them: "Most especially, we wish to know if you, Venerable Brethren, with your learning and prudence consider that the bodily Assumption of the Immaculate Blessed Virgin can be proposed and defined as a dogma of Faith and whether in addition to your own wishes this is desired by your clergy and people." When the replies were collated, it was found that 22 bishops out of 1,181 dissented, but only 6 doubted that the Assumption was revealed truth. The other 16 simply questioned the opportuneness.

On November 1, 1950, by the Apostolic Constitution *Munificentissimus Deus,* Pope Pius XII defined the Assumption of Our Lady as a dogma of faith. He gave the reasons for this singular honour: "From all eternity the Mother of God is united in a mysterious way to Jesus Christ. Immaculate in her conception, a spotless virgin in her divine motherhood, the noble companion of the Redeemer who won a complete triumph over sin and its consequences, she finally obtained as a crowning glory of her privileges, preservation from the corruption of the tomb and was raised body and soul into the glory of heaven."

Theologically, the corruption of the body is a consequence of the corruption of original sin. But Mary was exempted from the corruption of original sin and it was most fitting therefore that she should be exempted from the corruption of the grave. In short, the Assumption is really a consequence of her Immaculate Conception. As Pius XII said: "These two singular privileges bestowed upon the Mother of God stand out in a most splendid light at the beginning and the end of her earthly journey." And as Alphonse Bossard also stated: "Her divine Motherhood is in utter harmony with her Assumption, as are her Immaculate Conception and her perpetual virginity. How could the body of her in whom 'the Word was made flesh' in order to save flesh have known the corruption of the grave? Or the body of her who totally escaped the power of sin?"

Now, the doctrine of the Assumption does not specify if Mary died. It merely states that after the completion of her life, she was taken body and soul into heaven. That Scripture omits to record the fact is no argument against it. Omission is not denial. Here, of course, we get into an entirely separate matter, the question of *sola scriptura*. Indeed, the Bible actually denies that it is the complete rule of faith. John tells us that not everything concerning Christ's work is in the Scriptures (John 21: 25), and Paul says that much of Christian teaching is to be found in the tradition that is handed down by word of mouth (2 Timothy 2:2).

Elijah and Enoch were assumed into heaven without dying, just as the righteous will be at the end of time (Genesis 5:24; 2 Kings 2:11; I Thess. 4:17; Hebrews 11:5). Why then is it so hard to believe that God gave his mother this privilege? Matthew 27:52 suggests a bodily assumption, and most Protestants believe in the "rapture," based on the events described in 1 Thess. 4:17 and 1 Cor. 15:52. Some argue therefore that Mary is simply the first woman to be "raptured."

Indeed, no city has ever claimed her body and there is no record of her relics or remains anywhere. Rome, for example, claims the tombs of Peter and Paul. Peter's tomb is under the High Altar of the Basilica that bears his name, and Paul is buried in the Basilica of St. Paul Outside the Walls. Other cities have claimed the remains of other saints, and we know that the bones of some saints were distributed to several cities. We also know that after the Crucifixion, Mary was cared for by the apostle John, and it is believed he went to live in Ephesus and that Mary accompanied him there.

Scripture, however, is silent on this, and there is some dispute about where she ended her life, perhaps there, perhaps in Jerusalem. Nonetheless, it is interesting that neither of those cities or any other has claimed her remains. Remember that in the early 15th century relics of saints were jealously guarded, highly prized. Here was Mary, certainly the most privileged of all the saints, but we have no records of her bodily remains being venerated anywhere. This certainly lends support to her Assumption.

And so, the Papal definition does not take a position on whether the Virgin Mary died and was assumed into heaven afterward or was transformed without going through death. It remains a question that theologians may freely debate. However, the opinion that Mary, like her son, passed through death in order to be raised up, immediately or after a short interval, has by far the strongest support in tradition. For although she was holy, innocent, and never committed a sin, it is believed that she died in order to be in union with Jesus. Jesus chose to die. In this regard she also accepted death as Jesus accepted death.

But what did the Protestant reformers have to say? On the issue of the Assumption, Luther does not speak precisely but is content to assert on August 15, 1522, the feast of the Assumption: "From this Gospel one cannot draw any conclusion about the fashion in which Mary is in heaven. It is not necessary any more to know the fate of the saints in heaven. It is enough to know that they dwell in Christ as it says in Matthew 22:32: 'God is not a God of the dead but of the living.' "

Bullinger, the successor of the Swiss Reformer Zwingli, wrote in 1568: "Elijah was transported body and soul in a chariot of fire. He was not buried in any church bearing his name, but mounted up to heaven so that on the one hand we might know what immortality and recompense God prepares for his faithful prophets and his most outstanding and incomparable creatures, and, on the other hand, in order to withdraw from men the possibility of venerating the human body of the saints. It is for this reason, we believe, that the pure and immaculate embodiment of the Mother of God, the Virgin Mary, the Temple of the Holy Spirit, that is to say, her saintly body, was carried up into heaven by the angels."

Chapter 26

1951-54. A Fifth and Final Marian Dogma?

Three months after the definition of the dogma of the Assumption, the date was February 11, 1951. It was the anniversary of the first day that she appeared to Bernadette Soubirous in Lourdes where she said on March 25, 1858: "I am the Immaculate Conception." It was on that same day, February 11 in the year 1951 that she gave her prayer to the world. She said to Ida: "I am the Lady, Mary, *Mother of all Nations*. You may say 'the *Lady of all Nations*' or *'Mother of all Nations,'* who once was Mary. I have come precisely on this day to tell you that I wish to be known as this. Tell all the children of men, the children of all the countries in the world, that they must be *one!*" Then she said: "All men must return to the Cross; and only then, will peace and tranquility reign. Repeat after me this prayer in front of the Cross. It is a trinitarian prayer:

> *"Lord Jesus Christ, Son of the Father, send now your Spirit over the earth. Let the Holy Spirit live in the hearts of all nations, that they may be preserved from degeneration, disaster and war. May the Lady of all Nations, who once was Mary, be our Advocate. Amen."*

She continued: "My child, this prayer is so short and simple that everyone can say it in his own language before his own crucifix, and those who have no crucifix can repeat it to themselves. This is the message which I have come to give to you today for I have now come to tell you that I want to save souls. Everybody should collaborate in this great work..."

Ida described how she recited the prayer to her: "Suddenly I noticed that the Lady was becoming even more beautiful than she already was. The light which always surrounded her became much brighter and sharper so that I could hardly bear to look at it. She raised her hands which were normally turned downwards, and joined them. Her face became so heavenly, so sublime, that one simply cannot express it in words. Her figure grew even more translucent and surpassingly beautiful. I stayed looking at her in rapture and wondered what would happen next. Then the Lady began to recite the prayer: *'Lord Jesus Christ, Son of the Father ...'* O, the way in which she said this! Never before did I hear anyone pray like this. *'Send now your Spirit,'* she said, stressing the *'now'*. *'Let the Holy Spirit live in the hearts of all nations,'* she continued, this time stressing the *'all'*. She also pronounced the word *'Amen'* so solemnly. No one could pray the way she did, so beautifully, so impressively."

At first, the words *'who once was Mary'* caused considerable surprise, even bewilderment. As Ida herself confessed: "I must admit that the words *'who once was Mary'* were very strange indeed. I said to myself but surely you always are Mary. Afterwards, when I passed on the prayer to Fr. Frehe, he said: 'What on earth is this *'who once was Mary*?' She can't have said this. She is and would always be Mary.' 'I do not know what it means,' I said, 'but I have got to pass it on faithfully just as she said it.'"

Indeed, when the text of the prayer was submitted to the ecclesiastical authorities for approval, they too complained that they were confused by those words. This explains why when the prayer was first printed the words *"who once was Mary"* were omitted. But the Lady did not approve of this omission: "No change must be made in the text of the prayer," she said to Ida. "The words *'who once was Mary'* must remain. Tell the theologians that I am not satisfied with the change in the prayer. *'May the Lady of all Nations, who once was Mary, be our Advocate'* must remain." Eventually the complete text of the prayer was approved and the Lady later said to Ida: "Tell your bishop that I am satisfied. The text of the prayer is now correct."

She added: "There is a shortage of priests, but of lay people there is no shortage. Let a great movement among the laity be

1951-54. A Fifth and Final Marian Dogma?

organized..." She ended her apparition by pointing to a globe and saying: "This time is our time. You, child, are the instrument chosen so that you may pass on these things. Tell them that I wish to be known as *Lady of all Nations*." She also said: "My sole purpose is to ensure that the will of the son is obeyed in these times... The spirit of untruth is making such appalling progress that it is necessary to act quickly. The whole world is degenerating and for this reason the son sends the *Lady of all Nations*, who once was Mary... Now I stand before the Cross, for I have suffered with my son, spiritually and above all, bodily... My son came into the world as the Redeemer of men and the work of redemption was the Cross, with all its sufferings both of body and spirit."

She appeared again to Ida and said: "See my image. Look at it well. Keep all of this in your memory. See, I am standing on the globe. My two feet are solidly planted upon it. You can clearly distinguish my hands, my face, my hair, and my veil, but all the rest is hazy. Take a good look at what protrudes above my head and from each side at the height of my shoulders." Ida responded: "It is a Cross. I could see the horizontal arms tipping out on each side and, above your head, the upright arm." Then the scene unfolded with the Lady removing her sash and demonstrating to Ida how she bound it around her: first a complete turn, then another. "Listen and remember what this signifies," she said. "This betokens the loin-cloth of my son [on the Cross]."

The Lady then said: "You would have a picture made of this. You would propagate it at the same time as the prayer which I gave you. Such is my wish today. The prayer is to be translated in various languages. My child, I emphasize that all of this must be done. I am going to tell you why I present myself in this way. I am the Lady standing in front of the Cross. The head, the hands, the feet are similar to those of man but the rest of the body bears evidence to the Spirit. The son came by the will of the Father, and now it is the Spirit who must come into the world." Then, tracing with a movement of her hand a semi-circle above her head from one arm of the Cross to the other, she showed an arc of a very special type of light in which were written words formed of black letters. From the left, "The Lady"; on the top "of all" and to the right, the word "nations." She said: "Never has the world known such times or such a decline in faith. I wish to be the *Lady of all Nations*. Not of one nation, but of *all* nations…"

She appeared in front of the Cross standing on the globe with her feet resting on the top of Europe. "The Low Countries (the Netherlands) are on the verge of corruption," she lamented, "and that is exactly why I have placed my foot upon the Low Countries. Yet it is from these Low Countries that my prayer would spread all over the world. Look where I am placing my feet. One is on Germany, the other on the Low Countries. Poor people of Germany! Have you not yet learnt your lesson? Christians of Germany, return to the Cross. The people of the Low Countries have likewise embarked upon the wrong path."

Around the globe were numerous sheep, both white and black. Many of the sheep are depicted looking up to the Cross. In other words, they were looking up at the Lamb crucified on the Cross; he who was the shepherd of the flock but was at the same time both priest and victim. The Ewe, the mother of the Lamb, was standing in front of the Cross. As she said to Ida: "The flock of sheep symbolizes the nations of the entire world who will not find rest except in lying down and peacefully contemplating the Cross, the central point of this world."

Ida then saw in the middle of each of the Virgin's hands what looked like a scar of a wound emitting three rays which appeared to shine on the sheep below. She smiled and said: "These three rays are those of grace, of redemption, of peace. By the grace of my Lord and Master, the Father, in his love for humanity, sent upon the earth his only son, the Redeemer. Both now wish to send the Holy and True Spirit. He alone can bring peace. So, grace, redemption, peace. However, in this era the Father and the son wish to send Mary, the Lady of all Nations, as *Coredemptrix, Mediatrix* and *Advocate*. Now I have given a clear explanation of the image. You, my child, are the instrument destined to transmit these things. Take good care that the prayer (it is short and powerful) be spread as speedily as possible. The picture would go from *nation to nation* and city to city. Act promptly and use modern methods."

Indeed, the propagation of the prayer, which was given enthusiastic approval in the Netherlands in 1951, developed into a worldwide movement in a short time. With the approbation of more than thirty bishops abroad, the prayer and the picture have found their way into millions of copies, in thirty-two languages, and into the farthest corners of the earth. Without any sort of publicity, requests for it were pouring and are still pouring in every day as the Lady had prophesied: "You will find that the prayer would spread on its own accord. In the same manner that snow flakes flutter about and fall upon the earth covering it with a thick blanket, so too would my prayer and the picture which now circulates throughout the world, spread into the hearts of all nations."

The task of painting the picture was entrusted to the German painter Heinrich Repke. Ida gave an account of it in her diary: "Time and time again I had to explain to the painter what the Lady was like. Of course, this was terribly difficult. I tried to explain to him as well as possible. However, the painter had an almost impossible job to do, especially painting the expression of her face, her eyes, her hands, the rays of light from her hands, the light surrounding her, and her translucent form. In the end I asked the Lady whether the picture had her approval, but she just smiled. I then told the painter: 'It is alright as it is. Do not do anything further to it.' In my opinion it is altogether impossible to picture Mary or to make a likeness of her as I saw her."

This reminds me of the painting of Jesus as the Divine Mercy. When Sr. Faustina Kowalska was dissatisfied with the painter's portrayal of his face, she wept in disappointment and complained to Jesus: "Who would paint you as beautiful as you are?" In answer Jesus said to her: "Not in the beauty of the color, nor of the brush lies the greatness of this image, but in my graces."

On April 29, 1951, Her Majesty revealed: "The new dogma will be the dogma of the Coredemptrix. I emphasize 'Co.' I have already said how much controversy this dogma would arouse. The Church of Rome will have a long struggle over it, but will finally proclaim it. I have said that these times are our times. Here is what it means. The world is in a state of corruption. It is becoming more and more superficial. It no longer knows where it is going. It is because of this that the Father has sent me in the capacity of Advocate in order to announce the coming of the **Holy Spirit**. The world will not be saved through violence. The world will be saved by the **Spirit**. *The image and its dissemination—this is the work prerequisite to the dogma.* Later, this image would be the emblem of the Coredemptrix. The Lady, the Mother, has suffered the sufferings of the son, both spiritual and corporal."

On July 2, 1951, she said to Ida: "Now, look and listen. What I am going to say is an explanation of the new dogma. I am standing on the globe in front of the Cross of the Redeemer in the capacity of Coredemptrix, Mediatrix and Advocate. By the will of the Father, the Redeemer came into the world. For that, the Father had recourse to the Lady. From the Lady, and from her alone — I stress the word, alone — the Redeemer took flesh and blood; that is to say, his body. From my Lord and Master, the Redeemer received his divinity. In this way the Lady became the Coredemptrix by the *will* of the Father. It was necessary to begin with the dogma of the Assumption. Then the last and greatest would follow. *Mankind has been entrusted to the Mother*. That was when the Son said: 'Woman, behold your Son,' and to John: 'Behold your mother.' Tell that to your theologians. I do not come to bring any new doctrine. The doctrine already exists. Say this to your theologians: 'Already, from the beginning, she was Coredemptrix.' "

Now, she emphasized the prefix "Co." It comes from the Latin word "cum" (also col-, com-, cor-). And so, in referring to Mary, it is not intended to mean "co-equal," but "cooperating with" and "companion of" the Redeemer in a supportive role but also completely subjugated to him. This, of course, is very unlike the second verse in the well-known Eucharistic hymn the *Tantum Ergo,* composed by St. Thomas Aquinas: "Glory be to God the Father. Praise to his co-equal Son." In short, "Coredemptrix" does not mean "Co-equal Redemptrix."

There is in addition this major difference between the two. God could have redeemed the world by himself and could have appeared on earth as Adam did—without a mother. But he chose otherwise. He chose to be made man through a woman. On the other hand, the Coredemptrix, his mother, Mary, could never, never have redeemed the world on her own. She was only the **co**mpanion of the

Redeemer just as the first Eve, as the Bible says, was the "companion" of the first Adam (Genesis 3:12). It was a woman and a man who sinned in the Garden of Eden, and in God's inscrutable, logical and providential plan, it therefore had to be a man *and* a woman to redeem the world. It is as simple as that. Everyone should also be able to understand this. It does not call for any theological sense. Common sense will do! It was to be the Redeemer and the Coredemptrix.

Now, she continued speaking to Ida: "From the beginning the handmaid of the Lord was chosen to be Coredemptrix. Tell your theologians that they can find this in their books and that you are not bringing a new doctrine. Tell the theologians I would see to its realization... O, you do not know what tremendous forces are threatening this world. I am now not speaking of modern humanism, atheism, modern socialism and communism. There are yet forces of quite a different nature that threaten this world. Nations, do search for the truth. Nations, unite. . . Satan is still the prince of this world. He holds on to everything he can. That then is why the Lady of all Nations had to come now, into these times for she is the Immaculate Conception and, as a consequence of this, she is the Coredemptrix, Mediatrix and Advocate. These three concepts are one. Is that clearly understood, theologians?"

But this has been "clearly understood" by many of us since 1830 when she appeared to St. Catherine Labouré in the Rue du Bac in Paris and showed her the Medal of the Immaculate Conception (the Miraculous Medal). In this medal are all the symbols that Mary is the *Coredemptrix, Mediatrix* and *Advocate*. Indeed, the 'M' under the Cross is as much for "Mother" as it is for "Mary."

On another occasion she explained: "It was with the departure of the Lord Jesus Christ, and only then, that the Lady became Mediatrix and Advocate. It was with the departure of the Lord Jesus Christ that he made a gift to the nations of the *Lady of all Nations*. Never has Mary officially been called Coredemptrix. Never has she officially been called Mediatrix. Never has she officially been called Advocate. These three functions form one whole. It would constitute the keystone of Marian doctrines."

On the fiftieth apparition, on May 31, 1954, she said: "I have chosen this day because on this day the Lady will receive what would later be her coronation. Theologians, and you apostles of the Lord Jesus Christ, I have given you the justification of the dogma. Work then for this dogma. This is the date when the *Coredemptrix, Mediatrix* and *Advocate* would receive her title, duly proclaimed, of the *Mother of all Nations*." Indeed, on May 31, 1996, the public veneration of the Mother of God under the title the *Lady or Mother of all Nations* was officially approved by the two bishops of Haarlem (Netherlands), Bishop Hendrick Bomers and his Assistant Bishop Mgr. Josef Punt. Her prophecy of May 31, 1954 was thus fulfilled! May 31 is a very historic date. It is also the last day in the month dedicated to Mary. Interestingly, the Church also once celebrated the feast of *Mary, Mediatrix of all Graces*, on May 31, and later on it became the feast of Mary, Queen of the Universe. Today, May 31 is the feast of the Visitation.

She also warned: "You apostles, you nations, fall upon your knees before your Lord and Creator. Express your gratitude. The scientists of the world have turned men away from gratitude. They no longer know their Creator. So you nations, be warned. Bow down before your Creator. My child, do you realize what times you are living in? Never in its history has the world experienced a time like the present one — such a decline in faith… How thoroughly Satan holds the world in his clutches, only God knows! He now sends to you, to all the nations, his mother, the *Lady of all Nations*. She will vanquish Satan, as has been foretold. She shall place her foot upon Satan's head."

Then on another occasion she warned: "The enemy of the Lord Jesus Christ has done his work slowly but persistently. The posts are manned. His preparations are nearly finished. Nations, be warned! The spirit of lies and deceit is seducing many. It won't be long before the breaking of the storm. Great evils threaten the world. The Churches would be undermined even further. Please realize why I come as the *Lady of all Nations*. I come to assemble all nations in the Spirit, the Spirit of Truth, the Holy Spirit…The sheep must be gathered together into one flock, one great community. My prophecy 'from hence forth all generations shall call me blessed' will be fulfilled more than ever before once the dogma has been proclaimed... When the dogma, the last dogma in Marian history, has been proclaimed, the *Lady of all Nation*s will give peace, true peace. I repeat, true peace to the world. The nations, however, must say my prayer in union with the Church. . ."

On May 31, 1957, she said to Ida: "Before the Lord Jesus Christ died his bodily death; before the Lord Jesus Christ ascended to the Father. . . he gave you the great mystery, the great miracle of every day, every hour, every minute. He gave you himself. No, nations, [she shook her head vehemently as she said this] not merely a remembrance. No, nations, listen to what he said: not just an idea, but himself, under the appearance of a little piece of bread, under the appearance of wine. This is how the Lord wants to come among you, day after day. Do accept it. He gives you the foretaste, of eternal life."

Now, she was seen in front of the Cross with her hair loose and falling down beyond her shoulders. In other words, she "let her hair down," literally and figuratively. This "hairdo" fascinated me. And then I found out that there was a possible biblical significance to this. In the Book of Judges there is the "Song of Deborah," which was sung to celebrate the great victory of the army of the Israelites over the powerful pagan army of Sisera. The song describes the hairstyle of the Israelites: "That the warriors in Israel unbound their hair, that the people came forward with a will, for this bless Yahweh!" (Judges 5:1-2). According to the Jerusalem Bible, this was a well-known custom in battle and it is said that the modern Bedouin still observe this ritual of war. And so, she appeared in "battle array" (Song 6:10) in front of the Cross, threw down the gauntlet to her enemy, and called for the dogma which would officially recognize her victory over Satan as Coredemptrix, as promised in Genesis 3:15.

Let me finally expand on another historic relevance of the date, May 31. After the defeat of Louis Napoleon in the Franco-Prussian war of 1870, a vicious revolution exploded in Paris, and which called itself the *Commune* of Paris. Before the terrible weeks were over, the churches of Paris would be desecrated and clergy arrested by the dozens. Sr. Catherine Labouré and her Sisters of Charity were in the heart of the city and one morning she told her Superior of a dream she had during the night. It was that the Blessed Virgin had come to the Community advising them to leave Paris and that she would guard their house until they returned on May 31.

They left the following morning for Versailles and Catherine took with her the crown from Our Lady's statue in the chapel of the Rue du Bac. In removing it, she had promised Her Majesty that she would return to crown her. The deaths of Monseigneur Darboy, the Archbishop, and of seventy hostages, priests and laymen, marked the end of the *Commune*. When passions had died down the Sisters of Charity returned to Paris on May 30. At Mass on the morning of May 31, Sr. Catherine carried out the little crowning ceremony she had promised Her Majesty: "I told you, my good Mother, that I would return to crown you on the thirty-first of May," she said with great veneration and love.

In her 50th apparition in Amsterdam on May 31, 1954, Our Lady said to Ida: "I have chosen this day because on this day the Lady will receive what would later be her coronation. Theologians and you apostles of the Lord Jesus Christ, I have given you the justification for the dogma. Work then for this dogma. This is the date when the Coredemptrix, Mediatrix and Advocate will receive her title, duly proclaimed, of the Mother of all Nations." Then on May 31, 1969, Ida was in the chapel in the Rue du Bac. She wrote in her diary: "I saw a light while receiving Holy Communion and was given a very realistic perception of the Lord's presence. Then the following words impressed themselves very strongly upon me, although they were not uttered: 'What began here [in the Rue du Bac] will be continued by the Lady of all Nations.' "

And so, her prophecy of 1954 was fulfilled on May 31, 1996 by the bishops of Amsterdam. "What began here [in the Rue du Bac] would be continued by the Lady of all Nations," she said. Indeed, in chapter 13 on the Medal of the Immaculate Conception, it was shown that the medal contained all the symbols of Mary as Coredemptrix, Mediatrix and Advocate!

Chapter 27

1961. Mary's Warnings in Garabandal

Between June 18, 1961 and June 18, 1965, four young children from Garabandal in Spain claimed to be receiving apparitions of the Virgin Mary and Michael the Archangel. Dr. Celestino Ortiz Perez of Santander, a pediatrician specializing in child psychology, examined them when they were in a state of ecstasy during the apparitions. He concluded: "In this state of ecstasy, they gave proof that it is beyond the explanation of medical science and all natural laws. They showed no reaction to pain, pin pricks, et cetera. Once out of their trances however, they reacted immediately. The four little girls, from a pediatric and psychiatric point of view have always been and continue to be normal. The trances in which we have observed these young girls do not fit into the framework of any psychic or any psychological pathology presently known. Our conceit falls apart when we are faced with this kind of dilemma which God has bestowed on us in order to point out our medical limitations."

San Sebastian de Garabandal

San Sebastian de Garabandal is a tiny village in Spain. It is in the province of Santander in the heart of the Cantabrian mountains. It is a village where the people shared intense religious beliefs. The diocese of Santander is considered in Spain as being extremely Catholic, in fact, the most Catholic in Spain and San Sebastian de Garabandal has always been considered the most religious village of the dioceses. In 1961, there were about 300 inhabitants in this poor little village of 70 stone houses. They were mostly farmers. Customarily, each year on July 18, the feast day of St. Sebastian, there would be a great celebration when the statue of the saint would be processed around the village.

The chapter on Garabandal opened on June 18, 1961, on a Sunday at 8:30 in the evening. June 18 was the feast of St. Aubert, Bishop of Avranches in France, to whom Michael the Archangel had appeared in the year 706, requesting him to construct a sanctuary in his honour on Mount Tombé in Normandy. It was also on June 18, 1010, that the relics of St. Aubert were found. The word "coincidence" would not be found in the heavenly dictionary. June 18 was also the anniversary of the first apparition of the angel, believed to be Michael, to St. Catherine Labouré in the convent chapel of the Rue du Bac in Paris in 1830. It was there that the Virgin showed this nun of the Visitation Order the design of the Miraculous Medal with two Hearts beneath a large M surmounted by a Cross, one surrounded with thorns, the other pierced by a sword.

On that Sunday there was a sudden clap of thunder before the young girls saw a very bright and beautiful figure surrounded by a brilliant light. He looked liked a child about nine years of age, but at the same time appeared to be extremely powerful. He was wearing a long blue seamless robe and had wings which were large and pinkish. It was Michael, the same Michael, the angel of the first and the last decisive battles. On Saturday, July 1, he spoke to the children for the first time. July 1 was the feast of the Most Precious Blood of Our Lord Jesus Christ, a feast instituted in 1849 by Pius IX. "Do you know why I have come? It is to announce to you that tomorrow, Sunday, the Virgin Mary will appear to you as *Our Lady of Mount Carmel*." He talked to them for a while, and then said: "I shall return tomorrow with the Blessed Virgin."

Our Lady of Mount Carmel

The next day, July 2, 1961, was then the feast of the Visitation. As promised by the Archangel, it was on this day that the Virgin "visited" the children for the first time. The site was Los Pinos, a plateau on a hill with nine beautiful tall pine trees. Her Majesty was surrounded by a brilliant light and on each side of her stood an angel, one of whom was recognized as Michael. "She appeared in a white garment and blue mantle with a crown of golden stars on her head (Rev. 11:19;12:1). Her hands were ever so delicate but her feet were not visible. The scapular she wore on her right wrist was of a brown colour with a small mountain designed on it. Her hair was of a deep chestnut colour, long, slightly waved and parted in the middle as appeared in Amsterdam in 1945. Her complexion was tan but lighter than that of the angel; her voice was different from the angel's; a voice so very sweet and unusual that it is hard to explain. "There is no other woman who resembles the Blessed Virgin, either in her face, voice or anything," said Conchita. She seemed to be about eighteen years of age.

In the beginning of June 1963 one of the visionaries, Conchita Gonzales, announced that she was told that after the death of Pope John XXIII, there would only be three more Popes and then "will come the end of time, which is not the end of the world, but the "end of an epoch." Questioned about this Conchita declared that she did not understand the meaning of the Blessed Virgin's remark. The Virgin also told the children that, among the saints in heaven, an exceptional veneration is paid to St. Joseph "as the spouse of Mary." She also taught them how to say the rosary from the heart. As Conchita said: "When the Virgin recites the 'Gloria' at the end of the decade of the rosary, she does it with extraordinary reverence."

The Warning

Nearly four years later, on January 1, 1965, the feast of the Mother of God, the Blessed Virgin told Conchita about a warning which would be given to the world. She said that the warning was to be followed by a great miracle which would take place within a year of the warning and then a permanent sign would be left at the pines. If the warning and the miracle did not change people and turn them towards God, then a terrible and "fiery" chastisement will befall mankind. The year of the warning was revealed to the visionary Mari Loli, the date of the miracle, only to Conchita.

It is said that the warning will be experienced by everyone in the world and will be felt interiorly. It will be like a personal judgment when everybody will see the consequences of his or her own sins, a purification in preparation for the grace of the great miracle to follow. We will, as it were, find ourselves all alone in the world no matter where we are at the time, alone with our conscience before God. It will be for the conversion of the world and will be the expression of God's great mercy towards us. Reactions to this, some quite distressing, will vary from person to person.

According to the visionaries, before the warning, there would be a pre-warning: "There would come a Bishop who will not believe in these events at first, but the Blessed Virgin will give him a sign. The warning would then be very close." Conchita also said: "If I did not know about the other chastisement to come, I will say that there is no greater chastisement than the warning. Everybody would be afraid, but Catholics would bear it with more resignation than others. It would last for only a short time. The warning comes directly from God and it would be like an interior realization of our sins. Believers as well as unbelievers, wherever they are at the time, would see and feel and suffer it whether in the daytime as well as the night, whether we are in bed or not. It would be a horror of the worst kind. If I could only tell you how the Virgin described it to me! But the chastisement would be worse."

In the time of the warning, everything would stop—even the planes in the air.

Conchita knows the exact time of the Miracle and will announce it eight days in advance. The predicted miracle will be greater than that of Fatima. It would be visible in Garabandal, and from the mountains surrounding the village, and would take place at 8:30 in the evening on the feast of the martyr who had a great devotion to the Holy Eucharist. It will coincide with an important event in the Church and will last ten to fifteen minutes.

The sign

A sign will remain at the pines, which would be a miraculous phenomenon. It would be able to be photographed or filmed, but not felt or touched. Those present at the time would be cured and non-believers would be converted. Padre Pio is said to have seen it before he died. This great miracle would be sent as proof of the tender love of God and his Blessed Mother for the world. Afterwards, if the world does not reform, God will send a terrible chastisement.

Mari Loli described the chastisement: "It was horrible to see. We were absolutely terrified. I cannot find the words to explain it. We saw the waters in the rivers turn to blood. Fire was falling from heaven and something worse still which I cannot reveal at this time." Conchita in a letter to a priest also said: "I cannot disclose the nature of the chastisement although the Virgin has revealed it to me as well as to Loli and Jacinta. I can only say that it would be a direct intervention from God, which makes it more fearful than anything that you can imagine. This chastisement, if it comes— and I believe it would come would take place *after* the miracle."

She also said later on: "The chastisement, if we do not change, would be horrible, as we would deserve. We have seen it but we cannot reveal the nature of it, because I do not have permission from the Blessed Virgin. When I saw it, I experienced a great fear despite the fact that I could see the Blessed Mother at the same time." In another letter Conchita wrote: "I saw the chastisement and I can assure you that if it happens, it would be worse than if we were engulfed in flames; worse than if we had cinders or hot pitch under our feet and on top of our head. I do not know the length of time which would elapse between the miracle and the chastisement."

Conchita wrote a letter to a Fr. Laffieneur, and in his notes, he recorded: "By direct intervention from God, Conchita means that everyone would see that it is God himself who sends us the chastisement. It would not be produced, like wars or revelations which are caused by direct acts of men, by their ambition, their pride or their hardiness." In another note (undated), Conchita stated: "The future miracle will come before the chastisement and if people change their lives, the chastisement would not take place... The chastisement remains *conditional*, depending on whether or not humanity will comply with the demand of the Blessed Mother's message and on whether or not they believe in the miracle.

According to Mari Loli: "At a certain time, not a single motor or machine would operate; a terrible heat wave will come down on the earth and men will start to experience a great thirst. They will search desperately for water, but due to the heat, the water would evaporate. Finally, we saw a large number of people in flames. They were running to throw themselves into the sea and the lakes, but as they were entering the water, the water seemed to boil and instead of putting out the flames, it made them worse. It was so horrible that I asked the Blessed Virgin to take with her all our little children so that this would not happen to them, but the Virgin told us that when this day comes, the children would have already grown."

To a group of Americans Conchita also once said: "The Virgin would ask God to perform a miracle so as to avoid the chastisement, but the chastisement cannot be avoided, because we have lost even the meaning of sin. Now, we have reached such an extremity that God had no choice but to send the chastisement. As the result of the chastisement, those who survive would change enormously and then they shall truly live for God until the end of time."

On the second day of her apparitions, July 3, she brought the Child Jesus with her. On October 18, 1961 she said to the children: "You must make many sacrifices, perform much penance and visit the Blessed Sacrament frequently, but first, you must lead good lives. If you do not, a chastisement will befall on you. The cup is already filling up and if people do not change, a very great chastisement will come upon them."

The Miracle

The great miracle will take place within twelve months of the warning and it will be so spectacular that all who see it will believe. Conchita will announce the date of the miracle eight days before it is due to occur. According to her, the miracle will coincide with a feast of a saint-martyr of the Eucharist, and will last about fifteen minutes. It will take place in March, April or May at 8:30 on a Thursday evening. Notably, it was also at 8:30 p.m. that the first apparition of Michael had occurred. Significantly also, according to a few mystics who have been shown in visions the life of Jesus and his mother, the institution of the Holy Eucharist at the Last Supper in the upper room on Maundy Thursday took place at 8:30 p.m. This certainly leads us to conclude that the miracle will be Eucharistic. In fact, Conchita had always said that the Eucharist is a key feature of Garabandal, and at various times Michael himself appeared to the girls and gave them Holy Communion.

The Communion Host

On June 22, 1962, the Archangel told Conchita that not only would he give her Communion but that the Host would be visible to all. Later, the Blessed Virgin told Conchita that the date for this would be the 18th of July, and that she should announce it publicly fifteen days in advance. When Conchita did make the announcement, the news spread quickly throughout Spain and certain other parts of Europe and many people went to Garabandal to see what was to take place on that day. It was the feast day of San Sebastian. However, after waiting all day many of the people went home disappointed because the event had not occurred.

But after midnight Conchita left her home in ecstasy and several people immediately began to follow her. Soon after Michael then performed a miracle at one o'clock in the morning. Interestingly, she had gone to Mass and Holy Communion on the morning of July 18, but Church law at that time did not permit one to receive Holy Communion more than once a day. Therein lies the explanation. Obviously, Michael complied with Church law and waited until after midnight to give Conchita the Sacred Host. Alejandro Damians, a businessman from Barcelona, caught with his camera the last seconds of the miracle of the Host on her tongue. This was the evidence that so many people were looking for. The photograph circulated and more and more people then began to believe the children.

The Permanent Sign

Following the miracle, it is said that a permanent sign will remain at the pines. One will be able to "see it, photograph it, but not touch it." It will be miraculous and will stay in the Pines permanently. Interestingly, on November 18, 1961, a shepherd named Ramon Gonzales testified that he saw a *column of smoke* in the day and a fire at night, close to the nine pines! They were also seen from the village for two or three months in the autumn of 1962 and on November 25, 1965, by four reliable French witnesses.

The Message of October 18

On June 18, 1965, nearly four years later, St. Michael delivered this message on behalf of the Virgin: "As my message of October 18, 1961 has not been complied with and has not been made known to the world, I am advising you that this is the last one. Before, the cup was filling up, now it is flowing over. Many cardinals, bishops and many priests are on the road to perdition and are taking many souls with them. Less and less importance has been given to the Eucharist. You should turn the wrath of God away from yourselves by your efforts. If you ask His forgiveness with sincere hearts He will pardon you. I, your Mother, through the intercession of St. Michael the Archangel, ask you to mend your lives. You are now receiving the last warnings. I love you very much and do not wish your condemnation. Pray to us in sincerity and we will grant your request. You should make more sacrifices. Think about the Passion of Jesus."

The Two Hearts

Then in her last apparition to the children of November 13, 1965, Mary's closing remarks to Conchita were: "Conchita, why do you not go more often to visit my Son in the Tabernacle? He waits for you there, day and night." Then she said: "Remember what I told you. When you present yourself before God, your hands must be filled with good works done for your brothers and for the glory of God. But at present time, your hands are empty." It was only after reading this months later that I came to understand why Conchita inscribed words in Spanish on the front page of a book on Garabandal which she gave to me as a gift when I was a dinner guest at her home on August 29, 1989: "With love, it is my wish that the Blessed Virgin would be your Light to lead you to eternal happiness, and that on the way you will bring many souls to her. Pray for me — Conchita."

It was on November 17, 1988, that I first visited Garabandal. Curiously, I was the only pilgrim in the lonely village that day. Among many points of interests, I noticed that in the little church in the village the beautiful main altar was flanked on both sides by two lifesize statues, one of the Sacred Heart of Jesus and the other of the Immaculate Heart of Mary!

The Apocalyptic Photograph

There was an apocalyptic background to the apparitions in Garabandal and two photographs which I took there when I was leaving the Pines, after spending an hour on that holy ground, appear to be a depiction of an apocalyptic prophecy. As I reached the foot of the hill leading up to the Pines, I saw a large ceramic plaque with the traditional portrayal of the fallen angel Satan vanquished at the feet of the victorious Archangel Michael. His wings extended up to Michael's knees. Below the plaque was the following inscription: "On Sunday, June 18, 1961, the Archangel Michael appeared for the first time to the children."

It was a bright sunny November day and I took two photographs of the plaque fifteen seconds apart, one closer up than the other. When the films were developed, the first print showed the plaque as described above. In the second close up photo, a cloudy shaft of light appeared, completely obliterating the image of Satan, including his wings which had reached up to Michael's knees. Experts in photography outruled an artifact. To many, it was a dramatic and symbolic depiction of the prophecy of Genesis 3:15: "I will put enmity between you and the woman, and between your seed and her seed; (s)he will crush your head..." It was a depiction of the forthcoming decisive victory of the Woman over the ancient serpent; the victory of light over darkness.

With respect to these two photographs and the others which I will show in the chapter on *Marian Symbols in Medjugorje*, I ensured that professional photographers certify to me that the impositions on the films were not artifactual. Indeed, many people have been receiving such and other types of unusual phenomena on photographs, especially in Medjugorje; some artifactual, I am sure, but many are not.

Garabandal

Our Lady of Garabandal

The nine pine trees of Garabandal

Conchita serving at her dinner party (1986)

The first photograph of the plaque

The other photograph seconds later

Chapter 28

1973. Akita:
"Fire will fall from the sky"

A statue of the Virgin Mary wept in the convent of the Institute of the Handmaids of the Eucharist in Akita, Japan. It first happened on Friday, June 29, 1973. It was the feast of the Sacred Heart. Sister Agnes Sasagawa was praying in the convent chapel when she suddenly saw a brilliant light shining from the tabernacle, and then several angels appeared chanting: "Holy, Holy, Holy," as they faced the Blessed Sacrament. Suddenly, she heard an angelic voice to the right of her, praying the daily prayer of the Handmaids of the Eucharist, which was composed for them by the former Bishop of Niigata, Bishop John Shojiro Ito, who later gave ecclesiastical approval to the Akita events:

> "Most Sacred Heart of Jesus, present in the Holy Eucharist, I consecrate my body and soul to be entirely one with your Heart, being sacrificed at every instant on all the altars of the world and giving praise to the Father, pleading for the coming of His kingdom. Please receive this humble offering of myself. Use me as you will for the glory of the Father and the salvation of souls. Most Holy Mother of God, never let me be separated from your divine Son. Please defend and protect me as your special child. Amen."

Now, 56 years earlier in 1917, and this is of major importance, Her Majesty appeared in Fatima on May 13, the feast of Our Lady of the Blessed Sacrament or Our Lady of Eucharist, to warn us, among other things, about World War II. Her apparitions in 1917 were preceded in 1916 by the apparitions of the Angel of Peace, said to be Michael himself, to the three little children. He taught them to adore Jesus present in the tabernacles and gave them this prayer: "Most Holy Trinity, Father, Son, and Holy Spirit, I adore You profoundly. I offer You the most Precious Body, Blood, Soul and Divinity of Our Lord Jesus Christ, present in all the tabernacles of the world, in reparation for the outrages, sacrileges, and indifferences by which He is offended. By the infinite merits of His Sacred Heart and the Immaculate Heart of Mary, I beg of you the conversion of poor sinners."

Twenty-eight years later, in 1945, towards the end of World War II, Our Lady appeared to Ida Peerdeman in Amsterdam and this time her series of apparitions there *ended* with Ida having "Eucharistic Experiences" from July 17, 1958 onward. Another 28 years later, she appeared in Akita with an apocalyptic warning in the Convent of the Handmaids of the Eucharist whose main devotion is adoration of Jesus in the Eucharist and Blessed Sacrament, and whose Eucharistic prayer is very similar to that of the Angel of Peace of Fatima. The significance of this cannot be overemphasized and its message should be crystal clear!

Mary, indeed, gave birth to the Bread of Life who chooses to appear as a humble piece of bread, in fact, unleavened bread (not puffed up) in the tabernacles of the world and in Holy Communion. As she is the mother of Jesus Eucharist, the Church therefore calls her Our Lady of the Blessed Sacrament or Our Lady of the Eucharist. Let us also recall that her last message to Conchita in Garabandal in 1963 was: "Conchita, why do you not go more often to visit my Son in the tabernacle. He waits for you there day and night."

The feast of the Sacred Heart was, therefore, a most appropriate day for this first event. The vision disappeared when the prayer was over, and on the following day, June 30, Sr. Agnes felt a severe pain in the palm of her left hand, then a wound about 2 cm. wide and 3 cm. long appeared in the center of her hand. It was as though a cross had been engraved in her skin. On Thursday, July 5, a little hole then appeared in the center of the two branches of the cross from which blood began to flow.

In the early morning of Friday, July 6, Sr. Agnes saw an angel who smiled at her and said: "I am the one who is with you and watches over you." The angel then beckoned her towards the chapel. In a place of honour in the chapel was a wooden statue of the Blessed Virgin, sculpted by a famous Japanese sculptor, Saburo Wakassa, and fashioned after the image of the *Lady of all Nations,* which Her Majesty called herself when she appeared to the visionary Ida Peerdeman in Amsterdam in 1945.

As Sr. Agnes entered the chapel, she felt that the statue of the Virgin, now bathed in a brilliant light, had come to life and was about to speak to her. The voice was indescribably beautiful: "My daughter, do you say well the prayer of the Handmaids of the Eucharist? Then let us pray it together." As Our Lady began the prayer, the angel also joined in. Sr. Agnes then started to pray together with them: "Most Sacred Heart of Jesus, present in the Holy Eucharist..." At this point, the Virgin suddenly interrupted her, saying: "**truly present**. From now on you will add **truly**." From that day on, the prayer as been changed to "Most Sacred Heart of Jesus, **truly** present in the Holy Eucharist, I consecrate my body and soul..."

When the prayer was finished, the angel disappeared and the statue resumed its normal appearance. That same day the other nuns in the convent noticed the appearance of an identical wound and blood flowing from the right hand of the statue of the Blessed Virgin. Three months later, on September 29, the feast of Michael the Archangel, the wound in the statue disappeared. One day when Sr. Agnes was speaking to a stranger who visited the convent, she described the beautiful voice as "a voice which certainly could not have come from this world." The visitor then asked: "Was it comparable to that of the angel?" She replied: "The two voices are beautiful, but the voice of Mary is something more divine. One can say that the voice of the angel resembles a song and that of Mary, a prayer!"

However, it was on October 13 of that year that *Our Lady of Akita* gave this apocalyptic warning and prophecy: "My dear daughter, listen well to what I have to say to you. You will inform your superior. As I told you, if men do not repent and better themselves, the Father will inflict a terrible punishment on all humanity. It will be a punishment greater than the Flood, such as one will never have seen before. **Fire will fall from the sky** and will wipe out a great part of humanity, the good as well as the bad, sparing neither priests nor faithful. The survivors will find themselves so desolate that they will envy the dead. The only arms which will remain for you will be the rosary and the sign left by my son. Each day recite the prayers of the rosary. With the rosary, pray for the Pope, the bishops and the priests. The work of the devil will infiltrate even into the Church in such a way that one will see cardinals against cardinals, bishops against other bishops. The priests who venerate me will be scorned and opposed by their confreres, churches and altars sacked: the Church will be full of those who accept compromise and the demon will press many priests and consecrated souls to leave the service of the Lord. The thought of the loss of so many souls is the cause of my sorrow. If sins increase in number and gravity, there will no longer be pardon for them."

It is most interesting that after the first atom bomb fell in Hiroshima, Robert Oppenheimer, director of the Manhattan Project, exclaimed: "We have done the devil's work." Indeed, it is recorded that he wondered whether the dead of Hiroshima and Nagasaki were not more fortunate than the survivors whose exposure to the bomb would have lifetime effects!

The date the Virgin chose to give this apocalyptic message to Sr. Agnes was October 13. It was the anniversary date of her last apparition in Fatima, 56 years earlier in 1917, when the great atomic reactor, the sun, came hurling down to earth. Its significance is clear. However, comets and meteors falling to earth can also be like "fire falling from the sky," causing catastrophic destruction.

On January 4, 1975, the statue in Akita wept for the first time. This phenomenon of tears was observed on 101 separate days over a period of six years before the weeping finally stopped on September 15, 1981, the feast of *Our Lady of Sorrows*. Bishop Ito was himself a witness of the weeping on four occasions and he had the tear liquids examined on two occasions. Scientific investigations by Professor Sagisaka of Japan, an expert in forensic medicine, proved that the liquid was identical with human tears. The weeping was once seen on television by millions of Japanese, but it seems to have had little lasting effect!

On September 28, 1981, Sr. Agnes suddenly felt the presence of the angel at her side during adoration of the Blessed Sacrament. It was the feast of Michael the Archangel. She did not actually see the angel in person, but a Bible appeared open before her eyes and she was invited to read Genesis 3:15: *"I will bring enmity between you and the woman: and between your seed and her seed; (s)he will crush your head ..."* Then the angel explained that this passage in Scripture was relevant to the tears of Mary: "There is a meaning of the figure 101. This signifies that sin came into the world by a woman and it is also by a woman that salvation came to the world. The zero between the first and the second [figure] one signifies the Eternal God who is from all eternity until eternity. The first one represents Eve and the last the Virgin Mary." So said, I certainly understood the significance of the zero. A circle has neither beginning nor end!

It is significant that the Blessed Virgin appeared in Fatima in 1917 towards the end of World War I. Twenty eight years later, in 1945, towards the end of World War II, she appeared in Amsterdam. She then appeared once more 28 years later in 1973 in Akita, Japan, where the atom bomb was previously unleashed in 1945 and warned that "fire will fall from the sky if men do not repent." These 28 year intervals attracted my attention. Twenty-eight years after 1973 is the year 2001. Indeed, in my book *A scientist Researches Mary, Mother of All Nations,* I did write that something significant may happen in the year 2001. It did! On September 11, 2001, two fuel-filled planes were deliberately crashed into the World Trade Centre in New York. It may be said that "fire fell from the sky," and 6,000 people were instantly killed in a most unprecedented carnage of Americans on American soil. Perhaps this is a herald of yet another but even greater "fire to fall from the sky."

In an attempt to interpret the possibility that these 28-year intervals were not coincidences and seeking an explanation, I researched several sources. Among them was Graham Hancock's book *Fingerprints of the Gods.* He had previously researched the history and possible whereabouts of the Ark of the Covenant in his book *The Sign and the Seal. Fingerprints* is another intriguing piece of historical sleuthing, which, among other things, researches the so-called myths of civilizations of remote antiquity, unearthing in the process evidence of their vast sophistication, technological advancement, and surprising scientific knowledge. In the journey of his research he concludes that it appears that a warning has been handed down to us, a warning of a terrible cataclysm that affects the Earth in great cycles at certain intervals of time—a cataclysm that may be about to recur.

He discovered, for example, that, like many different peoples and cultures that had preceded them in Mexico, the Aztecs (to whom the Blessed Virgin appeared on Tepeyac hill in Mexico in 1531) believed that the universe operated in cycles or "suns," and that there is a major cataclysm about every 4000 years since the creation of the human race. "Cycles or suns!" How could this be linked with the 28-year cycle, I wondered? Now, a solar (sun) cycle is 28 years. This so-called solar cycle is the period of years after which the days of the seven-day week are repeated exactly on the same dates. Since one year contains 52 weeks of 7 days plus one day (365 days), the exact days of the week throughout a year would repeat every seven years were no leap year to intervene. As a Julian calendar leap year cycle is 4 years, the days of the week would therefore repeat on the same dates every 4 x 7 = 28 years. Indeed, I checked this with a computerized calendar which I have. Could we then surmise that the year 1917 when World War I was in progress symbolically represented the first epoch or sun: 1945, the second; 1973, the third and 2001, the fourth? One certainly is entitled to surmise and there it stops with me!

Now, like the ancient Maya, who were convinced that the end of the world or more correctly an "epoch" or "cycle" (The Flood, for example, was not the end of the world. It was the end of an epoch) is coming in the year 2000 *y poco* (*and a little*), the Hopi Pueblo Indians, distantly related to the Aztecs of Mexico, believe that we are walking in the last days with a sword of Damocles hanging over us. According to their myths, "the first world" was destroyed as a punishment for human misdemeanours, by an all-consuming fire that came from above. The second world ended when the terrestrial globe toppled from its axis and everything was covered with ice, and the third world ended in a universal flood. The present world is the fourth. Its fate will depend on whether or not its inhabitants behave in accordance with the Creator's plans. Indeed, a 96-year-old Hopi elder and a leading spokesman for his people once quoted his grandfather's prophecy: "If people do not change their ways then the spirit that takes care of the world will become so frustrated with us that he would punish the world with fire."

As the old negro spiritual *"I got a home in that rock"* says: "God gave Noah the rainbow sign; no more water, the fire next time." The Scripture source for this prophecy of world destruction is to be found in 2 Peter 3:6,7 when Peter warned: "The world at that time was destroyed by being flooded by water. But by the same word, the present sky and earth are destined for fire... Since everything is coming to an end like this, you should be living holy and saintly lives... You have been warned about this, my friends; be careful not to be carried away by the errors of undisciplined people, from the firm ground that you are standing on."

And as Hancock wrote: "When human beings from around the globe, and from many different cultures, share a powerful and overwhelming intuition that a cataclysm is approaching, we are within our rights to ignore them. And when the voices of our distant ancestors, descending to us through myths and sacred architecture, speak to us of the physical obliteration of a great civilization in remote antiquity (and tell us that our own civilization is in jeopardy), we are entitled, if we wish, to stop our ears... So it was, the Bible says, in the antediluvian world: 'For in those days, before the Flood, people were eating, drinking, taking wives, taking husbands, right up to the moment that Noah went into the ark, and they suspected nothing till the flood came and swept all away. In the same manner it has been prophesied that the next global destruction will fall upon us suddenly at an hour we do not suspect, like lightning striking in the east and flashing far into the west... The sun will be darkened, the moon will lose its brightness, the stars will fall from the sky and powers of heaven will be shaken... Then of two men in the fields, one is taken, one left; and of two women at the millstone grinding, one is taken, one left...' What has happened before can happen again. What has been done before can be done again. And perhaps there is, indeed, nothing new under the sun…"

In short, like all the messages of Her Majesty, her warning in Akita must be taken seriously. It is the concern of a mother for her children. Indeed, she has been crying tears of blood. It is Rachel weeping for her children. But why are we not listening?

The Handmaids of the Eucharist in Akita

1973. Akita: "Fire will fall from the sky"

The statues of Amsterdam and Akita

The weeping statue in Akita

Chapter 29

1981. The Ten Secrets of Medjugorje

Yugoslavia was comprised of a mosaic of denominations and faiths which was unique in the world. Five nationalities were recognized; Serbs, Croats, Slovenes, Macedonians and Montenegrans. The major religious identification of the population was Serbian Orthodox 34%, Roman Catholics 26% and Muslims 10%. Indeed, Balkan nationalism is one long history of conflicts which once culminated in the assassination in Sarajevo of the Austrian Archduke Franz Ferdinand, the heir to the Austro-Hungarian empire, and his wife Sophia on June 28, 1914. It was the beginning of a progression of events which directly led to World War I, then, in turn, to World War II and possibly, though hopefully not, a World War III.

The assassin, Gavrilo Princip, belonged to a Serbian nationalist secret society. The Serbs apparently wished to drive the Croats away from their provinces in order to amalgamate them into Serbia. The plan was to create a "Greater Serbia." This is nothing new. As far back as 1849, there was an elaborate Great Serbian Plan for the annexation of Croatia and Bosnia-Hercegovina, which was outlined in an essay called "The Serbs altogether and everywhere."

Around 1990 and onward, the atrocities in Yugoslavia became a tripartite conflict, a so-called ethnic cleansing with Orthodox Serbs, Catholic Croats and Muslims maiming and killing one another on an unimaginable scale which astonished the world. Indeed, a scenario then unfolded where former neighbours and friends became bitter enemies. The senselessness of it all was illustrated by a remark of Nikifor Simsic, a journalist from Sarajevo, who, referring to his own family as an example, once said: "My father is a Serb, my mother is a Catholic, my wife is a Muslim. So what are my children?"

Before 1981, the Croatian village of Medjugorje was virtually unknown throughout the world. It lies between two mountains. A huge mountain overlooking the Church of St. James is about 2,000 feet high and is known as Krizevac or "the Cross mountain" because in 1933, the people of the parish erected a great concrete cross,14 meters high, on its summit, to celebrate the nineteen hundredth anniversary of the Passion of Our Lord. The other smaller mountain is called Podbrdo. On June 24, 1981, the feast day of John the Baptist, six young witnesses maintained under oath that they saw the Blessed Virgin on Podbrdo hill. They were Marija Pavlovic, Ivanka Ivankovic, Vicka Ivankovic, Mirjana Dragicevic, Jakov Colo and Ivan Dragicevic. The visionaries related that the Madonna or "Gospa," as they call her in Croatian, is indescribably beautiful. Her eyes are blue and her feet are always covered by a little grey cloud. She wears a luminous grey dress, while on her head is a crown of twelve stars in suspension.

I interpret the little grey cloud (pregnant with rain) which covers her feet as symbolic of the cloud which Elijah saw on Mount Carmel and which appeared in the shape of a foot. It was the bearer of the rain which brought water to the parched land after the three-year drought in Israel (1 Kings 18:44-46). Indeed, in Mariology, the foot-shaped cloud has been seen by some as a symbol of Our Lady of Mount Carmel, the Woman of Israel, and a prototype of the Holy Virgin who, through her son, crushed the head of the serpent with her foot and brought the "water of life" to our arid souls. The twelve stars depict the Woman of the twelve tribes of Israel, the Woman of Revelation 11:19; 12:1.

This first encounter with the children was one of total silence as she repeatedly covered and uncovered the child she held in her arms. Since then she has been appearing every day in Medjugorje. As Fr. Richard Foley, a Jesuit priest and Mariologist in London, once said: "Medjugorje is a virtual Mariopolis, a city of Mary." The Madonna (Gospa) always begins her conversation with the phrase: "Praised be Jesus Christ," an old Franciscan greeting since the days of St. Francis of Assisi, and she ends, saying: "Go in the peace of God." And how often has it been said that the Blessed Virgin always comes to us on behalf of her son and not to glorify herself!

When the visionaries asked her on the third day, June 26, why she had come and what she wanted, she replied: "I have come because there are many believers here. I want to be with you *to convert and reconcile everyone.*" As they were being doubted and jeered by some skeptics, on the fourth day the children pleaded with Our Lady to give some sign to prove to the world that she was truly appearing. She replied that those who do not see should believe as though they were seeing her. She was thus echoing her son's response to the doubting Thomas: "Blessed are they who have not seen and have believed" (John 20:29). On the fifth day, when the visionaries asked her what she wanted of them, she replied: "Faith and respect for me!" Then, on another day, one of the visionaries enquired: "Gospa, how is it that you are so beautiful?" She smiled: "I am beautiful because I love. Love, and you too will be beautiful."

It was on that June 26 that she identified herself: "I am the Blessed Virgin Mary. Peace! Peace! Peace! Be reconciled!" And on August 6 she declared: *"Ja sam krljica mira" ("I am the Queen of Peace").* It was on the feast of the Transfiguration when her son was seen in all his glory on Mount Tabor. She was at that time on Mt. Podbrdo facing the "Cross mountain." Symbolically, I view Podbrdo as the mountain of Mary and the large Krizevac or Cross mountain as the mountain of her son.

Now, she told the children that she would impart to them ten confidential revelations (secrets), apparently admonitions, which were to be revealed to the world three days before the various events. It brings to mind the ten plagues of Egypt in the Old Testament (Exodus 7). Three of the visionaries have already received all ten prophecies and no longer see Our Lady daily. The other seers have so far received nine secrets and still continue to see her. We are told that the ninth and tenth secrets are particularly grave. They concern a chastisement for the sins of the world, and the visionaries say that after these ten events the world will change.

Our Lady also promised to leave a visible sign on Podbrdo hill after the apparitions have ended. It is meant especially to convert those who do not believe and will be a final call to return to the faith. But she also warned: "You faithful must not wait for the sign to convert yourself. Do not delay in converting yourselves. When the sign comes it will be too late for many." It is also said that a chastisement for the sins of the world is inevitable as we cannot expect the whole world to be converted. It can, however, be diminished or lessened by prayer and penance but it cannot be eliminated. After the first admonition, the others will follow in a rather short period and people will have some time for conversion. For that reason the Blessed Virgin invites us to urgent conversion and reconciliation.

In 1982 she gave in substance the following extraordinary revelation: "You must know that Satan exists. One day he asked to test the Church for a certain time. God gave him leave to try the Church for one century. Satan then chose the twentieth century. When the secrets confided to you are revealed, his power will be destroyed. Even now he is beginning to lose his power and has become aggressive. He is destroying marriages, creating divisions among priests, and is responsible for obsessions and murder. You must protect yourself against these things through fasting and prayer, especially community prayer. Carry blessed objects on yourself. Put them in your houses. Bring back the use of holy water."

It is also recorded in Fr. Svetzovar Kraljevic's book *Apparitions of Our Lady at Medjugorje* that the Madonna once told the children: "In God differences do not exist among his people, and religion need not separate people. Every person must be respected despite his or her particular profession of faith. God presides over all religions as a king controls his subjects through his priests and ministers. The sole mediator of salvation is Jesus Christ. However, it is not equally efficacious to belong to or pray in any church or community, because the Holy Spirit grants his power differently among the churches and ministers, for all believers do not pray the same way. It is intentional therefore that all apparitions are under the auspices of the Catholic Church."

According to the visionaries, these apparitions of Mary are her last apparitions on earth *in this era*. Indeed, she once said: "I came to Lourdes in the morning, to Fatima at noon, and to Medjugorje in the evening time." Although this has been interpreted in a figurative sense, meaning that she came to Medjugorje in what may be called "the final hour" of our time, it was also literally true in that in Lourdes her first appearance to Bernadette was at 7 o'clock in the morning; in Fatima she appeared to the children just after noon, and to the visionaries in Medjugorje at 6:15 p.m. in the evening!

On June 25, 1991, the day which the Blessed Virgin had requested that the Church celebrate a new feast of Mary as Queen of Peace, Croatia and Bosnia-Hercegovina declared their independence from the Central Communist Government. Suddenly on June 26, war escalated while I was in Medjugorje. It was a war which, in certain ways, was more atrocious than the massacres of Hitler's Second World War. Hundreds of churches and mosques were destroyed. However, while all around was being bombarded, pillaged and demolished, Medjugorje was untouched by the war. In fact, I never had the slightest fear of that—not when Her Majesty was still appearing there! Indeed, if Medjugorje and its church were destroyed that probably would have swayed me into believing that she was not appearing there at all!

Now, there are those who also criticize and dogmatize that the many apparently-miraculous events in Medjugorje are the works of Satan. If so, on behalf of the thousands of us who have been converted because of Medjugorje, I wish to express my sincere appreciation and thanks to Satan for those conversions!

But why would the Blessed Virgin choose this small village in Yugoslavia to appear as the "Queen of Peace," and for so long, indeed, for a longer period than any of all the known apparitions in Marian history? Medjugorje is in Croatia whose capital is Sarajevo, and we believe that it is probably partly because the Balkans has been the flash point of wars and conflicts for centuries and the events triggered two world wars. And so, it is all about "war and peace." She is appearing extraordinarily frequently there because of the seriousness of her warnings and their consequences if we do not do as she requests.

That Her Majesty chose to appear in Medjugorje for the first time on June 24, the feast of John the Baptist, is also not without relevance and significance. Just as the Baptizer prepared the way for the first coming of Jesus by fasting and preaching penance and conversion, Louis Marie Grignion de Montfort (1673-1716) has always taught that Mary's role is to prepare the world for the second coming of her son. As he wrote in his classic book *True Devotion To Mary*: "The providential function of Mary in the latter times is to make Jesus known, loved and served. God, then wishes to reveal and make known Mary, the masterpiece of his hands, in these latter times. Being the way by which Jesus comes to us the first time, she will also be the way by which he will come the second time, though not in the same manner."

And so, in these "latter times" she is preaching the same message of "cousin John." In fact, Medjugorje is Mary's school of prayer, fasting, conversion and reconciliation. We are hard-headed people and so it is her repetitive message there. But it is also a message of "PEACE" from the Queen of Peace.

St. James Church in Medjugorije

1981. The Ten Secrets of Medjugorje

Vicka, Ivan and Marija during an apparition

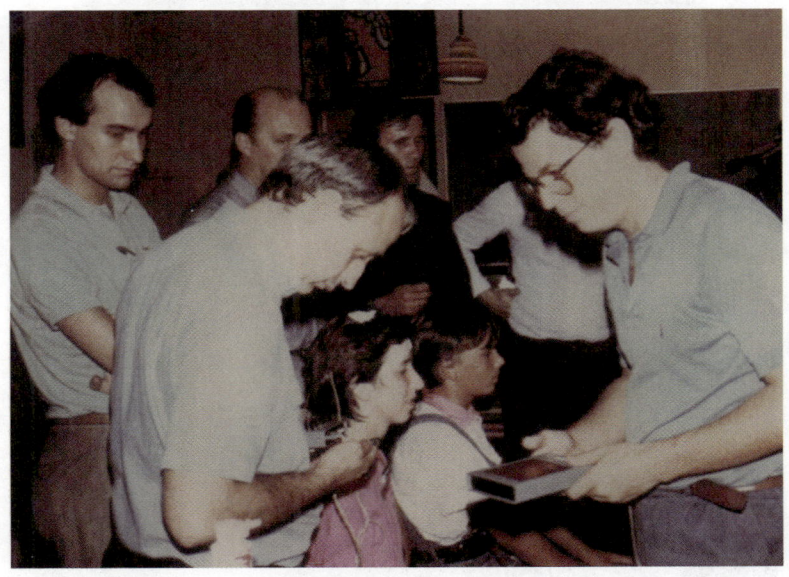
The visionaries examined by Italian and French scientists

Fr. Slavko and the author in 1990

Marija and the author in 2001

Chapter 30

Old Testament Marian Symbols in Medjugorje

Throughout the history of mankind God has sometimes chosen to manifest his presence by physical signs and miracles so that people will believe. While it is often stressed that the importance of Medjugorje does not lie in the physical and mystical signs which are not infrequently seen there, nonetheless, these signs must be important or else God would not have shown them. Like in the days of old, they are meant to strengthen our feeble faith.

The Burning Bush

A number of unusual phenomena have occurred on Krizevac and many people, for example, have seen the Cross change into a bright white column of light. Yet another miraculous sign of great importance, which occurred very early in the history of the apparitions, took place on October 28, 1981. On that day a fire of unknown nature broke out on the bushy hill at the site of the first apparition on Podbrdo. It lasted for about fifteen minutes and was seen by several hundred people. At that time the hill was still under guard by the Communist authorities and one guard, who had been stationed at the foot of the hill to prevent the pilgrims from climbing to the top, later investigated the site. The burning bush was brightly lit, yet there was no trace that the fire had burnt the bush. During the evening apparition it is recorded that the Blessed Virgin said to the visionaries: "This is one of the heralds of the great sign (to come)."

I was deeply curious about the significance of this statement and recalled that in his book *St. Mary in the Orthodox Concept*, Father Tatrous Malaty lists some of the titles given to Mary in the

Coptic Orthodox Church, and among the many symbols of Mary in the Old Testament is that of the *Burning Bush*. The Roman Church also identifies the *Burning Bush* as a Marian symbol (*Dictionary of Mary*, Catholic Book Publishing Company).

Mary as the *Burning Bush* relates to Moses' encounter with God at Horeb, the mountain of God (Exodus 3:2-6): "There the angel of Yahweh appeared to him (Moses) in the shape of a flame of fire, coming from the middle of the bush. Moses looked; there was the bush blazing but it was not being burnt up. ' I must go and look at this strange sight,' Moses said, 'and see why the bush is not burnt'... and God called to him from the middle of the bush: *'Come no nearer. Take off your shoes for the place on which you stand is holy ground. I am the God of your father, God of Abraham, the God of Isaac and the God of Jacob.'* At this Moses covered his face, afraid to look at God."

Father Malaty then quoted part of the Theotokia or Coptic Orthodox hymns, singing praise to Mary: "The bush which Moses saw in the wilderness was flaming but the branches were not consumed. It is a type of Mary, the spotless Virgin. The Word of God came and he was incarnated of her but the fire of his divinity did not consume her womb, and she was virgin even after her childbirth." He then recalls the words of St. Ephrem (306-373 AD): "She bore Christ in her virginal womb as the bush on Mount Horeb bore God in its flame."

And so, it is interpreted that the burning bush on the hill of Podbrdo was not only a symbol of Yahweh, the Covenant God, but also of the Virgin, the Ark of the Covenant. The visionaries revealed that Our Lady said that the fire which was burning on the hill of Podbrdo is "one of the heralds of the great sign to come, and which will be left on the hill permanently."

The Mystical Rose

Fr. Slavko Barbaric and the visionary of Medjugorje, Marija Pavlovic, once gave me photographs taken on December 7, 1987 by a Canadian pilgrim from Quebec. It was a photograph of a rose growing out of a stone wall in a house in Medjugorje at a time of year when roses do not bloom, reminiscent of the miracle of the roses in Guadalupe, Mexico. In the center of this red rose was a beautiful face of a lady with a veil on her head. This is one of Fr. Slavko's favourite photographs, depicting, we believe, one of the Old Testament symbols and titles of Mary—the Mystical Rose.

The Ark of the Covenant

When at the Exodus the Israelites left Egypt at night, "the Lord went in front of them in a pillar of cloud by day to lead them along the way, and a pillar of fire by night to give them light, so that they might travel by day and by night. Neither the pillar of cloud by day nor the pillar of fire by night left its place in front of the people" (Exodus 13:21-22).

After the terms of the covenant were given by Yahweh to Moses on Mount Sinai, he also described to Moses how the Ark or chest for the tablets of the covenant, the Ten Commandments, written in the hand of God, was to be built. Two cherubim extended over the propitiatory of the Ark, spreading their wings and covering the slab. There, between the golden wings of the cherubim and above the ark, rested the cloud, the visible presence of Yahweh. It was a cloud by day and a fire by night, who spoke to the prophets from the propitiatory or throne of mercy. Indeed, in the Old Testament there was no object so sacred and holy as the Ark of the Covenant.

During the Sinai trek the cloud in the shape of a pillar occasionally descended to stand at the door of the Tabernacle or Tent of Meeting when there was conversation between Yahweh and Moses. This visible appearance of God in the form of a cloud the Jewish writers called the *Shekinah*. This word is not found in the Bible and most of the references to the *Shekinah* are found in the Haggadah, the non-legal portion of the Rabbinical literature. It is from the Hebrew word "to appear," "to dwell." It was Yahweh himself dwelling among his chosen people.

Now, the Ark of the Covenant was intended to contain only the tablets on which the Law was written, namely, the Ten Commandments. However, upon subsequent command, a golden vessel containing some of the miraculous manna which fell from heaven during the wanderings of the Hebrews across the Sinai desert (Exodus 16:34) and the miraculous rod of Aaron were also enclosed in the Ark (Hebrews 9:4). However, according to Catholic theology, the Old Testament Ark was only a herald of the great living Ark to come, Mary. It was at the Annunciation that Her Majesty then became the living Ark of the Mediator of the New Covenant, the Ark who sheltered and contained the Uncontainable. She was the Womb of God and, like the ancient Ark of Noah which saved his family, she then became the new Ark of Salvation.

Now, just as the ancient Ark of the (Sinai) Covenant was made of an incorruptible acacia wood, so was the Her Majesty immaculate and incorrupt. There is also the indication that the incorruptible wood of the Ark would eventually signify the Virgin's immunity from the corruption of the grave. Indeed, according to the great mystic Mary of Agreda: "Among the titles of the most holy Mary none was more expressive then the Ark of the Covenant...The ancient Ark was a prototype of this Lady and of what she was to do in the new church of the Gospel... The finest and purest gold which was on the outside and inside of this ancient Ark certainly indicated the most perfect and exalted graces and gifts which shone forth in her heavenly thoughts, in her works and activities, so that in no exterior or interior of this mystical Ark could be discerned anything which was not entirely covered by the gold of the most explicit and finest carat." St. Alphonsus Liguori added his touch to this veneration. He declared that Mary was the "House of Gold which eternal Wisdom chose for his dwelling on earth." And I then said to myself: "No wonder she always wears a gold gown on her feast days in Medjugorje!"

And so, just as the ancient Ark contained the Law, the Ten Commandments, Mary contained in her virginal womb the Lawgiver himself. As David brought the Ark with the tablets of the Law to Jerusalem from Kiriath-jearim, so did Mary carry her God from Nazareth to Jerusalem. David leapt with joy in front of the Ark before it was brought to Jerusalem, so did the unborn John the Baptist leap with joy in his mother's womb when Mary arrived at the house of Zacharias (Luke 1:44). Elizabeth's exclamation at the appearance of the living Ark of the Covenant at her doorstep: "Who am I that the mother of my Lord should come to me?" (Luke 1:43) recalls David's query when the Ark came to him from Kiriath-jearim: "How can the ark of the Lord come to me?" (2 Samuel 6:9-10)

The analogies do not stop there. The Ark remained in the house of Obededom for three months and God blessed Obededom. Likewise, Mary brought blessing to the house of Zacharias and Elizabeth and stayed for three months until John the Baptist was born. Finally, just as the ancient Ark contained a ciborium with some of the manna which fell from heaven and which fed the Israelites in their trek through the desert, with her 'yes' to Gabriel and God, Mary then contained in her womb the true Bread of Life come down from heaven to nourish our immortal souls. The plan unfolds. The Old Testament is fulfilled in the New. As St. Augustine of Hippo once said: *"Novum Testamentum in Vetere Latet et Vetus in Novo patet."* "While the New Testament lies hidden in the Old, the latter is revealed in the New."

In the Book of Revelation, the Ark is eventually seen in heaven: "The sanctuary of God in heaven opened, and the Ark of the Covenant could be seen inside it... Now a great sign appeared in heaven: a woman adorned with the sun, standing on the moon, and with twelve stars on her head for a crown" (Rev. 11:19; 12:1). According to Catholic theologians, this certainly could not be the ancient Ark in the desert since that Ark lies hidden somewhere on earth. It can only refer to Her Majesty, the Godbearer, the Theotokos.

The Pillar of Cloud

One of the earliest symbols which I myself received in Medjugorje was a prominent white pillar which appeared on a photograph of Podbrdo Hill. At that time I did not appreciate its biblical significance until I received another similar imposition on one of my photos taken in Egypt. It all began on my return flight home after my second visit to Medjugorje in October 1987. I read the booklet *When Millions saw Mary* by Francis Johnston and I was so impressed with the testimony of the apparitions of the Virgin Mary in the book that I had a strong urge to visit the church of St. Mary in Zeitoun, just outside of Cairo, where the apparitions took place.

I arrived in Cairo on March 2, 1988 and soon visited the church, and on March 5, 1988, I attended evening Mass in the Church of the Annunciation in Cairo. It was an Armenian Church "In union with Rome" and the service was very similar to the Latin Rite. Armenia is the oldest Christian country. Significantly, the small congregation was reciting the rosary before Mass. At the end of the Mass, at about 7 p.m., as I was leaving the church, I was attracted by a beautiful arch and two pillars which were at the entrance of an alcove or tabernacle containing a statue of Our Lady of Lourdes with the inscription around her head: "I am the Immaculate Conception." I took a few quick photographs and the role of film was developed in London two days later. It was then that I saw something remarkable.

In one of the photographs the pillar at the entrance of the tabernacle to the left of the statue was covered with a white cloud, the top of which leaned towards the image of "the Immaculate Conception." The following day I showed the photograph to Fr. Richard Foley, the Jesuit theologian in Farm Street, London. "My dear Courtenay," he exclaimed, "This is the *Shekinah,* the divine Presence! It is in Exodus 33:9." The text relates that whenever the people of Israel set up camp during the Sinai trek, Moses would take the sacred tent and put it up some distance from the camp. It was called the tent of the Lord's presence and contained the Ark of the Covenant, and anyone who wanted to consult the Lord would go out to it. Whenever Moses went to it, the people would stand at the door of their tents and watch Moses until he entered it. After Moses had gone in, the *pillar of cloud* would come down and stay at the door of the tent, and the Lord would speak to Moses from the cloud.

It was interpreted, therefore, that the photograph depicted and symbolized the *pillar of cloud* in front of the living *Ark of the Covenant* in the tabernacle or tent. In addition, the photograph showed the cloud *leaning* towards Mary and was indicative of the *Shekinah* "leaning" affectionately towards his dove. This unusual photograph was taken in the Church of the Annunciation. It was at the Annunciation, and immediately following her consent, that Mary conceived and became the *Ark of the Covenant*!

Now, whereas the feast of the Annunciation celebrates the beginning of Mary's motherhood, the great feast of the Assumption celebrates the end of her earthly sojourn in this "desert" and her bodily Assumption into heaven. The Marian year which began on the feast of the Annunciation on March 25, 1987 was due to end on that August 15. I arrived in Medjugorje on the evening of August 14, and at 4 p.m. on the feast day, to my surprise, I was invited by Fr. Slavko Barbaric to be with the visionaries, Marija, Ivan and Jakov, for the apparition in the church at 5:40 p.m. At the appointed time, the visionaries walked over to the corner of the choir loft where the apparitions take place, and after a short prayer they suddenly knelt down in unison. She had appeared.

They knelt facing a wall upon which hung a canvas painting of *Our Lady of Medjugorje*. When the apparition occurred, I remember silently asking the Madonna: "I know I am not allowed to see you, but I wonder if you would be so kind as to show me, as you did in Egypt, *the pillar of cloud* in front of you." I then furtively and quickly took four photographs of the hallowed wall in front of which she appeared. The apparition lasted for about five minutes and it was an unforgettable experience and a great privilege to be so close to the invisible (to me) Queen on that day of her great feast. Immediately afterwards Drew Mariani, who was allowed to video tape the event in the choir loft that day, later interviewed me for what became his popular videos *Transforming Your Heart* and *Marian Apparitions of the 20th Century*.

I began my long return journey to Trinidad on the following day. This time the roll of film was developed in Trinidad. All the thirty-plus photographs which were taken of various scenes in Medjugorje developed normally. However, on the photograph taken in the choir loft at the time of the apparition, a *pillar of cloud*, which was obviously not on the original painting of *Our Lady of Medjugorje*, appeared in front of the image of the Madonna, *Ark of the Covenant*.

In Egypt the photographic symbol of the pillar of cloud in front of the *Ark of the Covenant* was seen in photographs taken in the Church of the Annunciation, the church in honour of the moment when she became the living *Ark of the Covenant*. This last photographic repetition of the *pillar of cloud* in front of her image on the wall occurred on the feast, which celebrates the assumption of the Ark into heaven. The Book of Revelations records her presence in heaven: "Then the sanctuary of God in heaven opened, and the A*rk of the Covenant* could be seen inside it... Now a great sign appeared in heaven: a woman adorned with the sun, standing on the moon, and with twelve stars on her head for a crown" (Rev.11:19, 12:1). Since then the pillar of cloud in front of the Ark of the Covenant was seen in several other photographs taken by myself and many other people over the years.

The Column of Smoke

Another Marian symbol which is not well known to many Catholics, yet well recognized in both the Roman and Eastern Churches, is the "Column of Smoke." *The Dictionary of Mary* lists it among other less well-known Marian symbols like "The flower of Sharon" (Song 2:1), "The sachet of myrrh" (Song 1:12) and "The best myrrh" (Sirach 24:15).

I, too, was unacquainted with this Marian title and symbol, "Column of Smoke," until yet another lesson on Mary in the Old Testament was taught to me through other mystical photographs. Once more the schoolroom was Medjugorje. I was there for the feast of the Exaltation of the Cross on September 14, 1988 which is so special to the Croatians of Medjugorje, and on September 13, having scaled a circular iron railing surrounding her statue in the courtyard of St. James Church, I placed a bouquet of seven roses at the feet of the statue of *Our Lady of Medjugorje*. These beautiful roses were given to me to take to Medjugorje by a medical colleague. She chose seven roses in honour of the feast of the Seven Sorrows of Our Lady, which is celebrated on September 15, the day following the feast of the Exaltation of the Cross.

It was a bright sunny day and I took a photograph of the statue of the Madonna, then, after placing the flowers, I took three other photographs in rapid succession. When the film was developed certain unusual phenomena were seen. The first photograph showed the statue of *Our Lady of Medjugorje* against the bright and sunny background with the Crucifix on the iron railing directly in front of her. The second was a close-up photo of the seven roses at her feet. The third photograph was most unusual in several aspects. Suddenly, the background was no longer bright and sunny, as it actually was on that day, and a cloudy haze in the sky with a black *column of smoke* and blue-tinted edges appeared in the photograph in front of the upper portion of the statue. In the fourth photograph the black *column of smoke* was fully formed, *leaning* obliquely from above the head of the statue down to the arm of the crucified Christ on the iron railing surrounding the statue.

I did not understand the significance of this curious imposition on the photograph and thought that perhaps the black carrying-cord of the camera had moved in front of the lens. However, several commentators on the photographs did not favour this interpretation. Nonetheless, should there be an artifactual recurrence, and to avoid any possible debate in the future, I cut off the carrying-cord of the camera. I now had, as it were, a bob-tailed camera!

One month later, on October 13, the anniversary of Our Lady's last apparition in Fatima, I was once more in Medjugorje en route to a medical conference in Tanzania. I had climbed Krizevac Hill in the cool, early hours of the morning to spend an hour there. Just as I was about to begin the downhill journey to the home of my host Jozo Vasilj, I took a few photographs of the large concrete Cross and the huge copper plaque nearby, depicting the fifteenth station of the Cross—the resurrected Christ. What appeared on that print left no doubt that the previous black column seen in front of the statue was not an artifact, for coursing across the arm of the Cross on Mount Krizevac and *leaning* towards the "resurrected Christ" was a similar black *column of smoke* with a blue tint at its edge, this time horizontally, not vertically!

Seeking an explanation for this *column of smoke,* I recalled a book entitled *The Sermons of St. Francis de Sales on Our Lady*. Some of the sermons preached by this great Marian Doctor of the Church between 1602 and 1622 were faithfully recorded in this book by his Visitation nuns. In a sermon given nearly four hundred years ago on the feast of the Assumption, August 15, 1602, he started with a quotation from the *Song of Songs*, betraying his well known predilection for a Marian mystical interpretation of

Solomon's *Song of Songs*. It was a quotation of Song 8:5: "Who is this coming up from the desert, flowing with delights, *leaning* upon her Lover? Later on, he quoted another passage: "Who is this coming up from the desert like a *column of smoke*, perfumed with myrrh and frankincense?" (Song 3:6).

According to the *Catholic Encyclopedia* Vol. 7, incense, with its sweet-smelling perfume and high-ascending smoke, is typical of prayer which rises up as a pleasing offering in God's sight. As prescribed by Yahweh Himself, an altar of incense was positioned directly in front of the curtain which separated the Holy of Holies containing the sacred *Ark of the Covenant* from the outer court.

With this background, let us now return to Francis de Sales. Following his quotation from the *Song of Songs*, he began his sermon with this account: "The *Ark of the Covenant* had been kept under tents and pavilions for a very long time when the great King Solomon placed it in the rich and magnificent Temple which he had prepared for it (1 Kings 8). The rejoicings in Jerusalem were so great at this time that the blood of the sacrifices flowed in the street, *the air was filled with clouds from so much incense and perfume.*"

This, therefore, seems to be the explanation for and interpretation of the cloudy haze of the atmosphere which appeared on the third photograph of Our Lady of Medjugorje in the courtyard of the Church of St. James, taken on September 13, 1988. It was meant to signify the smoke from the incense burnt in the front of the *Ark of the Covenant*.

Francis de Sales adds: "But let us look at the remainder of the sentence we have chosen for our subject. It says that this holy lady coming up from the desert flowing with delights, is *leaning* upon her Lover... All the saints do the same, and particularly the Virgin. All her perfections, all her virtues, all her happiness are referred, consecrated and dedicated to the glory of her son, who is their source, their author and finisher. If you call her a rose because of her most excellent charity, her colour will only be the blood of her son. If you say that she is a *column of smoke*, sweet and pleasing, say at once that the fire of this smoke is the charity of her Son; the wood of his Cross. In brief, in all and through all, she is *leaning* upon her lover."

This then appears to be the reason why the blue tinged *columns of smoke* in the photographs were both obliquely positioned. They were meant to be symbolic of Mary, the *column of smoke*, whose prayers are also like incense to God, *leaning* on the arm of her beloved son. It was a photographic lesson on Song of Songs 3:6 and 8:5.

Indeed, both the mystic the Venerable Mary of Agreda and the stigmatist and visionary Anne Catherine Emmerich have seen in their visions that Our Lord accompanied his Blessed Mother when she was bodily assumed into heaven. In her chapter in the *City of God* on the Assumption of the Blessed Virgin, Mary of Agreda wrote: "Christ our Saviour came back up to heaven, and at his right hand the Queen, clothed in the gold of variety, was so beautiful that she was the admiration of the heavenly court. All of them turned towards her to look upon her and bless her with songs of praise. Then were heard those mysterious eulogies recorded by Solomon: 'Who is she that comes from the desert like a column of all the aromatic perfumes? Who is she that comes up from the desert *resting* upon her Beloved and spreading forth abundant delights?' "

Now, what is little known is that just before Her Majesty appeared to the young children on October 13, 1917 in Fatima, a bluish-tinted *column of smoke* was seen above the heads of the visionaries in the dull, grey atmosphere of that rainy day. This phenomenon was witnessed by many people and is recorded in Francis Johnston's book *Fatima: The Great Sign*. He quoted the testimony of another scientist, Dr. Joseph Garrett, Professor of Natural Sciences, at Coimbra University in Portugal (see chapter 20): "It must have been about half past one when there rose up, on the precise spot where the children were, *a column of smoke, a delicate, slender, bluish column* that went straight up to about two metres and then evaporated. The phenomenon lasted some seconds and was perfectly visible to the eye. It was repeated yet a second and third time. On these three occasions, and especially on the last one, the slender posts stood out distinctly in the *dull grey atmosphere."* It was the calling card of Her Majesty, the *column of smoke*.

I cannot help but wonder, therefore, if the great sign to be left in Garabandal and Medjugorje may not be the Marian sign, the *burning bush* or the *column of smoke*, or perhaps the *pillar* of cloud by day and the *pillar* of fire by night, which always preceded the *Ark of the Covenant* in the Sinai trek.

The Church of Annunciation in Cairo

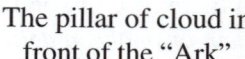

The pillar of cloud in front of the "Ark"

Old Testament Marian Symbols in Medjugorje

A pillar of cloud appears in front of the painting

A close up view of the pillar in front of the Ark

Her Majesty Mary, Queen of Peace

The statue. A bright sunny day

The crucifix in front of the statue

Old Testament Marian Symbols in Medjugorje

A column of smoke begins to appear

The column is fully formed

The horizontal column of smoke

A pillar of fire and a pillar of cloud in Betania
(courtesy R. Martinez)

Column of cloud and
image of
Our Lady of Fatima
(courtesy Dr. J. Fida)

Chapter 31

2000 AD.
The Third Fatima Secret Revealed

As I said in chapter 21, the first and second parts of the "secret" heard by the two young children (not by Francisco) during the apparition of July 13, 1917 in Fatima were not written down and made public until July-August 1941. It was when Lucia, who had entered religious life and had already learned to read and write, began documenting her recollections of the apparitions at the request of her superiors. She wrote that the secret is made up of three distinct parts. The first part of the secret was that the Blessed Virgin had shown the children a vision of hell "where the souls of poor sinners go." The second part was that God wanted devotion to her Immaculate Heart and that the Pope should consecrate Russia to her Immaculate Heart *in union with all the world's bishops.*

The third part would remain secret. It was what came to be known as the "third secret of Fatima." In fact, Lucia did not write down the "third secret" until January 3, 1944, twenty-seven years after the apparitions of 1917. This was written at the request of Bishop José da Silva of Leiria (the diocese where Fatima is located). He made this request after Lucia contracted a serious illness in the summer of 1943, prompting fears that she might die without ever revealing the message. Before giving the sealed envelope containing the "secret" to the bishop on June 17, 1944, Sr. Lucia wrote on the outside of the envelope that it could be opened only after 1960.

We are told that the bishop did not open the letter or read it. The letter was sealed with wax and placed in a double envelope in a safe in his episcopal palace. However, in 1957, Rome requested the text of the "third secret." It has been reported that the request was made because Rome had some concern that the letter might "fall into the wrong hands." When, years later, the question was asked why "only after 1960," and was it Our Lady who fixed that date? Sr. Lucia replied: "I fixed the date because I had the intuition that before 1960 it would not be understood, and that only later would it be understood. I wrote down what I saw, *however it was not for me to interpret it.*"

Bishop da Silva's sealed envelope reached Pope Pius XII (1939-1958) on April 16, 1957. It seems that he too never opened the envelope, probably waiting until 1960, and died in 1958 without having read the text of the secret. By all accounts, the first time the envelope was opened was in August 1959 when Pope John XXIII (1958–1963) called for it while he was at the Papal summer residence at Castelgandolfo. However, rather than publishing the contents of the secret, he chose to close the envelope again (in fact, we could now understand why he did not want to reveal that a Pope would be killed). On February 8,1960, to the disappointment of so many, the Vatican then announced that the secret would not be published. After the death of Pope John XXIII, Pope Paul VI (1963-1978) read it in March 1965 after he had been Pope for two years. His successor, Pope John Paul II also read the secret, but only after the attempt on his life, two weeks later on July 18, 1981. He was to be the one to reveal it.

Now, it is noteworthy that in a letter to Pope John Paul II, dated May 12, 1982, Sr. Lucia gave the following commentary on the third part of the "secret": "The third part of the secret refers to Our Lady's words: 'If not Russia will spread her errors throughout the world, promoting wars and the persecution of the Church. The good will be martyred; the Holy Father will have much to suffer and various nations will be annihilated' (July 13,1917). The third part of the secret is a symbolic revelation, referring to this part of the message, conditioned by whether we accept or not what the message itself asks of us. 'If my requests are heeded, Russia will be converted, and there would be peace; if not, she will spread her errors throughout the world, etc.' Since we did not heed this appeal of the message, we see that it has been fulfilled. Russia has invaded the world with her errors. And if we have not yet seen the complete fulfillment of the final part of this prophecy, we are going towards it little by little with great strides, if we do not reject the path of sin, hatred, revenge, injustice, violation of the rights of the human person, immorality and violence, etc. And let us not say that it is God who is punishing us in this way; on the contrary it is people themselves who are preparing their own punishment. In his kindness God warns us and calls us to the right path, while respecting the freedom he has given us; hence people are responsible."

Then, in a special meeting which took place on April 27, 2000 in the Carmel of St. Teresa in Coimbra, Portugal between Sr. Lucia, Archbishop Bertone, Secretary of the Congregation of the Faith and Bishop Serafín, when asked: "Is the principal figure in the vision the Pope?" Sr. Lucia replied at once that it was, then added: "We did not know the name of the Pope; Our Lady did not tell us the name of the Pope. We did not know whether it was Benedict XV or Pius XII, Paul VI or John Paul II. But it was the Pope who was suffering and that made us suffer too."

On Saturday, May 13, 2000, Pope John Paul II journeyed to Fatima to beatify the two shepherd visionaries, Jacinta and Francisco. At the end of the Papal Mass, Cardinal Angelo Sodano made this announcement concerning the third secret of Fatima to a large anticipative congregation: "The vision of Fatima concerns, above all, the war waged by atheistic systems against the Church and Christians, and it describes the immense suffering endured by the witnesses to the faith in the last century of the second millennium. It is an interminable Way of the Cross led by the Popes of the 20th century... After the assassination attempt of May 13, 1981, it appeared evident to His Holiness that it was a mother's hand that guided the bullet's path, enabling 'the Pope in his throes' to halt at the threshold of death... Even if the events to which the third part of the 'secret' of Fatima refers now seem part of the past, Our Lady's call to conversion and penance, issued at the start of the twentieth Century, remain timely and urgent today... In order that the faithful may better receive the message of Our Lady of Fatima, the Pope has charged the Congregation for the Doctrine of the Faith with making public the third part of the secret, after the preparation of an appropriate commentary..."

Some days later the text of the "third secret" which was written by Lucia, now Sr. Lucia of the Immaculate Heart of Mary, was released. It read: "I write in obedience to you, my God, who commands me to do so through His Excellency the Bishop of Lieria, and through your Most Holy Mother and mine. After the two parts (of "the secret") which I have already explained, we saw at the left of Our Lady and a little above, an angel with a flaming sword in his left hand; flashing, it gave out flames that looked as though they would set the world on fire; but they died out in contact with the splendour that Our Lady radiated towards him from her right hand. Pointing to the earth with his right hand, the angel cried out in a loud voice: 'Penance, Penance, Penance!' And we saw in an immense light that is God (something similar to how people appear in a mirror when they pass in front of it) a Bishop dressed in white; we had the impression that it was the Holy Father. Other Bishops, men and women Religious going up a steep mountain, at the top of which there was a big Cross of roughhewn trunks as of a cork-tree with the bark; before reaching there the Holy Father passed through a big city half in ruins, and half trembling with halting step, afflicted with pain and sorrow, he prayed for the souls of the corpses he met on his way. Having reached the top of the mountain, on his knees at the foot of the big Cross, he was killed by a group of soldiers who fired bullets and arrows at him, and in the same way there died one after another Bishops, priests, men and women Religious, and various lay people of different ranks and positions. Beneath the two arms of the Cross there were two angels each with a crystal aspersorium in his hand, in which they gathered up the blood of the martyrs and with it sprinkled the souls that were making their way to God" (Tuy 3-1-1944).

Chapter 32

2000 AD.
Cardinal Ratzinger's Interpretation

In his "theological commentary" under the caption *An attempt to interpret the "secret" of Fatima,* Joseph Cardinal Ratzinger, Prefect of the Congregation for the Doctrine of the Faith, wrote: "A careful reading of the text of the so-called 'third secret' of Fatima would probably prove disappointing or surprising after all the speculation it has stirred. No great mystery is revealed; nor is the future unveiled. We see the Church of the martyrs of the century, which has just passed representing in a scene described in a language which is symbolic and not easy to decipher. Is this what the Mother of the Lord wished to communicate to Christianity and to humanity at a time of great difficulty and distress? Is it of any help to us at the beginning of the new millennium? How should we understand the vision? What are we to make of it.

"The keyword of this third part (of the secret) is the threefold cry 'Penance, Penance, Penance!' To understand the signs of the times means to accept the urgency of penance—of conversion and of faith. This is the correct response to this moment of history, characterized by the grave perils outlined in the images that follow... Let us now examine more closely the single images. The angel with the flaming sword on the left of the Mother of God recalls similar images in the Book of Revelation. This represents the threat of judgment, which looms over the world. Today the prospect that the world might be reduced to ashes by a sea of fire no longer seems pure fantasy; man himself, with his inventions, has forged the flaming sword. The division then shows the power which stands opposed to the force of destruction—the splendour of the Mother of God and, stemming from this in a certain way, the summons to penance...

"Let us now consider the individual images which follow the text of 'the secret.' The place of the action is described in three symbols; a steep mountain, a great city reduced to ruins and finally a large rough-hewn Cross. The mountain and the city symbolize the arena of human history, but at the same time a place of destruction, where man actually destroys the fruit of his own work... On the mountain stands a Cross — the goal and guide of history. The Cross transforms destruction into salvation. At this point human persons appear; the Bishop dressed in white, other Bishops, priests, men and women Religious, and men and women of different ranks and social positions. The Pope seems to precede the others, *trembling and suffering* because of all the horrors around him. Not only do the houses of the city lie half in ruins, but he makes his way among the corpses of the dead.

"The Church's path is thus described as a Via Crucis, as a journey through a time of violence, destruction and persecution. The history of an entire century can be seen represented in this image, just as the places of the earth are synthetically described in the two images of the mountain and the city, and are directed towards the Cross, so too time is presented in a compressed way. In the vision we can recognize the last century as a century of martyrs, a century of suffering and persecution for the Church, a century of World Wars and the many local wars which filled the last fifty years and have inflicted unprecedented forms of cruelty. In the "mirror" of this vision we see passing before us the witnesses of the faith decade by decade.

"Here it would be appropriate to mention a phrase from the letter which Sr. Lucia wrote to the Holy Father on May 12, 1982: 'The third part of the 'secret' refers to Our Lady's words: 'If not, Russia would spread her errors throughout the world, causing wars and persecutions of the Church. The good would be martyred; the Holy Father would have much to suffer; various nations will be annihilated.' The Via Crucis of an entire century, the figure of the Pope has a special role. In his arduous ascent of the mountain we can undoubtedly see a convergence of different Popes. Beginning from Pius X up to the present Pope, they all shared the suffering of the century and strove to go forward through all the anguish along

2000 AD. Cardinal Ratzinger's Interpretation

the path which leads to the Cross. In the vision, the Pope too is killed along with the martyrs. When, after the attempted assassination in 1981, the Holy Father had the text of the third part of the 'secret' brought to him, was it not inevitable that he should see in it his own fate? He had been very close to death, and he himself explained his survival in the following words: 'It was a mother's hand that guided the bullet's path and in his throes the Pope halted at the threshold of death' (13 May 1994). That here, a 'mother's hand' had deflected the fateful bullet only shows once more that there is no immutable destiny, that faith and prayer are forces which can influence history and that in the end prayer is more powerful than bullets and faith more powerful than armies...

"The concluding part of the 'secret' uses images which Lucia may have seen in devotional books and which draw their inspiration from long-standing intuitions of faith. It is a consoling vision, which seeks to open a history of blood and tears to the healing power of God. Beneath the arms of the Cross angels gathered up the blood of the martyrs, and with it they give life to the souls making their way to God. Here, the blood of Christ and the blood of the martyrs are considered as one: the blood of the martyrs runs down from the arms of the Cross. The martyrs die in communion with the Passion of Christ, and their death becomes one with his... 'The blood of the martyrs is the seed of Christians,' said Tertullian. As from Christ's death, from his wounded side, the Church was born, so the death of the witnesses is fruitful for the future life of the Church. Therefore, the vision of the third part of the 'secret,' so distressing at first, closes with an image of hope; no suffering is in vain, and it is a suffering Church, a Church of martyrs, which becomes a sign-post for man in his search for God...

"And so, we come to the final question: What is the meaning of the 'secret' of Fatima as a whole (in its three parts)? What does it say to us? First of all we must affirm with Cardinal Sodano: '... the events to which the third part of the 'secret' of Fatima refers now seem part of the past.' Insofar as individual events are described, they belong to the past. Those who expected exciting apocalyptic revelations about the end of the world or the future course of history are bound to be disappointed. Fatima does not satisfy our curiosity in this way, just as Christian faith in general cannot be reduced to an object of mere curiosity. What remains was already evident when we began our reflections on the text of the 'secret': the exhortation to prayer as the path of 'salvation for souls' and, likewise, the summons to penance and conversion.

"I would like finally to mention another key expression of the 'secret' which has become justly famous: 'My Immaculate Heart will triumph.' What does this mean? The Heart open to God, purified by contemplation of God, is stronger than guns and weapons of every kind. The *fiat* of Mary, the word of her heart, has changed the history of the world, because it brought the Saviour into the world — because, thanks to her, Yes, God could become man in our world and remain so for all time... From that time forth, the word that prevails is this: 'In the world you will have tribulation, but take heart; I have overcome the world' (John 16: 33). The message of Fatima invites us to trust in this promise" (Joseph Card. Ratzinger, Prefect of the Congregation for the Doctrine of the Faith).

Chapter 33

The Apocalypse. Chapters 8 and 13

Cardinal Ratzinger's analysis was captioned: "An interpretation of the third secret." It was a prudent caption and suggests that he was not claiming a dogmatic analysis. As Robert Moynihan wrote in *Inside the Vatican* (June-July, 2000), there can be no doctrinal certainty in this interpretation and this is probably why, during the May 12-13, 2000 papal trip to Fatima, it was Cardinal Angelo Sodano, Vatican Secretary of State, and not the Pope himself, who announced the Pope's decision to publish the third secret. Vatican watchers see the choice of Sodano to read the text, rather than having the Pope read it himself, as one reflecting curial caution—the desire to make sure that no suggestion of papal infallibility may ever be given to the understanding of the meaning of the secret.

For this same reason the long explicatory commentary on the text of the secret was entrusted to Cardinal Joseph Ratzinger and his doctrinal congregation, not to a papal discourse. Both decisions emphasize this key point regarding the entire subject of the "third secret of Fatima": that no aspect of the secret or its interpretation belongs to the deposit of the faith.

So said, there have been many people who are not convinced that "insofar as individual events are described, they belong to the past." Indeed, those who expected apocalyptic revelations about the end of the world or the future course of history have so expected them in light of the threat of a possible "annihilation of various nations," as predicted by Our Lady in the second part of the secret; by the apocalyptic significance of the miracle of the sun, and finally by the alleged statement of Sr. Lucia about the third secret: "It is in the Gospel and the Apocalypse. Read them." She later added: "Chapters 8 and 13." That expectation was also influenced by the warnings of Our Lady in Garabandal, Akita and Medjugorje. Surely these extraordinary and frequent apparitions since the second half of the 20th century must be of major significance. However, as to the end of the world, many of us are aware that Our Lady has clarified in Medjugorje and elsewhere that it is not going to be the end of the world but the end of an era or epoch. We were also aware that the possible chastisement and its extent was *conditional*.

Now, with respect to chapters 8 and 13 in the Book of Revelation to which Sr. Lucia referred, a section of Chapter 8 reads: "Next, I saw trumpets being given to the seven angels who stood in the presence of God. Another angel, who had a golden censer, came and stood at the altar. A large quantity of incense was given to him to offer with the prayers of all the saints on the golden altar that stood in front of the throne [of God]. Then the angel took the censer, filled it with live coals ["fire" in the Jerusalem Bible] from the altar, and hurled it down to the earth. When the first angel blew his trumpet, there came hail and then fire, mixed with blood, which was hurled down to the earth. A third of the earth was scorched, along with a third of the trees and every green plant. When the second angel blew his trumpet, something like a huge mountain all in flames was cast into the sea. A third of the sea turned to blood, a third of the creatures living in the sea died, and a third of the ships were wrecked. When the third angel blew his trumpet, a huge star burning like a ball of fire crashed down from the sky. It fell on a third of the rivers and the springs. The star's name was '*Wormwood*' because a third part of all the waters turned to wormwood. Many people died from this polluted water. When the fourth angel blew his trumpet, a third of the sun, a third of the moon, and a third of the stars were hit hard enough to be plunged into darkness, the day lost a third of its light, as did the night" (Rev. 8:3-12).

Let us now attempt to link the "third secret" to Revelation 8. "The angel took the censer, filled it with live coals [fire] and hurled it down to the earth" (Rev. 8:5).

But who can interpret the Book of Revelation with any certainty? Certainly not I! Be that as it may, an atom bomb fell on Hiroshima and Nagasaki in August 1945. It was like "live coals" or "fire" falling down to earth, and within seconds 200,000 people were burnt to charcoal. Could this be a prototype and herald of things to come?

When the first angel blew his trumpet there came "hail and then fire," mixed with blood, which was hurled down to the earth, a third of the earth was scorched along with a third of the trees and every green plant (Rev. 8:7).

Interestingly, the seventh plague of Egypt was "the hail." "Throughout the land of Egypt the hail struck down everything in the fields, man and beast; it struck all the crops in the field, and it shattered every tree in the fields" (Exodus 9:25-26). However, I sometimes wonder whether this "hail **and** fire" could possibly refer to the effects of a comet. Hail is frozen pellets of rain, and a comet is, simply speaking, a snowball. It is made mostly of ice and dirt (a dirty snowball), however, its impact on earth could "set the world on fire," and depending on its size, it can be more explosive than many atomic bombs. Indeed, it does seem possible and even probable that a comet-collision with the earth, with an equivalent energy of about a million megatons of TNT destroyed the dinosaurs 65 million years ago!

Revelation 8 continues: "A huge star burning like a ball of fire crashed down from the sky…The star's name was 'Wormwood' because a third part of all the waters turned to wormwood. Many people died from this polluted water, because it was made bitter" (Rev 8:10).

Relevant to this, on a Saturday marking the beginning of the Orthodox Holy Week in Russia on April 26, 1986, an explosion occurred at the Chernobyl nuclear power plant in the Soviet Ukraine. Over 100,000 people were evacuated from the surrounding areas in the Ukraine and Byelorussia and there were more than 30 deaths and countless radioactive exposures, which could lead in time to cancers and leukemias. As Fr. Robert J. Fox wrote in his book *Mary Through the Ages:* "The English translation of Chernobyl is 'Wormwood'," an Old World plant known for its bitter taste. Following the disaster there was some discussion in the Soviet Union concerning the following passage from the 8th chapter of Revelation. In an interview with the influential Soviet periodical Literaturnaya Gazeta, the Russian Orthodox Metropolitan of Kiev rejected any connection between this scripture passage and the Chernobyl disaster. A panel of scientists later announced in Moscow that several hundred new wells have been dug in Ukraine, in the event the river water became contaminated due to radioactive runoff!"

It also reminds me of Czeslaw Milosz's poem, *The Wormwood star*: "Under the Wormwood star bitter rivers flowed. Man in the field gathered bitter bread. No sign of the divine care shown in the heavens. The century wanted homage from the dead."

"The fourth angel blew his trumpet, and a third of the sun, a third of the moon and a third of the stars were hit hard enough to be plunged into darkness; the day lost a third of its light, as did the night "(Rev 8:12).

Now, as Carl Sagan estimated, a massive nuclear exchange or comet/asteroid impact would produce between 300-400 million tons of smoke, 30% of which would be strongly light-absorbing carbon, and hardly any sunlight would be coming through. Indeed, there could be the much-touted "three days of darkness"—and many more! Let us not forget that the ninth plague in Egypt was three days of darkness: "...for three days there was deep darkness over the whole land of Egypt" (Exodus 10:22-23)!

Of further interest, and especially because of recent history, the sixth plague of Egypt was "the boils," and over the millennia the "boils breaking into sores on man and beast" have been attributed to be caused by anthrax. In fact, anthrax is one of the oldest recorded diseases in history, most commonly occurring in cattle, sheep and goats. The name "anthrax" is derived from the Greek word *anthrakis*, meaning "coal," and refers to the black sores seen on affected areas in the skin. And so, it seems that Old Testament plagues appear to be plaguing us now, albeit in a different way! Let us now return to the "third secret" and my attempt to interpret it further and in more detail in the light of the Book of the Apocalypse.

Chapter 34

An Attempt to Interpret Further the Third Secret

Now, the third part of the secret begins with the vision: "We saw at the left of Our Lady and a little above, an angel with a flaming sword in his left hand; flashing, it gave out flames that looked as though they would set the world on fire, but they died out in contact with the splendor that Our Lady radiated towards him from her right hand."

In concert with Sr. Lucia's parallel of this part of the secret with the Book of the Apocalypse, John Haffert, the co-founder of the Blue Army and a great American ambassador of the messages of Our Lady of Fatima, recently wrote before he died: "The angel with the flaming sword recalls the images in the Book of Revelation. This represents the threat of judgment over the world. Today the prospect that the world might be reduced to ashes by a sea of fire is no longer pure fantasy. Man himself, with his inventions, has forged the flaming sword. The angel of God's justice was about to strike the world with fire but the Mother of God (the Mother of Mercy), standing beside the angel prevents the strike. However, the interpretation by Sr. Lucia would seem to indicate that we are nearing a deadline, after which it could be too late."

Indeed, I see the *"angel with the flaming sword in his left hand"* as representing God's left hand of justice and *"the splendor that Our Lady radiated towards him from her right hand"* as representing God's right hand of mercy. And so, mercy tempered justice! Probably pertinent to all of this, in the land where the first atom bomb was dropped in 1945, the Blessed Virgin is said to have given this warning to the world 28 years later, in 1973 in Akita, Japan: "As I told you, if men do not repent and better themselves, the

Father would inflict a terrible punishment on all humanity. It would be a punishment greater than the flood, such as one would never have seen before. *Fire will fall from the sky* and will wipe out a great part of humanity, the good as well as the bad, sparing neither priests nor faithful. The survivors will find themselves so desolate that they will envy the dead. The only armour which would remain for you will be the rosary and the sign left by my son. Each day recite the prayers of the rosary. With the rosary, pray for the Pope, the bishops and the priests…"

Undoubtedly, a heavy nuclear exchange would certainly "set the world on fire." That Akita warning was given on October 13, 1973, the anniversary date of the "miracle of the sun" in Fatima on October 13, 1917 when the nuclear reactor which we call the sun retreated to its celestial abode, as it were, in contact with "the splendor of Our Lady." This was symbolically akin to the Jewish Queen Esther of the Old Testament who saved her people from annihilation on the 13th day of the month (Esther 9:17).

Now, the third part of the secret should also be placed in the context of the first two parts of the secret. So said, on July 13, 1917, the Lady of the Rosary of Fatima warned: "The war is going to end soon. *But if people will not stop offending God,* another and more terrible war will begin during the reign of Pius XI." People did not stop offending God and World War II came to pass. Later on in the warning, mention was made of *"the annihilation of various nations."* Fifty million people died in World War II, but there was no *annihilation of various nations.* In fact, I believe that this word "annihilation" should be taken literally as it implies a much greater cataclysmic "fire" to come. Impossible in 1917, this tragic threat is no longer far-fetched for us in today's nuclear age.

The third part of the secret continued: "Pointing to the earth with his right hand, the angel called out in a loud voice: 'Penance, Penance, Penance!'" And so, thrice the angel called for "Penance." But to appreciate and fully understand the angel's cry, I believe that it is necessary to detail the full meaning of the word "Penance." Section Two, Chapter Two, Article 4 of the *Catechism of the Catholic Church* does so: "Those who approach the *sacrament of Penance* obtain pardon from God's mercy for the offenses committed against him, and are, at the same time, reconciled with the Church which they have wounded by their sins... It is called the *sacrament of conversion*, the first step in reuniting with the Father from whom one has strayed by sin... It is called the s*acrament of confession*, since the disclosure or confession of sins to a priest is an essential element of this sacrament..., a confession of the holiness of God and of his mercy toward sinful man. It is called the *sacrament of forgiveness*, since by the priest's sacramental absolution God grants the penitent 'pardon and peace'." This then is about what the angel was calling. It is all about God's merciful response to penance and repentance. It is all about confession of one's sins which is being practised less and less by more and more of the faithful.

But it was not only "the angel of the third secret" who has thrice called for "Penance." In one of her apparitions to Bernadette Soubirous in Lourdes on Friday, February 26, 1858, Our Lady said three times to Bernadette: "Penance! Penance! Penance!" She then made this request to her: "You will kiss the ground for sinners." In his book, *We Saw Her*, B.E. Sandhurst wrote: "We knew later that it was an act of penance asked for by the Lady on behalf of sinners." The angel therefore was simply repeating the call, sixty years earlier, of his Queen, Her Majesty. The Church recognizes Mary as the Queen of the angels because her mission is higher than theirs. They are God's servants whereas she is the Mother of God.

> *"And we saw in an immense light that is God... a Bishop dressed in white; we had the impression that it was the Holy Father, other Bishops, men and women Religious going up a steep mountain at the top of which there was a big Cross."*

In 1597, 26 Christian martyrs were marched to the steep Nishizaka hill in Japan, not far away from present-day Nagasaki railway station. It was their Mount Calvary. There, 26 neatly sawn crosses ran from the top of the hill down towards the harbour so that every one could see the spectacle. The victims were fastened to the crosses by iron rings and straw ropes, and two Samurai stood beneath each cross with an unsheathed bamboo lance, waiting to run their weapons up under the rib cages of the Christians. All of a sudden a Franciscan priest on one of the crosses began to sing repeatedly: *"Jesus, Mary...Jesus, Mary..."* The others on their crosses and the Christians in the large crowd then chanted *repeatedly* in unison, 4,000 of them: *"Jesus, Mary...Jesus, Mary..."* And the refrain went on and on.

I saw a deep meaning to this. These 16th century martyrs probably appreciated that Mary was also a martyr standing under the Cross, except that she was not allowed to die. In fact, early in the first century of the Christian era the word "martyr" had the connotation of giving testimony to one's faith in Christ, at the risk of being forced either to give up one's convictions, or to expose oneself to the punishment of death. It was only by degrees that the term "martyr" came to be exclusively applied to those who actually died for the faith. As St. Augustine (354–430 AD) once said: "It was the martyr's privilege to join the Master in the perfect sacrifice, as a burnt offering, a holocaust. Mary is the martyrs' Queen in suffering, for she shared more intensely and more intimately in Jesus' pains by her inner union with him on the Cross than did all the martyrs by their bloody affliction. It is beautifully expressed in the *Stabat Mater*."

But in the twentieth century, certainly much more than in the 16th century, and perhaps even more frequently than in the period of the early Church, many were called to prove their loyalty to Christ with heroic suffering. As Antonio Gaspari, writing in *Inside the Vatican*, said: "Many martyrs refused to bow to the idolatrous cults of the twentieth century or fall victim to Communism or Nazism." Indeed, the largest number of innocent dead in the 20th century were victims of Communism. If we take the Soviet Union alone, it is estimated that more than one million Christians went to their death, most of whom will remain nameless. In fact, the Catholic martyrs of the twentieth century, by any measure, present a brutal spectacle that may be remembered historically as one of the darkest periods of martyrdom."

"Before reaching there the Holy Father passed through a

big city half in ruins and half trembling with halting step, afflicted with pain and sorrow, he prayed for the souls of the corpses he met on his way."

I do not believe that this text was meant to infer that the Pope was trembling, say, *because* of fear from the carnage around him. The Pope was not "trembling" but *"**half** trembling with halting step."* This is the classical medical description of hemi-Parkinson's disease from which the Pope has suffered for several years. It was originally a one-sided *hemi-tremor* of the left hand and a slight rigidity of the left leg, accompanied by a *halting step*, typical of the Parkinsonian gait.

He was "afflicted with *pain and sorrow."* Apropos this, in the December 1999 issue of *Inside the Vatican*, Dominic Morawski, in an article captioned *Suffering and Ecumenism*, relevantly quoted a reflection by Cardinal Ratzinger on the second decade of Pope John Paul II's pontificate, which was published in the July 1999 Cracow weekly *Tygodnik Powszechny* (Universal Weekly): "Pain is constantly written on the Holy Father's face. His figure is bent, he moves with great difficulty and increasingly leans on his papal staff — the symbol of a shepherd leading his flock. Often during moments of physical exhaustion, particularly in public, he can barely speak. John Paul II is truly a figure of suffering and weakness." Indeed, his tremor has recently become bilateral—all part of his great suffering.

"Having reached the top of the mountain on his knees at the foot of the big Cross, he was killed by a group of soldiers who fired bullets and arrows at him and in the same way there died one after the other Bishops, priests, men and women Religious and various lay people of different ranks and positions."

"Bullets and arrows," it says. Indeed, three bullets were shot at the Holy Father by the Turk, Mehmet Ali Agca. But what about the arrows? Surely, we are not in medieval times, and so, the arrows in modern times must be explained. In fact, the Bible frequently refers

to spiritual "arrows." For example, Psalm 11:2 reads: "See how the wicked are bending their bows and stretching their arrows to the string, ready to shoot the upright from the shadows," and: "You need not fear the terrors of the night, the arrow that flies in the daytime" (Psalm 91:5). Finally, speaking on spiritual warfare, Paul, in his letter to the Ephesians, wrote: "So stand your ground, with truth buckled round your waist and integrity for a breastplate… and always carrying the shield of faith so that you can use it to put out the burning arrows of the evil one…" (Ephesians 6:14 –17). May I suggest therefore that the "arrows" could signify the "spiritual" darts of the principalities and spiritual wickedness in high places, the powers of darkness (Ephesians 6:12) ever at aim at the Pope, the clergy and the faithful laity. So said, Mehmet Ali Agca was only the "trigger" who, as suspected, fired the bullets on behalf of a group of military men (soldiers) in Bulgaria and Russia.

Now, Pope John Paul II read the third secret only after the attempted assassination on his life in 1981. Had he read it *before* the attempt on his life, like his predecessors Pope John XXIII and Pope Paul VI, he too probably would not have revealed it. Indeed, it is most likely that the other Popes did not reveal it because no Pope would want to publicly reveal in advance that a "Holy Father" would be "killed by a group of soldiers." Moreover, if he had read the secret *after* he already had Parkinson's disease and *before* he was shot, he probably would have definitely identified himself as being the Pope of the third secret who was "half trembling and with halting step." Heaven would not also have wanted that, as it would have been distracting for him in his mission. And so, his Parkinson's disease with its *half trembling* began some time *after* the attempted assassination, and *after* he had read the secret. It seems therefore that in the divine plan Our Lady's prophecy was therefore meant to be confirmed *post facto*. In short, it was a prophecy given in 1917 by Our Lady, the Queen of the prophets (as she is also called in the Litany of Loreto), identifying the fate of the seventh Pope after the year 1917 (the other six, including the reigning Pope Benedict XV, were Pope Pius XI, Pius XII, John XXIII, Paul VI and John Paul I). It was a prophecy made in 1917 about a Pope's fate 64 years hence, in 1981.

But the Holy Father was not killed and miraculously escaped death from bullets fired at close range, a survival, which, we are told, greatly surprised the would-be hired assassin. As Cardinal Ratzinger also wrote: "It only shows once more that there is no immutable destiny; that faith and prayer are forces which can influence history and that in the end prayer is more powerful than bullets and faith more powerful than armies." To quote a passage of John Paul II in his book *Crossing The Threshold Of Hope* and put it into this context, "Perhaps this is why it was necessary for the assassination attempt to be made in St. Peter's Square precisely on May 13, 1981, the anniversary of the first apparition at Fatima—so that all could become more transparent and comprehensible, so that the voice of God which speaks in human history through the 'signs of the times' could be more easily heard and understood."

Nonetheless, he did suffer much. Bishop Stanislaus Dziwisz, Personal Secretary of Pope John Paul II, recalled the event: "At five o'clock in the afternoon the Pope was to hold the usual Wednesday General Audience. At 5:17 p.m., during his second tour of the Square, the shots fired at John Paul II were heard. The shots injured the Holy Father in the stomach, on the right cheek and the index finger. A bullet passed through the Pope's body and fell between us. I was spared, but their force was such that they could have passed through more people. I asked the Holy Father: 'Where?' He answered: 'In the stomach.' 'Does it hurt?' 'It hurts,' he answered. At that instant he began to collapse. Standing behind him I was able to support him. He was drained of strength.

"We rushed him to Gamelli Hospital. He fainted on entering the hospital. As long as he could, he prayed in a whisper. It was a serious condition. At a certain point Dr. Buzzonetti, his personal physician, turned to me asking me to administer the Anointing of the Sick since the patient was in grave danger: his blood pressure was falling, and his heart beat very faint. The blood transfusion restored him to a condition in which it was possible to begin surgery, which was very complicated. The operation lasted five hours and 20 minutes. For two days after the operation, the Holy Father was in pain but his hopes of life were increasing. On the first day after the operation, the Holy Father received Holy Communion, and in the following days, he concelebrated the Eucharist in bed" (Dziwsiz, *Inside the Vatican*/July 2001).

Now, his blood was shed for Christ! He would have died, but "a mother's hand" saved him. That suffering mother too could also have died from unspeakable anguish at the foot of the Cross, but God preserved her from dying. He needed her to be with the apostles later. Yet the Church recognizes her as a martyr, in fact, Queen of the martyrs. Question? Is John Paul II not also a martyr—who was not allowed to die?

The secret concludes: *"Beneath the two arms of the cross there were two angels each with a crystal aspersorium in his hand, in which they gathered up the blood of the martyrs and with it sprinkled those souls that were making their way to God."* Indeed, on every continent and throughout the twentieth century there were Christians who preferred to be killed rather than give up their special mission, and men and women religious lived their consecrated lives by spilling their blood. In his encyclical *Tertio Millennio Adveniente*, Pope John Paul II made a point to remind the world of the old truth, "*the blood of the martyrs is the seed of Christians*" (Tertullian c.155-200s AD). He added: "At the end of the second millennium, the Church has once again become a Church of martyrs. The persecution of believers—priests, religious, and laity—has caused a great sowing of martyrdom in different parts of the world... This witness must not be forgotten."

Cardinal Ratzinger also associated this part of the secret with Tertullian's well-known saying. Tertullian was a pagan convert to Christianity in the early Church. His famous sentence was part of his defiant testimony, written with the usual ardour and impetuosity of his nature. He wrote: "Instead of being tortured until we confess, we are tortured until we deny. Crucify us, torture us, condemn us, destroy us! Your injustice is proof of our innocence. Your savage dealings accomplish nothing. We become more numerous every time you cut us down. *The blood of the martyrs is the seed of Christians...*"

Whereas the secret of Fatima certainly includes "a part of the past," and even perhaps most of it, it cannot be certain that the visions *all* " belong to the past. " Indeed, it is possible that the third secret of Fatima has not been fully unfolded. We are into the third millennium and the secret may not be limited to "the suffering endured by the witnesses to the faith in the last century of the second millennium." The martyrdom continues. It did not end with the twentieth century!

But didn't the Holy Father himself express his concern about the contents of the Fatima message and its relevance to these times? He wrote in his book *Crossing the Threshold of Hope*: "And thus we come to May 13, 1981 when I was wounded by gunshots fired in St. Peter's Square. At first, I did not pay attention to the fact that the assassination attempt had occurred on the exact anniversary of the day Mary appeared to the three children at Fatima in Portugal and spoke to them the words that now, at the end of this century, seem to be *close* to their fulfillment." His book was published in 1994, thirteen years after he had read the third secret of Fatima! Close to their fulfillment, yes—but not *the* fulfillment.

Let us recall that Sr. Lucia had given an indication for interpreting the third part of the secret in a letter to the Holy Father, dated May 12, 1982: "...And if we have not yet seen the complete fulfillment of the final part of this prophecy, we are going towards it little by little with great strides. If we do not reject the path of sin, hatred, revenge, injustice, immorality and violence, etc., let us not say that it is God who is punishing us in this way; on the contrary it is people themselves who are preparing their own punishment." Indeed, John Paul II himself, in his Act of Entrustment of the third millennium to the Immaculate Heart of Mary, said in St. Peter's Square on October 8, 2000 (and this was after the third secret of Fatima was revealed in May/June 2000!): "...We are men and women of an extraordinary time, exhilarating yet full of contradictions. Humanity now has instruments of unprecedented power: We can turn this world into a garden, or reduce it to a pile of rubble... Today, as never before in the past, humanity stands at a crossroads."

The great hope, however, lies in the fact that the terrible chastisement prophesied in the messages of Fatima, Garabandal, Akita and Medjugorje are all *conditional*, and can be lessened or prevented *if we do as she says*. This is what, for example, Her Majesty was saying through the miracle of the sun in Fatima when it retreated to its heavenly abode. As the Queen of Peace, she also said in Medjugorje: "You have forgotten that through prayer and fasting you can avert wars and suspend the laws of nature" (July 21, 1982). But she has also often said that she has been holding back the hand of justice of her son, but that if people do not convert, she will no longer be able to do so. Unfortunately, we have not been listening to her and this is the reason for her many tears in so many of her apparitions recently.

"Many nations will be annihilated." However, *"to prevent this"* (July 13, 1917*)* calls for adoration of the Sacred Heart of Jesus in the Blessed Sacrament, and devotion to the Immaculate Heart of Mary and her five First Saturdays. It calls for a Rosary Crusade as was requested in 1571 by St. Pope Pius V during the battle of Lepanto. It calls for wearing her medal of the Immaculate Conception and her scapular. It calls for "Penance, Penance, Penance." Indeed, this is the most important statement I have to make in this book. It is such an urgent appeal. It is the appeal of the third secret of Fatima!

A monument to the 26 martyrs in Nagasaki

An Attempt to Interpret Further the Third Secret

A painting of Polish nuns martyred in World War II

Pope John Paul II immediately after being shot

The Pope and Mehmet Agca. Forgiveness

Chapter 35

2000 AD. Millennium Entrustment to the Immaculate Heart

Now, you will recall that on July 13, 1917, the Lady of the Rosary of Fatima said to the children: "The war is going to end soon, but if people will not stop offending God, another and more terrible war will begin during the reign of Pius XI... *To prevent this,* I shall come to ask for the consecration of Russia to my Immaculate Heart and the Communion of Reparation on the five First Saturdays. If my requests are granted, Russia will be converted and there would be peace..."

Twelve years later, on June 13, 1929, Her Majesty appeared privately to Lucia and said: "The time has come when God asks the Holy Father, *in union with all the bishops of the world,* to make the consecration of Russia to my Immaculate Heart, promising to save it by these means." Now, the Fatima apparitions were not finally approved by the Church until 13 years later, on October 13, 1930. Then on October 31, 1942, Pope Pius XII solemnly consecrated the world to the Immaculate Heart of Mary. Russia, however, is not expressly mentioned, and in an interview several years later, Sr. Lucia stated: "What Our Lady wants is that the Pope and all the Bishops in the world shall consecrate Russia to her Immaculate Heart on one special day. If this is done, she will convert Russia and there will be peace. If it is not done, the errors of Russia will spread throughout every country in the world..."

Ten years later, in July 1952, in an apostolic letter *Sacro Vergente Ano,* Pope Pius XII once more explicitly entrusted and consecrated "in a very special way to the Immaculate Heart of Mary all the peoples of Russia." That letter was issued on the feast of Sts. Cyril and Methodius (826-883 AD), two brothers who are patrons of the Unity of the Eastern and Western Churches. However, it was not a Collegial Consecration with all the Bishops of the world.

Following the assassination attempt on his life on May 13, 1981, Pope John Paul II immediately thought of consecrating the world to the Immaculate Heart of Mary, and he himself composed a prayer, which he called an "Act of Entrustment." This was celebrated in the Basilica of St. Mary Major in Rome on June 7, 1981, the Solemnity of Pentecost, and, significantly, the 1550th anniversary of the Council of Ephesus. This Council declared the first Marian dogma, Mother of God, in 431 AD. However, since the Pope was unable to be present as he was in Gamelli Hospital recovering from the near-fatal attempt on his life, his recorded address was broadcast.

The following is part of the text of that 1981 Act of Entrustment: *"Mother of all Individuals and peoples*, you who know all their sufferings and hopes, in your motherly heart you feel all the struggles between good and evil, between light and darkness, that convulse the world: accept the plea which we make in the Holy Spirit directly to your heart, and embrace with the love of the Mother and Handmaid of the Lord those who most await this embrace, and also those whose act of entrustment you too await in a particular way. Take under your motherly protection the whole human family, which with affectionate love we entrust to you, O Mother. May there dawn for everyone the time of peace and freedom, the time of truth, of justice and of hope." Now, there was another attempted Collegial Consecration of Russia to the Immaculate Heart of Mary on May 13, 1982 by Pope John Paul II. However, Sr. Lucia was later to say that it too was incomplete.

Indeed, the Collegial Consecration had to wait until 1984 to be accomplished as heaven requested. This was on March 25, 1984 in St. Peter's Square, when the Holy Father, John Paul II, *in spiritual union with the Bishops of the world,* who had been "convoked" beforehand, entrusted all men and women and all *peoples* to the Immaculate Heart of Mary. He said: "We have recourse to your protection, holy Mother of God… We find ourselves united with all the Pastors of the Church in a particular bond whereby we constitute a body and a college, just as by Christ's wish the Apostles constituted a body and college with Peter. *O Mother of all men and women and all peoples*, you who know all their sufferings and their hopes, you who have a mother's awareness of all the struggles between good and evil, between light and darkness, which afflict the modern world, accept the cry which we, moved by the Holy Spirit, address directly to your heart. Embrace with the love of the Mother and Handmaid of the Lord, this human world of ours, which we entrust and consecrate to you, for we are full of concern for the earthly and eternal destiny of individuals and peoples. In a special way we entrust and consecrate to you those individuals and *nations* which particularly need to be thus entrusted and consecrated...'We have recourse to your protection, Holy Mother of God!' Despise not our petitions in our necessities...' Enlighten especially the peoples whose consecration and entrustment by us you are awaiting. Help us to live in the truth of the consecration of Christ for the entire human family of the modern world. In entrusting to you, O Mother, the world, all individuals and peoples, we also entrust to you this very consecration of the world, placing it in your motherly Heart... From famine and war, deliver us. From nuclear war, from incalculable self-destruction, from every kind of war, deliver us..."

Now, for that 1984 consecration Pope John Paul II had written to all the Catholic bishops of the world, even to the Bishops of the Orthodox churches and to major Protestant leaders. According to Fr. Richard Fox in his book, *Fatima Today. The Third Millennium*, the Orthodox responded and even some of the non-Catholic or Protestant leaders joined the Pope in that Act of 1984. When Sr. Lucia was told that not every Catholic Bishop in the world joined in the consecration, she replied: "It is true that not every Catholic Bishop responded to the Pope's request. That is their personal responsibility. However, because of these Bishops, God did not refuse to accept the Act of Consecration of 1984 with the act of union which met the necessary conditions. It was done right in 1984 and Our Lord has accepted the Collegial Consecration." Indeed, it is said that a moral majority of the Bishops had in fact acted in union with Pope John Paul II, and an even greater majority of the world's Bishops joined the Pope on March 25, 1984 (than had in 1982) in renewing and reaffirming the Act of Consecration of Russia and the world.

Following debates whether the Consecration was done as

heaven had requested, in a letter dated November 8, 1989, Sr. Lucia personally confirmed that this 1984 solemn and universal Act of Consecration, while, admittedly, not mentioning Russia by name, was accepted by Our Lady. This would appear to be true since one year after the consecration, in fact, almost to the day, Mikhail Gorbachev rose to power in the Soviet Union and immediately introduced *glasnost* (openness) and *perestroika* (restructuring) which heralded the collapse of the Communist system. Then, on December 1, 1989, this leader of the Soviet Union, once the world's most militant atheistic state, met with Pope John Paul II at the Vatican, the first meeting ever between a General Secretary of the Communist Party of the Soviet Union and a Supreme Pontiff of the Roman Catholic Church. Communism fell in Russia three years later on August 22, 1991. Religion was allowed to be practised again. God was once more alive in Russia. Indeed, on March 3, 1992, Gorbachev praised Pope John Paul II in a copyrighted article published in major newspapers around the world. He said that Pope John Paul II played a major role in the collapse of Communist in Eastern Europe. However, full religious "openness" and "restructuring" would take some time!

JOHN PAUL II ENTRUSTS THE THIRD MILLENNIUM TO MARY

It was a most important event in Marian history. On Sunday October 8, 2000, in a moving and momentous ceremony, and with 1,500 Bishops, and 4,000 priests present, John Paul II entrusted humanity and the third millennium to the protection of the Virgin Mary. The Pope announced the solemn words before the original image of the statue of the Virgin of Fatima, which was brought to St. Peter's Square for the occasion. Sr. Lucia also travelled from Portugal to Rome for that most significant event. In the statue's crown was the bullet that almost ended the Pope's life on May 13, 1981. Indeed, recognizing the importance of that "Entrustment," I travelled to Rome for the occasion. St. Peter's Square was a sea of people. At noon the Pontiff pronounced the "Act of Entrustment" of all humanity to the Virgin Mary at the dawn of the third millennium:

"Woman, behold your Son!" (John 19:26), he said. As we near the end of this Jubilee Year, when you, O mother, have offered us Jesus anew, the blessed fruit of your womb most pure, the Word made flesh, the world's Redeemer, we hear more clearly the sweet echo of his words entrusting us to you, making you our Mother: 'Woman, behold your Son!' When he entrusted to you the Apostle John, and with him the children of the Church and all people, Christ did not diminish but affirmed the role which is his alone as the Saviour of the world. You are the splendor which in no way dims the light of Christ; you exist in him and through him... Here, then, are your children, gathered before you at the dawn of the new millennium. The Church today, through the voice of the Successor of Peter, in union with so many Pastors assembled here from every corner of the world, seeks refuge in your motherly protection and trustingly begs your intercession as she faces the challenges which lie hidden in the future... Today we wish to entrust to you the future that awaits us, and we ask you to be with us on our way. We are the men and women of an extraordinary time, exhilarating yet full of contradictions. Humanity now has instruments of unprecedented power. We can turn this world into a garden or reduce it to a pile of rubble. We have devised the astounding capacity to intervene in the very well-springs of life: man can use this power for good, within the bounds of the moral law, or he can succumb to the short-sighted pride of a science which accepts no limits, but tramples on the respect due to every human being. Today as never before in the past, humanity stands at a crossroads. And once again, O Virgin Most Holy, salvation lies fully and uniquely in Jesus, your Son...To you, Dawn of Salvation, we commit our journey through the new Millennium, so that with you as guide, all people may know Christ, the light of the world and its own Saviour, who reigns with the Father and the Holy Spirit forever and ever. Amen."

Indeed, the wording of these consecrations and entrustments also strongly *suggests* to me that the Holy Father is fully aware of the significance and importance of the Amsterdam apparitions and the prayer of the Lady or Mother of all Nations or of all Peoples. Not once, for example, did he call the Blessed Virgin by her name "Mary." It was always "Mother" or "Mother of all individuals and peoples" or "Mother of all men and women and all peoples."

In Amsterdam, Her Majesty did not want to be called Mary but the Mother of all Nations or Peoples (who once was Mary). Her prayer which she wishes to be recited "in these times" throughout the world is: "Lord Jesus Christ, Son of the Father, send now your Spirit over the earth. Let the Holy Spirit live in the hearts of all nations that they may be preserved from degeneration, disaster and war. May the Lady of all Nations who once was Mary be our Advocate. Amen."

Statue of Our Lady of Fatima in St. Peter's Basilica.
October 7, 2000

2000 AD. Millennium Entrustment to the Immaculate Heart

Veneration of Our Lady of Fatima in St. Peter's Square.
October 8, 2000

Pope John Paul II entrusts the millennium to Mary

1984 Act of Consecration in St. Peter's Square

Chapter 36

What is the Triumph of the Immaculate Heart?

The triumph of Mary has been promised by God to mankind since the fall of Adam and Eve in the garden of Eden: "I will put enmity between you and the woman; between your seed and her seed. She will crush your head" (Genesis 3:15). Ever since then the battle has been raging. Indeed, the Madonna has warned us on several occasions during her many apparitions on earth about how powerful is her adversary Satan.

Now, in Fatima she requested the consecration of Russia to her Immaculate Heart and in one of her letters to her confessor, dated May 18, 1938, Sr. Lucia confirmed that the Lord himself said to her: "I want my whole Church to acknowledge that consecration as a triumph of the Immaculate Heart of Mary so that it may extend its cult later on, and put the devotion to the Immaculate Heart beside the devotion to my Sacred Heart." We should note that Our Lord said that the conversion of Russia must be recognized as "a" triumph (not "*the*" triumph) of her Immaculate Heart. And so, apparently, the triumph is not simply "a" single event. Of course, it isn't that the country Russia *per se* was all that important. It is what Russia stood for, namely, the rejection of God, as dictated in the communist manifesto, and the subsequent "scattering of her errors throughout the world." In fact, Lenin's compatriot Zinovieve once said: "We will vanquish God in his highest heaven."

After several attempts, the consecration of Russia to the Immaculate Heart of Mary was eventually confirmed by Sr. Lucia as being accepted by God. The acceptable words of the consecration were spoken by Pope John Paul II in St. Peter's Square on March 25, 1984, the feast of the Annunciation. This confirmation, it would seem, was true, if only by the fact that one year less two weeks later, on March 11, 1985, Mikhail Gorbachev attained supreme power in the Soviet Union, becoming head of the Communist Party on the death of Konstantin Fachernencko. He was seen as an openminded Kremlin leader with an interest in reform and introduced two revolutionary concepts into the Russian political language and policy: *glasnost* (openness) and *perestroika* (restructuring). It was a reformation which heralded the collapse of the communist system. What seemed impossible for seventy years certainly happened over night. The Communist Party collapsed without a shot being fired. Religion and God were once more given visas to enter Russia. This was a major triumph of the Immaculate Heart of Mary. Heaven chose the day for the triumph of its Queen over the satanic ideology of atheistic Russia. It was on August 22, 1992, the feast of the Queenship of Mary. Now, how could anyone consider that to be a coincidence?

Then, in October 1992, nine hundred Marian pilgrims accompanied the famous International Pilgrim Virgin statue of Our Lady of the Rosary of Fatima, which was blessed by Pope Pius XII in 1954 as representing the image of Our Lady and was commissioned to be carried abroad and help spread the message of Fatima worldwide. Pope Pius XII dubbed her "the Messenger of Mary's Royalty." He stated: "In the doctrine of the Queenship of Mary lies the world's greatest hope for peace."

We traveled from New York in two Boeing 747 jumbo jets to Russia, led by John Haffert, the co-founder of the Blue Army, and Dr. Rosalie Turton of the 101 Foundation. We flew over the Kremlin and arrived at Moscow's airport on October 16. Now, on Friday, October 16, 1917, three days after the miracle of the sun in Fatima, St. Maximillian Kolbe, that great devotee of Mary, whom he called "the Immaculata," made a prophecy that "one day the cavaliers of Our Lady will carry her statue over the heights of the Kremlin and into the heart of Moscow." That prophecy was therefore fulfilled 75 years later in 1992.

October 16 was also the feast of St. Margaret Mary Alacoque, the nun to whom Jesus appeared as the Sacred Heart in 1673 in Paray le Monial, France. And so, the Pilgrim Virgin statue of Our Lady of the Rosary of Fatima, which is the messenger of the devotion to the Immaculate Heart of Mary, arrived in Moscow on the feast of that great saint who promoted the devotion to the Sacred Heart of Jesus. The propriety of this date was further accentuated by the fact that the official theme of the pilgrimage was "The Alliance of the two Hearts," and printed on the left side of our blue jackets was a rosary in the shape of a heart, which, in turn, encircled two hearts linked together. Above it was written the words *Unus in Sui Amore* (one in their love).

The heavenly "coincidence" did not stop there. October 16 was also the 14th anniversary of the election of Cardinal Karol Wojtyla as Pope. He chose the name John Paul II and his motto was *"Totus Tuus"* ("I am all yours").

On Sunday, October 18, 1992, the 900 Marian pilgrims were allowed to pass the barriers to the entrance of Moscow's Red Square, which is prohibited to demonstrators and processions —a miracle in itself. I was there and it seemed as though the guards were totally mesmerized by some force and the stone at the entrance to the tomb of Lenin, as it were, was moved aside as if by some angel as we marched victoriously into the historic Square with two large icons of Christ the King and Our Lady of Guadalupe. As we reached the raised dais from which the decrees of Czas were proclaimed in the pre-communist days, a small statue of the Our Lady of the Rosary of Fatima was crowned there by John Haffert. The crown, in turn, was taken from a small statue of the Infant Jesus of Prague which one pilgrim had carried with her. It was as though Christ himself wished to crown his own mother "Queen" in Moscow's Red Square. It was good to be there!

Precisely at that moment, the mystic Janie Garza was privileged with a vision of Our Lady of the Rosary of Fatima over Red Square, wearing a crown. (In Fatima in 1917 she did not wear a crown, but on this occasion she chose to do so.) There were lights streaming from Her Majesty's heart. They flooded the Square and then bounced back upwards and outwards in all directions. Fr. Henry Bordeaux, Janie's spiritual director, later signed a statement saying that, "based on the humility, holiness and his personal knowledge of Janie, it is credible that her witness was true and that Our Lady did appear in Red Square in the manner described."

But heaven was not finished with its joyful bouquets of "coincidences." That Sunday, October 18, 1992, was the feast of St. Luke in the Roman Catholic Church, the biographer of the Annunciation of the Lord and of Mary's *Magnificat*, and in the Russian Orthodox Church, it was the great feast of the *Intercession of the Blessed Virgin*. Coincidence? That great Russian feast commemorates one of the greatest victories in Russian military history over the Tartars in 1552, and which was believed to have been accomplished through the intercession of the Blessed Virgin.

That night a second crowning took place. It was raining heavily and in the dark of the night we carried the true international Pilgrim Virgin statue of Our Lady of the Rosary of Fatima to the Square. Once more, to our surprise, the guards allowed us in. It was agreed that the crown would pass from hand to hand so that each one would physically participate in the crowning. It was midnight when the miraculous Pilgrim Virgin statue, which has been seen to weep tears several times throughout the years, was crowned by a sixteen-year-old Russian girl who has baptized only two weeks previously. Coincident with the crowning, there was a ceremony of the midnight changing of the guards in Red Square! The rain which was pouring all day stopped immediately after the crowning. Heaven had exhausted its tears of joy.

Bishop Paulo Hnilica, who flew from Rome solely for the great event that day, spoke to the peace pilgrims at the end of that ceremony. His voice choking with emotion, he said: "From today on, Russia belongs to Our Blessed Mother. Today is your hour, the hour of the apostles of Our Lady of Fatima, who have been prepared for years for these times, the times of the triumph of the Immaculate Heart of Mary. The essential part of Fatima's message is centered on the conversion of Russia. It was given to prevent a great catastrophic militant atheism and to announce the greatest grace of this century of ours —the triumph of the Immaculate Heart of Mary, the triumph of God's infinite mercy on Russia and upon the world through the tenderness of his mother's heart. Divine Providence has chosen the Holy Father, John Paul II, to fulfill the heavenly request made at Fatima. The attempt made on his life on May 13, 1981, and the Act of Consecration made on March 25, 1984, are all fundamental signs of his pontificate to help us recognize that he is the shepherd chosen to accomplish the promised triumph. It is, in fact, under his pontificate *Totus Tuus*, that the triumph of the Immaculate Heart of Mary must be realized."

Now, many Christian churches, particularly Catholic churches, were either destroyed or closed or used for other purposes during the 70-year reign of atheism in Russia, and after a decade of work, on December 12, 1999, the feast of Our lady of Guadalupe, Archbishop Tadeusz Kondrusiewicz, Apostolic administrator in the Latin-Rite Catholic Church in Russia, presided over the re-consecration of the Church of the Immaculate Conception of Mary in Moscow, the Catholic Cathedral in the Russian capital: "I come from Russia," he began, "a country whose name, until recently, was associated with the persecution of religion and the rights of man when totalitarianism was dominant. However, although Russia has really been the Golgotha of the 20th century, today the Church is being reborn. Today, in view of the new millennium, the testimony of the martyrs cannot be forgotten. This consecration fulfils the promise of Fatima: 'My Immaculate Heart will triumph'. Indeed, the church is dedicated to the Immaculate Conception. And so, 80 years after the Fatima apparitions, what was considered unlikely at the a time, if not impossible, in the once atheistic Russia, a church dedicated to Mary stands near the center of Moscow. It is the Church of the Immaculate Conception."

In 1858, she said to Bernadette in Lourdes: "I am the Immaculate Conception." As already said, the re-consecration of the church took place in December 12, the feast of Our Lady of Guadalupe, who first appeared to Juan Diego in Mexico in 1530, on the feast of the Immaculate Conception. But the Lady of Fatima, the Lady of Lourdes and the Lady of Guadalupe are one and the same!

In September, 2000, the religious developments in Russia which continued to signal an eminent revival of Christianity in that formally atheist state saw the consecration of a cathedral. On September 8, the feast of the birthday of Her Majesty, a new cathedral was dedicated to the Immaculate Heart of Mary. In a four-hour service, attended by 15 Bishops and 70 priests as well as representatives of other Christian denominations and former Siberian labour camp victims, East Siberia's new Cathedral was testimony of Russia's conversion. The Mass was celebrated by Cardinal Kazmierz Swiatek of Belarus and concelebrated by the Pope's representative, Cardinal Jan Schotte, secretary-general of the Synod of Bishops, and the Vatican's nuncio in Moscow, Archbishop Giorgi Zur. In his homily, Archbishop Tadeusz Kondrusiewicz said: "Although it once seemed nothing would ever change, the prophecy of Our Lady of Fatima has been fulfilled. Russia is being converted, and the faith is reviving here, as churches reopen and God returns." Indeed, it was so appropriate that the name of the Cathedral on that September 8 was the cathedral of the Immaculate Heart of Mary! What a birthday gift to Her Majesty.

Today, Russia has 220 Catholic parishes, 215 priests and 75 young men studying for the priesthood in St. Petersburg and there are about 500,000 Catholics in Russia. Indeed, the new President Vladimir Putin, I should emphasize here, has a reputation of being a church-going Christian, and he himself has confirmed that he is a believer. In fact, he, like Mikhail Gorbachev, has paid an official visit to John Paul II in the Vatican.

But Russia is not fully converted as yet, however, it is on its way for sure. On the occasion of the first Catholic Eucharistic Congress, held in Moscow from May 26-29, 2000, after 70 years of communist rule, Archbishop Kondrusiewicz, the Pope's Apostolic administrator of European Russia, told the gathering: "We pray for the arrival of the Pope. That would be another miracle, but here miracles do happen. We are praying for this as a grace from the Madonna of Fatima. It would, when it happens, signal the breathing of the Church with two lungs, the unity that is so wanted of the Orthodox and Christian churches."

But, to me, the final triumph of the Immaculate Heart of Mary will be the definition of the fifth and final Marian dogma. It is only then that the full mystery of Mary will be revealed and understood. This is the dogma which her adversary is fighting the hardest to prevent as shown by the opposition to it even in some hierarchical positions in Church. In fact, it is Satan's nemesis as it would then be officially recognized on earth as it is in heaven that the Woman of Genesis 3:15, the Mother of the Word, through her seed defeated him. It will be the dogma which confirms that the Mother of God (first dogma) is the perpetual Virgin (second dogma) and the Immaculate Conception (third dogma), who was assumed bodily into heaven (fourth dogma) and is the Coredemptrix, Mediatrix and Advocate. It is then that all generations will call her blessed and she will be able to shower all her graces on us. It will be the era of Mary in full bloom.

There are those who do not favour the definition of this dogma because of fear of misinterpretation, namely, that it may be interpreted by some that the Church will be deifying Mary as a fourth person of the Blessed Trinity as *Newsweek* once put it. Another concern is that of potential ecumenical discord. Surely, however, Mary's role as Coredemptrix is not new doctrine. The word "Coredemptrix" should not evoke any controversy whatsoever once it is clearly stated and understood that "Co" certainly does not mean "Co-equal." It means "cooperating with," and "companion of" and subjugated to the one Redeemer. For those who do not wish to accept this then, as far as I am concerned, and as Jesus once said: "Shake the dust off your feet as a testimony against them" (Luke 9:5).

With respect to ecumenical discord, history records that all the previous Marian dogmas were met with discord of one type or the other, including concern about ecumenism. They were defined! As John Paul II stated quite explicitly in *Ut Unum Sint:* "The obligation to respect the truth is absolute." Mary is indeed the Coredemptrix and truth must not be sacrificed on the altar of ecumenism.

Paul was not ashamed of the Gospel, neither should any Christian be ashamed to proclaim Mary as Mother and Coredemptrix. This is not the time for the faint hearted or of those who thrive on compromise. When the dogma is proclaimed then the whole mystery and truth about Mary would at last be revealed. Then and only then will she be given the leeway to shower all her graces upon us, all generations will call her blessed and it will hasten the day when all will be one.

Her Majesty Mary, Queen of Peace

Gorbachev visits Pope John Paul II in the Vatican

Lenin addressing the Russian masses

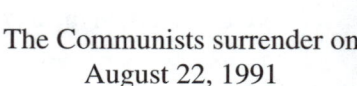

The Communists surrender on August 22, 1991

What is the Triumph of the Immaculate Heart?

The peace pilgrims march through Red Square in Moscow

John Haffert crowns small statue of Our Lady of Fatima

Her Majesty Mary, Queen of Peace

The midnight crowning of the
International Pilgrim Virgin Statue

What is the Triumph of the Immaculate Heart?

Fidel Castro welcomes John Paul II in Cuba

Vladamir Putin visits John Paul II in the Vatican

Chapter 37

Judaism, Christianity and Islam

But all are not one and there are divisions and even divisions within divisions in religion. Now, Jewish history dated from the day 4000 years ago when a man named Abraham had an encounter with God. Indeed, Judaism is the religion of the Jewish people, and it was the first great faith to hold that there is only one God. However, Judaism does not accept that Jesus is the Son of God and considers the doctrine of the Trinity to be polytheism and an absolute contradiction to the strict monotheism of Judaism. Judaism also rejects the inheritance of original sin and believes that man enters the world free of sin with a soul that is pure, innocent and untainted.

Throughout the turbulent history of the Jewish people, the belief in the coming of a personal Messiah has also been an integral part of their faith. The Messianic hope was that the Messiah, a son of David, having defeated their enemies, would restore Israel to its former glory and reconcile the people to God. Orthodox Jews are still awaiting that Messiah and do not believe, as Christians do, that Jesus was that person, neither do they believe that he resurrected from the dead. According to Moses Maimonides (1135–1224), said to be the greatest Jewish teacher of that age, "the Messiah will come, even if he is delayed."

CHRISTIANITY

Christianity is the faith which has the largest followering in the world and it is estimated that there are about one billion Christians today. It began in Israel with the story of its founder, Jesus of Nazareth. Christianity therefore sprang from Judaism, and he who encounters Jesus, encounters Judaism for according to his human nature, Jesus was a Jew. All Christians firmly believe that Jesus is the Son of God and that his miracles are some of the prophetic signs and manifestations of his divinity. A crucial Christian concept, the mystery of the Trinity, holds that while God is fully one, there are three Persons in the one God. Unlike Judaism, Christianity also believes in the doctrine of original sin and the need for baptism. As a consequence of this, the shared beliefs of Judaism and Christianity stop at the Old Testament.

ISLAM

Islam is the youngest of the three major religions discussed in this chapter and originated in the 7th century AD. It is the second largest religious faith and its conceptual roots are in Judaism and Christianity. It is estimated that there are about 850 million Muslims in the world today. Muhammad is the founder of Islam. He was born into the leading tribe of Mecca, the Koerish, in approximately 571 AD. He first worked as a camel driver, the animal which is ideally suited to the desert. Indeed, Islam was born in the desert region of Arabia and initially was considered an "Arab religion for the Arabs," just as Judaism was the religion of the Jews many centuries before. In fact, Muhammad called upon the "People of the Book" (Jews and Christians) to believe in him and to follow him. However, they did not obey his call and argued that the Scriptures did not announce the coming of the Arabian Prophet, said in the Koran to be "the seal of the prophets" (Koran 33:40), that is, the one who finally closed the series. He died on June 8, 632 AD.

Muhammad is considered to be a prophet, like Moses, who guided the Arabs towards monotheistic truth. According to Muslim tradition, the Koran is the infallible word of God revealed by the Angel Gabriel to the Prophet Muhammad one night in Ramadan about the year 610 as he was asleep or in a trance. However, there are major differences between the Koran and the Bible. Like Judaism, Islam rejects the divinity of Jesus and the doctrine of the Trinity. Islam honours Jesus as a true Prophet of God, but not as the Son of God. But the Christian Bible quotes the same Angel Gabriel as saying: "And so, the child will be holy and be called Son of God" (Luke 1:35)! Which therefore is the truth, and will the true

Gabriel please stand up?

Unlike Jesus, Muhammad had no miraculous powers and when asked by his fellow citizens to show them a miracle which would prove his right to claim the gift of prophecy, he confidently appealed to the Koran itself. The miracle, he said, was the Koran. The Koran, however, accepts the Immaculate Conception of Mary, and, according to the Koranic account of the Annunciation, Jesus was born without a human father and Mary remains a virgin. However, the Koran states very definitely that Jesus is only a creature. It rejects clearly the mystery of the Incarnation and states that Jesus "is no more than a mere mortal whom We favoured and made an example to the children of Israel (*Penguin Classics*. Koran 43:59). The Koran also adds that Jesus was not crucified but was taken up into heaven by God after another who resembled him was killed in his place: "They denied the truth and uttered a monstrous falsehood against Mary. They declared: 'We have put to death the Messiah, Jesus the son of Mary, the apostle of God.' They did not kill him, nor did they crucify him, but they thought they did (*or literally 'he was made to resemble another for them'*)... they did not slay him for certain. God lifted him up to Him; God is mighty and wise" (Koran 4:157-158).

Islam therefore rejects altogether all ideas of redemption. By rejection of the divinity of Christ its position is therefore close to that of Rabbinic Judaism. As Pope John Paul II says in his book *Crossing the Threshold of Hope:* "There is no room for the Cross and the Resurrection (in Islam). Jesus is mentioned, but only as a prophet who prepares for the last prophet, Muhammad. There is also mention of Mary, his virgin mother, but the tragedy of redemption is completely absent. For this reason not only the theology but also the anthropology of Islam is very distant from Christianity." In fact, although Muslims expect the return of Jesus before the end of the world, they do not look for any religious change from his coming. He will play only a subordinate part in the service of Islam.

With respect to the Christian doctrine of the Trinity, for the Koran there is only one unforgivable sin, namely, associating other beings with God and placing them on an equal with Him: "God will not forgive those who serve other gods besides Him; but He will forgive whom He will for other sins. He that serves other gods besides Him is guilty of a heinous sin" (Koran 4:48). Koran 4:171-172 reads: "Never has Allah begotten a son, nor is there any other god besides Him, were this otherwise, each god would govern his own creation, each holding himself above the other. Exalted be God above this falsehood" (Koran 23:91), and "O People of the Book, do not transgress the bounds of your religion; speak nothing but the truth about God. The Messiah, Jesus the son of Mary, was no more than God's apostle and His Word which He cast to Mary: a spirit from Him. So believe in God and His apostles and do not say: 'Three.' Desist, and it shall be better for you. God is but one God."

The Koran is a Law book and in this it is similar to several books of the Old Testament. As to polygamy, from early post-exile times and long before the birth of Christ, monogamy was generally accepted as the norm in Jewish society and in the year 1000 AD, it was ordained that polygamy was punishable by excommunication. Indeed, this was accepted by all but Jews living in Muslim countries. In fact, according to Jacques Jomier in his book *The Bible and the Koran*, the Law of the Koran has played a great part in the spread of Islam, and the right of women slaves, the possibility of divorce and the authorization of polygamy up to four simultaneous wives were taken into account by many new converts. On the other hand, Muhammad himself had ten wives and two concubines. When he was 25 years old, he married his first wife, a wealthy widow, Kadijah, aged 40. His second wife and the youngest, Aisha, was six years old when he married her (Maxime Rodinson, *Mohammed*, Penguin Books, 1961).

Islam believes in the resurrection of the body and retribution according to works and to the observance of a revealed law. With respect to marriage, Jesus Christ taught that there is no marriage in heaven: "At the resurrection men and women do not marry; no, they are like the angels in heaven" (Matthew 22:30). On the other hand, the Koran teaches that "they (the righteous) shall recline in couches arranged in rows. To dark eyed houris. We shall wed them... and there shall wait on them young boys of their own, as fair as virgin pearls" (Penguin Classics. The Koran 52:21-24). And in Koran 44:43-58: "As for the righteous, they shall be lodged in peace together amidst gardens and fountains arrayed in rich silk and fine brocade. Yes, and We shall wed them to dark eyed houris."

Moreover, because Islam, like Judaism, does not espouse the doctrine of original sin, there is also no rite of baptism. And so, these three major world religions have major differences in their beliefs. Indeed, even within the main religions there are splits and factions. For example, although it is very clear in Scripture and early Church history that Jesus Christ left only *one* Church, today there are over 20,000 denominations within that Church. But God is "a God of truth" (Deuteronomy 32:4) and truth cannot contradict itself. The day must therefore soon come when the truth, the whole truth, and nothing but the truth will be revealed and all will believe in the one truth and in the one true Church.

Pope John Paul II, in his encyclical *Redemptoris Missio* (Mission of the Redeemer), also warns against an attitude that "one religion is as good as another," and in his book *Crossing the Threshold of Hope,* he writes: "The Council remarks that *'The Catholic Church rejects nothing that is true and holy in these* (other) *religions.* The Church has a high regard for their conduct and way of life, for those precepts and doctrines which, although differing on many points from that which the Church believes and propounds, often *reflect a ray of that truth which enlightens all men.* However, the Church proclaims, and is bound to proclaim that Christ is *'the way and the truth and the life'* (John 14:6) in whom men must find the fullness of religious life and in whom God has reconciled everything to Himself'"(*Nostra Aetate* 2). He then ends his discourse, saying: "Christ came into the world for all peoples. He redeemed them all and has His own ways of reaching each of them in the present eschatological phase of salvation history."

And in the chapter *In Search of Lost Unity,* he wrote: "Christians are more deeply aware that the divisions existing between them are contrary to Christ's prayer at the Last Supper: 'May they all be one, as you, Father, are in me and I in you so that the world may believe that you sent me' (John 17:21). He (Christ) founded only one Church—the only one capable of speaking in his name. These divisions are certainly opposed to what Christ had in mind.

It is impossible to imagine that this Church, instituted by Christ on the foundation of the apostles and of Peter, should not be one... By the year 2000 we need to be more united, more willing to advance along the path toward the unity for which Christ prayed on the eve of his Passion. This unity is enormously precious. In a certain sense, the future of the world is at stake, and more than ever before! The future of the Kingdom of God in the world is at stake."

But the years 2000 and 2001 have come and gone and the world is even more militantly divided in its religious beliefs than ever before, including the emergence of a militant form of piety. Indeed, the future survival of the world is at stake.

A view of the city of Jerusalem

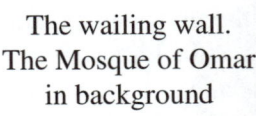

The wailing wall. The Mosque of Omar in background

Judaism, Christianity and Islam

John Paul II visits the wailing wall

Islam at prayer

Her Majesty Mary, Queen of Peace

A Christian procession in Jerusalem

The heads of Judaism, Christianity and Islam in Israel

Chapter 38

The Palestinian Problem

The Middle East crisis is a major threat to world peace and a potential trigger for another world war. Its extraordinary significance to me lies in the fact that it has a very important biblical background. In his book *The Palestinians,* published in 1979, Jonathan Dimbleby, the British television reporter, gave a history of the Middle East from a Palestinian point of view. In defense of the Palestinian, he wrote: "The Palestinian will fight Israel, and he will do so, if not with a gun, then with a bomb. The Israeli solders will seek to kill him. If they succeed, they will report that another 'terrorist' has been eliminated. And the PLO will announce that another 'martyr' has been born... It is now generally agreed that the conflict in the Middle East is, at root, a territorial dispute between two peoples: the Israelis and the Palestinians. The Zionist case for Palestine is well known. The Palestinian case is equally powerful, though it is still referred to, in terms which reflect the imbalance of our Western perception, as the Palestinian 'problem'."

"This book," he continued "is neither a hymn to terrorism nor an apologia for the PLO. It is, however, an attempt to redress our imbalance of perception... The most obvious symbol of this distortion is the use of the word 'terrorist' to distinguish Palestinian from Israeli atrocities. *'Terrorists' do not have jet planes to mutilate innocents from a distance*; they do it with bombs in markets. Is the former less heinous than the latter because it is sanctioned by an Israeli Cabinet? But again and again the Israeli authorities emerge morally inviolate from their military adventures while the PLO is compared to the Nazis or the Ku Klux Klan for refusing to give up guerilla war..."

Now, this was written in 1979. Twenty-two years later, on September 11, 2001, Arab "terrorists" did indeed use *"jet planes to mutilate innocents from a distance"* — but, to the shock of the world, with suicide bombers! Dimbleby was wrong!

Samuel T. Huntington, the Albert J. Weatherhead III University Professor at Harvard, wrote the lead article for *Newsweek* magazine of December, 2001: "An outbreak of violence is sweeping across the world. What are the root causes and will they erupt into a full-scale global conflict? The makings of a possible 'clash of civilizations' are present. Contemporary global politics is the age of Muslim wars. Muslim wars have replaced the cold war as the principal form of international conflict. These wars include wars of terrorism, guerilla wars, civil wars and interstate conflicts. These instances of Muslim violence could congeal into one major clash of civilizations between Islam and the West or between Islam and the Rest."

David Shipler, who received the Pulitzer prize for general nonfiction in 1987, wrote in his book *Arab and Jew*: "I am neither Arab nor Jew. By culture and creed, I should suffer neither pain nor passion over the causes and battles that entangle the two peoples... And yet I cannot help caring... At times a rush of anger would propel me to the conviction that, in their mutual hatreds, both sides deserve each other. And then at other moments I was enveloped by a sense that both sides were right. But I offer no solution to the problem. I have no prescription for peace." Shipler then ended his book with a comment of a young Jewish doctor in Israel: "There is a tremendous gap culturally, emotionally, and in mentality. I don't see how this gap is going to be bridged in a hundred years."

But to attempt to understand the problem is to beg the central question from which all others lead: "To whom does Palestine belong?" Now, the Middle East history really begins with Abraham around 2000 BC. Very briefly, his people wandered in the land of Canaan (Palestine) for decades, but in time the Pharaohs enslaved them in Egypt. Around 1200 BC, Moses then led the Hebrews out of Egypt and they wandered in the Sinai Desert. According to the Bible, the Hebrews at the time of the giving of the Law at Mt. Sinai numbered more than 600,000. They conquered the Canaanites in Palestine and King David (1010-975 BC) eventually captured Jerusalem, after which it was called the City of David. It was however decreed that his son Solomon should be the one to build the Temple to house the Ark of the Covenant.

Between 900-800 BC, Palestine was broken up into the kingdoms of Judah and Israel. But around 800 to 700 BC, the kingdom of Israel was conquered by the Assyrians and its people taken captive and dispersed. It was the end of the Israelites. From 600 to 500 BC, the kingdom of Judah also fell to King Nebuchadnezzar and the Jews were deported to Babylonia after the destruction of the Temple and the plunder of Jerusalem. However, between 500 to 400 BC, Cyrus, the King of Persia, defeated the Babylonians and the Jews were freed. Then followed the first return of the Jews from Babylonia to Palestine, and under Herod the Temple was rebuilt. Between 300 BC to 1 AD, Palestine was conquered, this time by the Romans, and the Emperor Titus destroyed the Temple by fire in 70 AD, as prophesied by Jesus (Mathew 24:2).

In the 7th century AD, Islam conquered Jerusalem but the Muslim conquerors were then ejected by the Crusaders in 1099 and they, in turn, drove out the Crusaders in 1187. Through the Ottoman Turks, the Muslims held Jerusalem until the end of World War I when the British took over and set the stage for the reestablishment of a Jewish nation. Of the 160,000 Arabs in Palestine in 1922, over 100,000 were desert nomads at that time. The rest were landless peasants. Then between 1918 and 1936, about 150,000 Jewish immigrants settled in Palestine. However, with the ascent of Hitler into German politics, a new type of Jew began immigrating to Palestine and by 1936 there were 60,000 German Jews in Palestine, providing her with much needed scientists, engineers, managers, chemists and researchers to increase her productive capacity and to improve the quality of her goods. Thus began the process of transforming the desert of Palestine into a "land of milk and honey" (Exodus 3:8). In fact, this little strip of real estate has been alternately called Canaan, Palestine, Judea, Judah, and Israel.

In later years, largely in reaction to pogroms in Germany and Russia, significant numbers of European Jews began to migrate to Ottoman-controlled Palestine, but the migration gained urgency when Hitler came to power and exterminated an estimated 6 million Jews in the cause of racial purity. Jews in Europe were flowing in from Nazi terror in increasing numbers and as the doors to other countries were closing to them, Palestine was their only hope. Indeed, out of the holocaust grew the international compassion for the purpose of a new Israel as a sanctuary for the Jews.

After World War II, on November 29, 1947, the General Assembly of the United Nations voted to internationalize Jerusalem and create a Jewish and an Arab state. The Jews accepted the decision; the Arabs defied it. The State of Israel was officially born on Friday May 14, 1948 with the establishment of a Jewish state in Palestine to be called Israel. It will be open to Jewish immigration and for the ingathering of the exiles. The dream was always that one day the children of Israel will return to the *"Promised Land,"* and secure their ancient claim to Palestine. In fact, until 1948, for close to 3,000 years, the Jews did not even have a country of their own, yet they preserved their ethnic identify among alien cultures. Indeed, in all the years of exile, the Jewish people never ceased to pray for their return to the land of Israel. However, to the Muslims it is Palestine. To the Jews it is Israel. That Friday evening the Israelis toasted their new homeland. The next morning they manned the front line for defence.

The Arabs rejected the new state and six Arab nations — Syria, Jordan, Egypt, Iran, Lebanon and Saudi Arabia, all invaded Israel and outnumbered the Jews 40 to 1. Israel defeated the Arab armies! However, the process of establishing an Israeli state was unfortunately achieved with the displacement and dispossession of the people who already lived there. Eight hundred thousand Palestinians were driven or expelled from their homes, and were dispersed throughout the Middle East. This dilemma was the womb which nourished the tragedy of the Middle East. Wars followed in 1956, 1967, 1973, and 1982. They are fighting for the same land on behalf of their people. The Palestine Liberation Organization or PLO was formed. But it is more than the liberation of Palestine. For some groups it is also all about the destruction of Israel. However, as one commentator on the Middle East once wrote, the hardships of the Palestinian Arabs in modern-history bear no resemblance in scope and depth to those of the Jews. The Arabs in this crucial country of Palestine have suffered powerlessness and deprivation of land, but never genocide.

Now, the Arabs claim the right to be the sole rulers of Palestine by virtue of Muhammad's conquest of that country in the seventh century AD and by virtue of constituting a majority of the population at the end of World War I. The Jews claim the right to Palestine by virtue of their conquest of that country in the 12th century BC, and by virtue of having been a majority in that country far longer than the Arabs. All else is rationalization. The City of David is also a major source of conflict. As Ariel Sharon said in an interview in *Newsweek* of December 17, 2001: "There are problems to which there are no answers: the question of Jerusalem. I believe Jerusalem is the capital of the Jewish people and the capital of the state of Israel, united and undivided forever. Of course, the Palestinians do not accept that. The other issue is the right of return of the Palestinian refugees."

Lance Lambert, writing from a biblical and Israeli point of view, in his book *The Uniqueness of Israel,* defends the Israeli claim to the land. He argues that for the Jews it is the country of the patriarchs. "It is the country of Moses and Joshua. It is the land where kings ruled from the country of David and Solomon. It is the land of the psalmist. It is a unique land and is the subject of a divine promise. Indeed, no other land on earth has ever been promised by God to one particular people."

It is supposed to be the legacy given to the seed of Abraham, the father of the Jews and the Arabs. It began with the barrenness of Abraham's wife Sarah and a prevailing custom which, because of her barrenness, sanctioned a union between Abraham and Sarah's Egyptian maidservant Hagar. Abraham was 86 years old when she conceived. However, once she conceived, her mistress was despised in her eyes and Hagar treated her with contempt. Mutual jealously, understandable enough, then led to Hagar's running away from the house after Sarah dealt harshly with her (Genesis 16:4-6). Hagar is then told by the angel of the Lord: "Return to your mistress and submit to her. I will so greatly multiply your offspring that they cannot be counted for multitude. Now you have conceived, and you will bear a son; you shall name him Ishmael, for the Lord has heard your cry of distress. A wild-ass of a man he would be, with his hand against everyone and everyone's hand against him, and shall live at odds with all his kin" (Genesis 16:9-12). Unfortunately, this image of the violet Arab reinforced by war and terrorism remains in the minds of many Israeli Jews.

Now, Abraham was 100 years old when Sarah eventually bore him a son, Isaac. The jealousies then deepened and Sarah sent away Hagar and her son Ishmael. After much suffering Hagar went through the desert to Paran and eventually returned to Egypt where she got a wife for Ishmael (Genesis 21:1-21) to the east of Egypt, on the way to Assyria. He did set himself to defy his brothers. The number of years he lived was one hundred and thirty-seven. Then he breathed his last, died, and was gathered to his people" (Genesis 25:17-18). However, God did make certain promises to Abraham regarding Ishmael: "And as for Ishmael, I have heard thee: Behold, I have blessed him and will make him fruitful, and will multiply him exceedingly; twelve princes shall he beget and I will make him a great nation. But my covenant will I establish with Isaac" (Genesis 17:20- 21). In fact, the Christian New Testament repeats the statement: "Does not the Scripture say: 'Cast out the handmaid and her son: This son of the handmaid shall not inherit with the son of the free woman' " (Galatians 4:30).

And so, according to Genesis, this was the land that God gave to Abraham and his seed through Isaac, and some of the Jews of modern Israel have articulated their biblical claim. Those Jews who relied on the biblical deed to the land take their history from the ancient period of 4,000 years or so ago, skipping over the centuries of Muslim rule that followed; those Arabs who regard history as their ally tend to begin with the Muslim conquest in the 7th century AD, blithely ignoring the Jewish kingdom that existed there 2,000 years before Muhammad made his appearance. As one author wrote: "It is clear from these Scriptures that whatever claims the Arabs—and the Palestinian Arabs in particular—may make upon the Holy Land, those claims have to be based upon political, historical or practical grounds and not upon Scripture. As far as the Word of God is concerned, the land has been specifically promised as an everlasting possession to the descendants of Abraham through Isaac and Jacob."

The Koran, on the other hand, directly contradicts this. From the Muslim point of view, the Jewish revelation was a divine revelation that was corrupted. Islam states that Abraham had only one son and that Isaac was born afterwards as a reward to him for his obedience to God's command to sacrifice Ishmael. The Koran says that Ishmael was "the son of the promise" (covenant), and not Isaac, as is said in the Jewish and Christian faiths. According to the Koran, Ishmael goes to Mecca. His descendents who grew up in Arabia are Muslims, whereas those of Isaac, who remained in Palestine, are the Jews.

This idea that Jews and Arabs were "cousins," who were descended from Isaac and Ishmael respectively, was accepted in Jewish writings and included by Muhammad in his teachings that became the Koran. As Prime Minister Shimon Peres said in a 1985 address to the United Nations General Assembly: "The sons of Abraham will have become quarrelsome, but remain family nonetheless." Indeed, it is written that at the death of Abraham, his sons Isaac and Ishmael buried him in the cave of Machpelah (Genesis 25:9-10).

But the conflict in the Middle East, which is fraught with the potential for a world conflagration, will be solved only when the Palestinians and Israelis recognize that each has an understandable claim upon Palestine. Now, the Koran was only written in 7th century AD, ages after the birth of Christ and aeons after the era of Abraham and Sarah. The Judeo-Christian Bible testifies that the Covenant God is the God of Abraham, his son Isaac and Isaac's son Jacob, who gave birth to the Israelites and the Jews. Through this bloodline came Jesus, the founder of Christianity. Indeed, the Gospel according to Mathew begins with the ancestry of Jesus: "A genealogy of Jesus Christ, son of David, son of Abraham..." (Matthew 1:1). What I am saying is that the recognition by the Palestinians and the Israelis that they both have a claim on Palestine will not be enough to bring forth peace. True peace will only come when the two, the Arabs and the Jews, will become "one" in faith (John 17:21) and adopt the one true religion, handed down by Jesus of Nazareth, son of God, son of David, and son of Mary, daughter of Abraham. The same can be said for all the nations of the world.

Indeed, the Palestinian problem is of immense importance in that it had its origins in the Covenant which Yahweh made with Abraham, Isaac and Jacob. The Jews see Palestine or Israel as an essential part of the Covenant. It is the *Promised Land*. In this land, for them, there is an all-pervading sense of religious centrality that just does not exist in other lands. As I said before, this is the key for understanding the Jewish point of view. Indeed, their historic tie with Israel, and in particular Jerusalem, is exemplified by their longing for that city which is repeated and expressed each year at the closing of the Passover Seder meal when the people pray: "Next year in Jerusalem."

But it is the Holy City, not only to the Jews, but also to Christians and Muslims as well. However, as I have also said before, the similarity between Judaism and Christianity stops at the New Testament. Indeed, Jesus tearfully lamented: "Jerusalem, Jerusalem, you who killed the prophets and stone those who are sent to you! How often have I longed to gather your children, as a hen gathers her chicks under her wings, and you refused! So be it! Your house will be left to you desolate, for, I promise, you shall not see me any more until you say : 'Blessings on him who comes in the name of the Lord!' "(Matthew 23:37-39). In this closing remark he was quoting Psalm 118:25-26. It reads: "Please, Yahweh, save us. Please, Yahweh, please give us prosperity. Blessings on him who comes in the name of Yahweh." According to the footnote of the Jerusalem Bible, this last remark may possibly refer to the reconciled Jews who will eventually acclaim that Jesus is the Messiah.

In the New Testament, Paul, speaking about the remnant Israel, wrote: "Let me put a further question then: is it possible that God has rejected his people? Of course not. I, an Israelite, descended from Abraham through the tribe of Benjamin, would never agree that God has rejected his people, the people he chose specially long ago... Let me put another question then: have the Jews fallen forever? Their fall, though, has saved the pagans in a way the Jews may now emulate. Think of the extent the world, the pagan world, has benefited from their fall and defection—then think how much more it will benefit from the conversion of them all... and the Jews, if they give up their unbelief, (will be) grafted back in your place. God is perfectly able to graft them back again" (Romans 11:1-24).

Now, Mary is given place in the Koran as the virginal mother of Jesus: "O, Maryam, God has truly chosen you; He has purified you; and He has chosen you above all women in the world" (Koran 3:40-45). In the year 770 AD, the year of the Battle of Roncevalles, the Emperor Charlemagne besieged the fortress of the town of Lourdes in France, which was under Muslim control. But the Muslims refused to surrender even during an enforced starvation. Charlemagne was then about to lift the siege when the Bishop of Le Puy, who was with him, had an inspired thought. It was that the Muslim Commander Mariat should be asked to surrender, not to the Emperor, but to Mary, the Queen of Heaven. This idea appealed to Mariat, who laid down his arms at the feet of the statue of the Virgin of Le Puy. It is said that he was eventually baptised and took the name Lores which was given to the town, and in time it eventually became "Lourdes."

The word *Islam* means *"submission,"* and so, it may be said that Mariat surrendered in "submission" to Her Majesty, the Queen of Heaven. Indeed, I envisage the day when present-day Islam will submit *in toto* to Her Majesty. In fact, she has appeared in most dramatic ways to millions of Muslims in Egypt—in Zeitun where multitudes have seen her on the roof of the Church of St. Mary, and more recently in the Church of St. Mark in Assuit.

The Apostle Paul once wrote: "I, an Israelite, descended from Abraham through the tribe of Benjamin, would never agree that God has rejected his people." But Mary, the daughter of Abraham, an Israelite, descended from Abraham through Kind David, is the mother who will bring her children back to the Father. She is the Woman of Israel and the Woman of Revelation 11:19;12:1 with a crown of twelve stars on her head. The twelve stars represent the twelve tribes of Israel and the Queen of the (twelve) apostles. Indeed, she appeared in Garabandal with such a crown of twelve stars and in Medjugorje she still appears with her crown.

Now, she is not known to have appeared in Israel, but how can this Woman of Israel forsake her children. In fact, she has been seen weeping all over the world in recent years. It is Rachel weeping for her children for they are no more (Matthew 2:18), and I envisage the day when, at an appropriate time of her choice, she will finally appear in the land of her birth and that of her son, the Holy Land, where he lived and died. It will be the prelude to the conversion and unity of all the children of Abraham who will then worship the Second Person of the Blessed Trinity as their God. The day will soon come when all nations will prostrate themselves before him. You see, the Woman of Israel is also the Lady of All Nations!

Chapter 39

God's Children at War

A new war has begun in this 21st century. It started on September 11, 2001. But the previous 20th century has seen more lives lost than in all the wars of past human history. The Church also has had more martyrs in that century than in all the 19 centuries since the first martyrdom of the founder of Christianity on Calvary.

The first war in creation history started in heaven between Michael and the obedient angels and Satan and his proud and disobedient followers. It was a war as a consequence of pride, jealousy, ambition and disobedience to authority. The fallen angels were then cast down to earth and since then the history of the human race has been one of war. Indeed, it is said that in the 17th century there were only seven calendar years without a major war between European states. The 18th century began with the wars of Louis XIV and ended with those of Napoleon. But in the 19th and 20th centuries wars were much more bloody and devastating as weaponry became more and more lethal, and as Winston Churchill once said: "Except for brief and precious interludes there has never been peace in the world... and murderous strife was universal and unending."

World War I was expected to be over by Christmas of 1914, and conscripts enlisted by the hundreds of thousands, bursting with burgeoning nationalism. The nation was supreme. When it ended on November 11, 1918, over 10 million lives were lost, many more maimed. World War I also made possible the Russian Revolution in 1917 and greatly contributed to the great depression of the thirties, the rise of communism, and the economic collapse which helped drive the Germans into Hitler's embrace. The onset of World War II resulted in part from the humiliation of Germany and the imperfect peace that ended World War I.

When World War II engulfed the world, it proved to be the bloodiest conflict ever in known history. Fifty million people, including 6 million European Jews, would die before Berlin fell to the Soviet Red Army on May 8, 1945. In August of that year, the United States dropped two atomic bombs on Japan, ending the war and changing the world. It was the birth of the apocalyptic nuclear age. Hiroshima and Nagasaki were turned into living hells. There were charred bodies all over the place and there were people walking like ghosts with their skin peeled and hanging like seaweed. But even as the guns fell silent in 1945, a new threat began to take shape. Soviet aggrandizement and Western resistance then triggered the Cold War. The Russians were bent on installing friendly regimes in the Eastern European lands which they had liberated, and so, an Iron Curtain descended, as Winston Churchill warned. It was also inevitable that the Cold War would turn hot. First in Korea, then in Vietnam, communist regimes in the North launched wars to capture by force the non-Communist South countries.

But there were other wars all over the world. When hard-line communist regimes collapsed, and we thought that freedom of religion and democracy would bring the world closer to God, they all seem not to do so in a similar way, and a kind of gangster capitalism emerged with a cadre of Mafia elites and the spawn of corruption and prostitution. It is the story of present-day Russia and other European communist countries. The murderous Khmer Rouge in Asia, for example, was no different. It was a sadistic revolution that left 1.7 million Cambodians dead. Now the red flag of so-called democratic Kampichena has given way to the red lights of massage palours and brothels. It was the fleshpot legacy of Pol Pot.

Meanwhile, in Algeria and other parts of Africa, colonialism was ended by wars of national liberation or by guerrilla movements, but those consequences were no less deadly. In fact, every nation in sub-Saharan Africa has either been devastated by war or borders a nation that has been. War erupted in Rwanda, Congo, Algeria, Angola, Uganda, Chad, Namibia, Zimbabwe, Burundi, Eritrea, Ethiopia, Sierra Leone, and some other countries. Furthermore, these wars often last a generation or more, and children who grew up surrounded by war now perceive it as a normal way of life. Indeed, everyday all around the world, children are abducted and recruited into the armed forces. An estimated 300,000 children are actively participating in 36 ongoing or recently ended conflicts in Asia, Europe, Africa, the Americas and the former Soviet Union. In Sierra Leone some 80% of all rebel soldiers are age 7-14, and in Cambodia one fifth of the wounded soldiers were between 10 and 14 years old.

There were also ethnic or religious wars in Israel, Sudan, India, Kashmir, Indonesia, Malaysia, Afghanistan, Sri Lanka, the Philippines, Northern Ireland, Nigeria and in Yugoslavia. In fact, Sarajevo, which the Pope refers to as "the Jerusalem of Europe," can be understood as a world in miniature, where the ideals of ethnic and religious harmony are being severely tested, and where there has been a pillage of most callous murders, rapes and destruction of houses and churches. Eleven thousand people died in Sarajevo; two thousand were children and the Balkan Peninsula is again nurturing conflicts that are centuries old. Meanwhile there were other wars in the Central and South American continents, including Nicaragua, Argentina, Chile, Colombia, Peru, Cuba and San Salvador.

Indeed, the 20th century, following an egoistic and hedonistic sexual revolution, also reached levels of permissiveness, promiscuity, openly displayed vulgarity, corruption and public shamelessness, which seem to have few parallels in known history. According, for example, to a recent report by the United Nations Children's Fund that called for a global campaign to eradicate the multi-billion-dollar sexual exploitation of young children, "millions of children throughout the world are being bought and sold like chattels and used as sex slaves. The report estimates that 400,000 children and women are subjected to commercial sexual exploitation in India, between 244,000 and 325,000 in the United States, 200,000 in Thailand and 175,000 Eastern and Central Europe. It estimates that 100,000 women and children are also sexually exploited in the Philippines, Taiwan and Brazil, and 35,000 in West Africa.

That century was also the most oppressive and bloody of all history, a century without respect for human life and without mercy.

We certainly cannot forget the horror of the extermination of the Jews, which can never be execrated sufficiently. But it was not the only extermination. No one remembers the genocide of the Armenians during the First World War. No one commemorates the tens of millions killed under the Soviet regime. No one ventures to calculate the number of victims sacrificed uselessly in the various parts of the earth to the communist utopia. Regrettably, no pen can adequately describe the savagery and suffering, the anguish and agony of the 20th century.

But it is the religious wars which are now threatening world peace as never before through divisions and the emergence of so-called militant fundamentalism, mimicking the fanatical passions of the Crusaders of yesteryears; passions which, like the Japanese Kamikazes, readily and willingly lead to suicidal missions and the death of others, all erringly in the name of God! Indeed, religious wars are superceding ethic, civil, and other wars in severity and in their potential for a total global disaster and conflagration.

Children soldiers in Africa

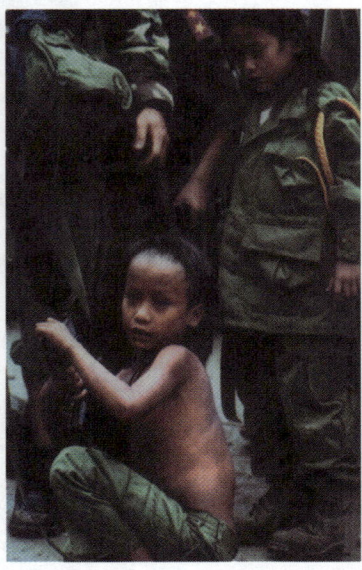

Children soldiers in Cambodia

Chapter 40

Her Majesty, the Queen of Peace

Before the Prince of Peace was born, the Virgin of Nazareth was only the "Queen-designate," but when she said "yes" to Gabriel and God, the Holy Spirit overshadowed her, she conceived, and then became the *Queen of Peace*. Nine months later, she gave birth to the Messiah. A first-century physician recorded the event: "In the countryside close by, there were shepherds who lived in the fields and took in turns to watch their flocks during the night. The angel of the Lord appeared to them and the glory of the Lord shone around them. They were terrified, but the angel said, 'do not be afraid. Listen, I bring you news of great joy, a joy to be shared by the whole people. Today, in the town of David a saviour has been born to you; he is Christ the Lord... and suddenly with the angel there was a throng of the heavenly host, praising God and singing: 'Glory to God in the highest heaven and peace on earth to men of goodwill' " (Luke 2:8-14).

But the event was prophesied by Isaiah: "For there is a child born for us, a son is given to us and dominion is laid on his shoulders; and this is the name they gave him: 'Wonder-Counsellor, Mighty-God, Eternal Father, Prince of Peace' (Isaiah 9:5 – 6). Then in his farewell discourse to his disciples at the Last Supper, the Prince of Peace said: "Peace I bequeath to you, my own peace I give you, a peace the world cannot give, this is my gift to you" (John 14:27). Paul later summarized his Lord's mission: "He came to bring the good news of peace, peace to you who were far away and peace to those who were near at hand" (Ephesians 2:17).

Her Majesty's mission is also one of peace. She not only gave birth to the Prince of Peace but she was at the foot of the Cross when he made peace between man and God. She appeared in the Rue du Bac in Paris in 1830 and in La Salette in 1846, and wept over the civil war which she prophesied would occur in France and other states in Europe. She appeared in Pontmain, France in 1874 towards the end of the Franco-Prussian war as the *Lady of Hope*, and saved the little prayerful town. She appeared in Fatima towards the end of World War I in 1917 as the *Lady of the Rosary*, in response to the prayers of Pope Benedict XV and the faithful, and promised that the war would end soon, but warned that another and more terrible war will come if men did not do as she says. World War II started in 1939. She appeared in Amsterdam towards the end of World War II in 1945 as the *Mother of all Nations* and also assured us that the war was shortly going to end, as she said, "thanks to the rosary." She then appeared in 1981 in Medjugorje, Yugoslavia as the *Queen of Peace* warning us again about war. Yugoslavia paid her little heed except the parish of Medjugorje and its environs. War broke out in Yugoslavia in 1992. She also appeared in Kibejo in Africa in 1981 and warned of war and bloodshed. Her call for prayer and conversion was not heeded. It came to pass.

Little Jacinta, one of the visionaries of Fatima, said to Lucia before she died in 1920: "Make it known that the Sacred Heart of Jesus wishes that the Immaculate Heart of Mary be honoured with him. People must ask for peace through the Immaculate Heart of Mary, for God has entrusted the peace of the world to her." Indeed, when, according to Sr. Lucia, Pope John Paul II's consecration of Russia to the Immaculate Heart of Mary in 1984 was accepted by the Lord, within two months, almost to the day, Mikhail Gorbachev came into power and introduced two new ideologies in Russia, *glasnost* (openness) *and perestroika* (restructuring). It was the beginning of the fall of Communism and its promotions of wars.

But Russia is not as yet fully converted. This may await the definition of the fifth and final Marian dogma—Mary, Coredemptrix, Mediatrix and Advocate. And so, we should do as she says and pray the prayer of the *Mother of all Nations*, which she said is the prerequisite to the dogma: "Lord Jesus Christ, Son of the Father, send now Your Spirit over the earth. Let the Holy Spirit live in the hearts of all nations that they may be preserved from degeneration, disaster and war. May the Lady of all Nations, who once was Mary, be our Advocate. Amen." Indeed, when the dogma, the last dogma in Marian history, is proclaimed, then more than ever before, all generations will call her blessed and she will be able to shower in abundance the graces of the Mediatrix, who advocates for us before the throne of God. She gained this privilege at the moment she said 'yes' to his wedding invitation; that moment in time when she became the Coredemptrix and Queen of Peace.

In an address to the United Nations on September 25, 1961, President John F. Kennedy said: "Unconditional war can no longer lead to unconditional victory. It can no longer serve to settle disputes. It can no longer be of concern to great powers alone. For a nuclear disaster, spread by winds and waters and fear, could well engulf the great and the small, the rich and the poor, the committed and the uncommitted alike. Mankind must put an end to war or war would put an end to mankind."

Kofi Annan, the Secretary-General of the United Nations was awarded the Nobel Peace Prize in Oslo on December 10, 2001. It was a significant and appropriate choice in this era of war. In his Nobel lecture he said: "We have entered the third millennium through a gate of fire. If today, after the horror of 11 September we see better, and we see further, we will realize that humanity is indivisible. New threats make no distinctions between races, nations or regions. A new insecurity has entered every mind, regardless of wealth or status… The 20th century was perhaps the deadliest in human history, devastated by innumerable conflicts, untold suffering, and unimaginable crimes. Time after time, a group or a nation inflicted extreme violence on another, often driven by irrational hatred and suspicion, or unbounded arrogance and thirst for power and resources. In response to these cataclysms, the leaders of the world came together at mid-century to unite the nations as never before. A forum was created, the United Nations, where all nations could join forces to affirm the dignity and worth of every person, and to secure peace and development for all peoples… In the 21st century I believe that the mission of the United Nations will be defined by a new, more profound, awareness of the sanctity and dignity of every human life, regardless of race or religion."

A *Reuter* report stated that the day after he had urged the world in apocalyptic terms to pull back from the brink of further conflict, apparently signaling his anxiety over the Afghan war, on December 8, 2001, the feast of the Nativity of the Blessed Virgin Mary, Pope John Paul II said in a speech in Rome: "Dark clouds are gathering on the horizon. Humanity, which greeted the dawning of the third millennium with hope, now feels weighted down by the threat of new shocking conflicts. World peace is at risk."

Now, on August 6, 1981, the feast of the Transfiguration, Her Majesty identified herself to the children in Medjugorje: "I am the *Queen of Peace*," and in the beginning of April, 1982, she made this request: "I wish a feast of the *Queen of Peace* on the 25th of June, the anniversary of the first apparition. When the *Holy Spirit* comes, peace would be established. When that occurs everything would change around you. I am asking you to spread peace and love. Pray for peace because Satan wants to destroy the little peace you have." It is to be noted that when she appeared in Amsterdam as the *Lady or Mother of all Nations*, the prayer which she composed for the world was also an appeal to the *Holy Spirit*: "Lord Jesus Christ, Son of the Father, send now Your *Spirit* over the earth. Let the *Holy Spirit* live in the hearts of all nations that they may be preserved from degeneration, disaster and war…"

This Queen of Peace is the Mother of all Nations and also the Mother of Unity, and her longing is for a world of united nations; nations with her children all of one faith. Our Lady's concern is therefore not confined to individuals. It embraces entire nations. World peace cannot be achieved unless the law of the Author of Peace is taken into account; until nations return to God and the reign of Christ is established among the nations. This is why she wishes to be called "in these times" the *Mother of all Nations*.

Because she gave birth to the Prince of Peace, I have selected all the messages which she has given to Maria Pavlovic-Lunetti of Medjugorje on each Christmas day over the past decade from 1990 to 2000: "Dear children, without peace you cannot experience the birth of the little Jesus, neither today nor in your daily lives. Therefore, pray to the Lord of Peace that he may protect you and that he may help you to comprehend the greatness and importance of peace in your heart. In this way, you shall be able to spread peace from your hearts throughout the whole world. Pray, because Satan wants to destroy my plans of peace. Be reconciled with one another and by means of your lives help peace to reign on the whole earth" (1990).

"Today in a special way I bring the little Jesus to you so that he may bless you with his blessings of peace and love. Give your love as an example to your families. You say that Christmas is a family feast, therefore, dear children, put God in the first place in your families so that he may give you peace and may protect you not only from war but also during peacetime, and protect you from every satanic attack. When God is with you, you have everything, but when you do not want him, you are then miserable and lost and you do not know whose side you are on. Therefore, little children, decide for God and then you will obtain everything (1991)."

"Dear children, today is the day of peace, but throughout the whole world there is a great lack of peace. Therefore, I call on you to build up a new world of peace together with me by means of prayer. Without you I cannot do that, and I therefore call all of you, with my motherly love, and God will do the rest. Do not forget that your life does not belong to you, but it is a gift with which you must bring joy to others and lead them to eternal life" (1992). "Today I rejoice with little Jesus and it is my desire that the joy of Jesus may enter every heart. I give you a blessing with my son Jesus so that in every heart peace may reign. I love you, little children, and I want you to come closer to me through prayer. You talk and talk but do not pray, therefore, little children, decide for prayer. Only in this way would you be happy and God will give you what you ask of him" (1993).

"Today I am joyous with you and I pray with you for peace; peace in your hearts, peace in your families, peace in your desires and peace in the whole world. May the King of Peace bless you today and give you peace" (1994). "Jesus is the King of Peace and only he can give you the peace that you seek. I am with you and I am presenting you to Jesus in a special way now in this new time in which one should decide for him. This is the time of grace" (1995).

"I am your mother and I wish to reveal to you the God of love and the God of peace. I do not want your life to be one of sadness but that it be realized in everlasting joy, according to the Gospel. Only in this way will your life have a meaning" (1996). "I desire that each of you reflect and carry peace in your heart and say: 'I want to put God in the first place in my life.' In this way each of you would become holy" (1997). "In this Christmas joy I give you the blessing of little Jesus. May he fill you with his peace. Today, little children, you do not have peace and yet you yearn for it. That is why, with my son Jesus, I call you on this day to pray, pray, pray, because without prayer you cannot have joy or peace or (a future). Yearn for peace and seek it, for God is true peace" (1998).

"Dear children, I am giving you the possibility to decide for peace. Through your 'yes' for peace and your decision for God, a new possibility for peace is opened. Only in this way, little children, will this century be a time of peace and well-being for you. Therefore, put little newborn Jesus in your hearts" (1999). "Dear children, today when God has allowed me to be with you with little Jesus in my arms, I rejoice with you and give thanks to God for everything he has done in this Jubilee year. I thank God especially for all the vocations of those who said 'yes' to God completely. I bless you all with the blessing of the newborn Jesus. I pray for all of you for joy to be born in your hearts so that in joy, you too may carry the joy which I have today. In this child I bring to you the Savior of your hearts and the One who calls you to the holiness of life. Thank you for having responded to my call" (2000 AD).

But she is truly the Queen of Peace. The United States entered World War II on December 8, 1942. It was an entry which won the war for the Allies. It was the feast of the Immaculate Conception. The war ended when Japan surrendered on August 15, 1945. It was on the feast of the Assumption of the Blessed Virgin Mary. Japan signed another formal pact in San Francisco pertaining to her surrender. It was called the Second World War Peace Treaty. It was signed on September 8, 1951, the feast of the nativity of the Blessed Virgin Mary. The signing of the Intermediate Range Nuclear Forces Treaty in Washington by Mikhail Gorbachev and Ronald Reagan, abolishing medium range missiles in Europe took place on December 8, 1987, the feast of the Immaculate Conception. The Communist Party in Russia suddenly and dramatically collapsed without a shot being fired on August 22, 1991. It was on a very special feast day of Her Majesty, the feast of the Queenship of Mary! This was a fitting day for the triumph of Her Royal Highness. As Albert Einstein once said: "God does not play dice!" On December 8, 1991, the feast of the Immaculate Conception, began the Commonwealth of Republics and the end of the USSR. Twelve days later, Yeltsin of Russia met with Pope John Paul II at the Vatican. Then on December 25, 1991, Christmas Day, the communist flag was taken down for the last time over the Kremlin and one year later, on December 25, 1992, once more on Christmas Day, Communism was declared illegal in Russia.

But peace is not simply the absence of war, and world peace must begin with the inner peace of all peoples and all nations, the peace of God in our consciousness. And so, as the song says: "Let there be peace on earth and let it begin with me. Let there be peace on earth, the peace that was meant to be. With God as Our Father, brothers all are we. Let me walk with my brother in perfect harmony. Let peace begin with me, let this be the moment now. With every step I take, let this be my solemn vow. To take each moment and live each moment in peace eternally; let there be peace on earth and let it begin with me."

When that moment comes, "The wolf shall lie with the lamb, the panther shall lie down with the kid; the calf and lion cub will feed together with a little child to lead them. The cow and the bear will make friends, their young shall lie down together. The lion shall eat hay like the ox. The baby shall play over the cobra's hole; and into the vipers lair the young child puts his hand. They shall not hurt nor harm in all my holy mountain, for the earth shall be filled with the knowledge of Yahweh as the waters swell the sea" (Isaiah 11:6-9), and "nation will not lift sword against nation, there will be no more training for war" (Isaiah 2:4).

Then it will be "as it was in the beginning." It is the everlasting wish of Jesus, the Prince of Peace, who has entrusted the peace of the world to his Mother and the Mother of all Nations, the Coredemptrix who gave birth to the Redeemer and King of all Nations—Her Majesty, the Queen of Peace.

Lady of All Nations

Her Majesty, the
Queen of the Angels

Her Majesty, the Queen of Peace

Queen of Peace
(St. Mary Major Church in Rome)

BIBLIOGRAPHY

1. Able, Dr. Robert Peter, Final Warning—The Legacy of Chernobyl, Warner Brooks, Inc., New York, 1988.
2. Agreda, Mary of, The Mystical City of God, Tan Books and Publishers, Inc., Illinois, 1978.
3. Albright, Judith M., Our Lady at Garabandal, Faith Publishing Co. Milford, Ohio, 1992.
4. Auclair, Raoul, The Lady Of All Peoples, Les Presses, Lithographiques, Inc., Quebec, 1978.
5. Ayo, Nicholas, The Hail Mary, University of Notre Dame Press, USA, 1994.
6. Bassilli, Mary & Armani, The Life of the Mother of God, The Virgin Mary, London, 1988.
7. Bartholomew, Prof. Courtenay, A Scientist Researches Mary Ark of the Covenant, The 101 Foundation, Asbury, NJ, USA, 1995.
8. Bartholomew, Prof. Courtenay, A Scientist Researches Mary Coredemptrix, Mediatrix and Advocate, The 101 Foundation, Asbury, NJ, USA, 1998.
9. Bartholomew, Prof. Courtenay, A Scientist Researches Mary Mother of All Nations, Queenship Publishing Co., Goleta, CA, USA, 1999.
10. Bonanno, Raphael, Jews, Moslems And Christians. Children Of God, Franciscan Printing Press, Jerusalem, 1988.
11. Breen, Eileen, Mary, The Second Eve, From the Writing of John Henry Newman, Tan Books, 1982.
12. Bunsón, Margaret R., John Paul II's Book Of Mary, Our Sunday Visitor, Inc., Indiana, 1996.
13. Carroll, Warren H., Our Lady of Guadalupe and the Conquest of Darkness, Christendom Publications, Virginia, 1983.
14. Carroll, Warren H., 1917: Red Banner, White Mantle, Christendom Publication, Virginia, 1983.
15. Chapman, Geoffrey, Catechism of the Catholic Church, A Cassell imprint, London, 1994.
16. Chettham, Nicolas, A History of the Popes, Dorset Press, New York, 1992.
17. Clark, Ronald W., Einstein: The Life And Times. Avon Books, New York, 1984.
18. Clarke, Dr. Peter, The World's Religions, The Reader's Digest Association Limited, USA, 1993.
19. Coe, Michael T., Breaking The Maya Code, Penguin Books Ltd., Middlesex, 1992.
20. Comay, Joan, The Jerusalem I Love, Peli Printing Works Ltd., Israel, 1976.
21. Cruz, Joan Carroll, The Incorruptibles, Tan Books and Publishers, Inc., Illinois, 1977.
22. Daughters of St. Paul, Women of the Gospel, St. Paul Editions, USA, 1975.
23. Dawood, N.J., The Koran, Penguin Books, London, England, 1993.
24. Dawn, Peter, St. Margaret Mary Alacoque, Catholic Truth Society, London, 1979.
25. de Montfort, Louis, True Devotion To Mary, Tan Books and Publishers, Inc., Illinois, 1941.
26. De Marchi, John, Fatima From the Beginning, Missoes Consolata, Fatima, 1983.
27. Dennis, Mary Alice, Melanie and The Story of Our Lady of La Salette, Tan Books and Publishers, Inc., Illinois, 1995.
28. Deiss, Lucien, Mary, Daughter of Sion, The Liturgical Press, Minnesota, 1972.
29. Delaney, John, A Woman Clothed With the Sun, Image Books, New York, 1961.
30. Derum, James, Patrick, Apostle In A Top Hat, Fidelity Publishing Co., Michigan, 1960.
31. Diaz, Bernal, The Conquest of New Spain, Penguin Books, London, 1963.
32. Dictionary of Mary, Catholic Book Publishing Co., New York, 1985.
33. Dimbleby, John, The Palestinians, Quarter Books Ltd., London, 1979.
34. Dirvin, Fr. I., Saint Catherine Labouré of the Miraculous Medal, Tan Books and Publishers, Inc., Illinois, 1958.
35. Divine Mercy in My Soul – The Diary of the Servant of God – Sister Faustina Kowalska, Marian Press, Massachusetts, 1987.
36. Dimont, Max, Jews, God And History, Penguin Books, Inc., USA, 1994.
37. Dolorous Passion Of Our Lord Jesus Christ: From the Meditations of Anne Catherine Emmerich, Tan Books and Publishers, Inc., Rockford, U.S.A.,1983.
38. Duffner, Rev. Father, Sorrowful and Immaculate Heart of Mary, World Apostolate of Fatima, Washington, New Jersey.